The True Story of a Muslim Middle Eastern Family in the United States

Betrayal of a Muslim-American Family by their Best Friends: Osama and Saad

PART 1

ADAM NOOR

PAGE PUBLISHING, INC.
Conneaut Lake, PA

First originally published by Page Publishing 2020

ISBN 978-1-68456-540-5 (pbk)
ISBN 978-1-64462-998-7 (digital)

Printed in the United States of America

ACKNOWLEDGMENTS

A year ago, I was sitting in Dr. Rick's office. I asked him, "What's next for me? What could I possibly do with my life?" I felt useless and without any purpose. I was damaged beyond repair. I really felt like I had nothing to live for.

"Adam…wish," Dr. Rick said to me.

"Wish for what?" I asked, completely baffled. "Wish for what? At this point, what could I possibly wish for in my life?"

I wondered, after all these years, was my doctor just plain wrong now?

I went home that night and went to bed. During my sleep, the word *wish* just kept repeating in my head over and over. I woke up with an idea. I was going to write a book about my experiences. I was going to write about everything that had happened to me. I was also going to detail what had happened to my father.

When I saw Dr. Rick again, I told him about my idea. He absolutely loved it. Dr. Rick thought it was a great idea. This whole book was born from what he said to me that day. Throughout the writing process, Dr. Rick was nothing but supportive. This book exists because he told me to have hope.

I would like to thank Senator Chris Smith. Without him, the media would have lost interest in my father's murder years ago. Without him, I wouldn't have had the opportunity to tell this story. His support has been invaluable. Senator Smith became one of the two people in my life that I regularly talked to. He became like a grandfather to my children. Frequently, my family and I would go to his house for cookouts. During the hot summers, my children would swim in his pool. Senator Smith is a valued friend. As this book was being written, his creative input was very helpful.

Senator Nick Allen's support was also amazing. He's a very brave man as well as a friend. When my father was killed, I had a very hard time. The support I received from Senators Allen and Smith was lifesaving.

Finally, I will never forget Pat from Social Services. When I was on the verge of getting evicted, she hugged my wife and me. She told me that if we were evicted, we would have a home with her. I will never forget her for this. She has continued to help my family whenever we needed it. She literally saved my family from having to live on the streets. At the last moment, she swooped in like an angel to help my family. I can never say enough about how much I owe her. My sincere thanks to a truly amazing woman.

Prologue

On a cold, brisk September day, I found myself walking in the cemetery that had become the home to my father's resting soul. A stiff breeze blew, forcing me to clutch my coat closer to my body to stay warm. Decaying dead leaves blew across the grass in between the tombstones. There was no one else at the cemetery on this day. My only company was the spirits of the dead. As I walked, I found myself gazing at the various tombstones. All of them were different shapes and sizes. Some were small, some large. Each one of them represented a story that no longer had the ability to be told. How many of their stories were left unknown? How many of their voices were never really heard? I was determined not to let that be my father's fate.

I arrived at my father's grave and stopped, my eyes misting slightly as I read his name on the marble stone. I stood there for a moment in silence, pondering. I came to America from my home country of Jordan, filled with high aspirations and hope for a better life. I came to this country seeking the land of freedom and opportunity. The optimism I held seemed like something from a long-ancient past. Now, it was a vague memory at best.

My mind wandered, pondering over the various surreal twists and turns that my life had taken to arrive at this exact point. A mugging and brutal beating that forever changed my life, a marriage to a woman I had never met—absolutely none of that hit as hard as the moment I learned of my father's death.

My mind refocused on the tombstone in front of me with the name of my father written on it. His name on the cold, hard marble stone—this was all I had left of the man I once loved and adored with everything that I was. A man that was kind, patient, and compassionate, he never failed to be there for me, even through the darkest times of my life.

My father
1942–2012

"Hi, Dad," I said to the open air. "Why are you here? Why aren't you with me?" I was hoping to get an answer but not really expecting one. "They took your money," I said with a heavy sigh, my slightly damp eyes getting more watery by the minute. "And then they killed you." I choked up. "Why? Why? Why?" I repeatedly asked, desperate for any answer. The cemetery stayed silent, failing to yield any of its secrets—either unable or unwilling to do so.

* * * * *

Ever since I was a little boy, it was my dream to live in the United States. As a kid, I wasn't concerned with who I was going to be or what work I was going to do. I had no dreams or aspirations higher than living in the United States. To me, America seemed magical, and I always pictured living there to be like living in heaven. I was not the only person from my part of the world to feel this way. If you had asked any of my friends, they would have told you that they would have loved to go to the United States, the land of freedom and opportunity. As Americans traveled around the world; people would look at them as though they had arrived from the stars. As a child, I would get excited to go downtown just to catch a glimpse of American tourists. Even the briefest sight of them was enough to make me happy.

Some of my family already lived in the United States. They would occasionally travel to Jordan for a vacation. When we talked to them and heard their stories, it sounded like they came from a land on a distant planet. Even when they were not wearing the nicest clothes, I liked how they looked because I believed this to be the "American style." No matter what happened, no matter what mistakes they made, I always gave Americans the benefit of the doubt. I thought of Americans as though they were different from other people. Americans were not liars! Americans could be trusted. Americans were good people!

People from all over the world go to the United States for a variety of reasons. Many plan to go to the US for the opportunity that the country represents as they struggle to live in their home countries. They can't make enough to provide for their families, so they go to the United States in search of a better life. My father was such a man. This was his lifelong dream. It was his dream to come to this country, work very hard, work his way up the ladder, and eventually own a business. It was a dream he would achieve very briefly, but at the cost of his own life.

My father instilled in me the idea that in America, if you worked hard, you would achieve your dreams. If you worked hard, you would find nothing but success. I believed wholeheartedly in my father's idealism. I believed wholeheartedly in the American Dream. Unfortunately, I would learn at a terrible cost that this was not always so.

I remember arriving in America, finally achieving what I had set out to do: joining my father in the United States. He had beaten me there by a good ten years. I arrived in JFK airport, in awe of its size and grandeur. I took in all the sights and sounds around me as I walked. Marveling at what, at long last, was my home. As I walked, I stopped in front of a large window in the terminal. It was my first actual glimpse of the United States. The sun beamed brightly through the window, forcing me to shield my eyes. I swore that in the bright lights, I could see my future. As far as the eye could see, there was nothing but hope.

I continued walking, and as I walked further into the terminal, I made a more concentrated effort to look for my family. The terminal was alive with the sound of talking and laughter. People were hugging and kissing all around, clearly having not seen each other for a long time.

I had not yet seen my father, and my heart raced with excitement as I continued to scan the crowd. And then I saw him! His hair was grayer. He had gained a few pounds. But it was unmistakably him. My father saw me, and the features on his face lit up. A bright smile stretched across his face. I picked up my pace as I moved faster toward him, anxious to feel his embrace once more. I reached him and wrapped my arms around him in a tight hug. We both laughed with joy.

"Hello, son." He beamed at me. "Welcome to America," he finished with pride.

Still holding on to each other, we began to walk. We exited JFK airport, hoping that a bright future awaited us both.

* * * * *

Back in the cemetery, my eyes were no longer just misting. I was weeping openly as I fell to my knees in front of my father's grave. My hands reached out to feel the cold stone, longing for a physical connection that I could no longer have. He was stolen from me. He was stolen from my family.

"Father, they killed you, thinking you were nothing. Because you were a Muslim man from a faraway country, they thought nobody would notice nor care. But, Dad, you wouldn't believe the support we've been getting—from the media, from the people of Massachusetts, everyone. The American people all know your story. They are all sad about your death. The support has been amazing and overwhelming."

I paused, gulping, finding myself unable to speak. I composed myself before continuing, "I met a man. A senator!" I paused again. "I know what you're thinking." I smiled through tears. "My son talking to senators? Unbelievable!" I said loudly. "But it's true. This man is Senator Chris Smith. He's going to help me find justice for whoever did this to you! He told me he would work hard to get to the bottom of this. He's a fantastic man. A lot like you actually. I promise you, Dad." I continued sobbing. "I will find out who did this to you. I will find out the reason you're no longer here with me. I will never stop until justice is served." But as I talked, my voice gained strength.

"You taught me to always keep going and to never give up. I never will, Father."

I pulled my hand back and kissed my fingers then once again put my hand back on his tombstone.

"I miss you," I cried. "I only have two people in this life that I can count on now—Senator Smith and my doctor. You remember him, Dad? Dr. Rick? He's been amazing in my time of grief."

I sat down on the ground and looked up at the graying sky, a stark contrast from my first day in this country. There were answers out there. I would find them no matter what the cost.

I would honor my father.

This is my father's story. This is my story.

CHAPTER 1

1998

I have always loved music. If you've ever had passion for something, then you know. You'd feel it in your bones. You would eat, sleep, and drink it. It would encompass your entire being. Music was my passion. I lived for music. I was never more alive than when I was performing. It was what kept me in my native country of Jordan even after my dad left for the United States to pursue a better life ten years earlier. He took two of my brothers and my sister with him. My mom stayed in Jordan for a while. But eventually, she went to the United States as well.

I wasn't a famous musician. I wasn't a superstar. But I was known well enough. My performances were not just confined to Jordan. I would often travel around the Middle East, playing in various Arabic nightclubs. I would work three nights a week: Wednesday through Friday. Those were usually the busiest nights. The rest of the week would be taken up by practicing.

When the venue where I was supposed to perform was close enough, I almost always chose to travel by foot. There was nothing I loved more than music, followed by nighttime walks.

I remember one particular night very clearly. I was walking home from a performance. It was a perfect night. It was neither too cold nor too hot. As was often the case, I found myself looking up at the stars. Looking at the stars in Jordan is not like looking at the stars in the United States. The stars shine brighter in Jordan because there is not nearly as much light pollution. Don't get me wrong. There are plenty of lights in Jordan, especially in my home city of Amman. But nowhere near the number that there are in the United States.

As I looked up at the stars, I often thought about how insignificant we all really are—you, me, everyone. We are so small compared to the rest of the universe. There are billions of stars. Maybe trillions. I always find that thinking about the vastness of space is really humbling. But that wasn't the only thing I saw when I looked up into the sky that night. I felt that I saw the future. When I looked up at the stars, I couldn't help but believe that my future was as bright and brilliant as the stars twinkling above my head. As I walked, staring up into the heavens, I happened to catch a glimpse of a shooting star. The sight made me smile brightly. I turned my attention away from the beautiful Jordan sky, and I started to sing quietly to myself. I sang all the way home.

Seeing myself these days, it's hard to imagine that the person in my memories was actually me. It was a time in my life when I saw my future as something other than a nightmare. When I was barely thirty years old, I was optimistic that eventually all my dreams would come true, that I would continue to shine as brightly as any star or planet you might see in the sky. Looking back today, that memory seems so long ago.

* * * * *

One fateful day, as I sat at my piano in the middle of my living room, I heard the phone ring. I jumped up quickly and ran to pick it up.

"Hello?" I said as I picked up the phone, curious as to whom it would be.

"Hello, son," I heard the gravelly tones of my father on the other end. I literally felt filled with joy upon hearing his voice, as I always did.

"Dad! How are you? How's life in America treating you?" I asked excitedly.

"Amazing, son. As always," my dad answered.

This was what he always said. He never had one negative thing to say about his new home. Whether that was really the truth, or just my father's belief in not complaining, I will never really know.

"Fantastic! Always good to hear," I replied.

"You should come and find out for yourself. The family all misses you down here," my father said warmly. He was always trying to convince me to join him in America.

"And I them," I started, "But you know I have my life here. My music career. One day I will join you guys. One day I will be a famous musician in America," I said confidently and enthusiastically.

"But of course, my son," my father replied kindly. "Let me give you a bit of fatherly advice though. Don't take too long. The years have a funny way of disappearing on you. Before you know it, you'll be an old man like me," he finished with a laugh.

"Oh, Dad, you are not old," I objected.

"Adam, my kind son as always. Unfortunately, the graying, wrinkled man I see in the mirror begs to differ." He laughed again. "Listen, son. I am going to take a vacation to see you in Jordan for at least a few months. I hope you wouldn't mind having me."

"Of course, not! My home is your home," I excitedly replied.

"It most definitely is," he said, his tone taking on a teasing tone. It was, in fact, my father's home. My dad owned the apartment as well as several others.

"It will be great to see you. It's been too long!" I replied enthusiastically.

"Indeed! I will also be bringing a woman with me," my father said cryptically.

"A woman?" I asked.

"Yes, a woman," my dad answered, offering no more new information.

"Who is she, Dad?"

"She's an American woman whom I've known for some time. She's like my best friend. She cooks like you wouldn't believe. And she cleans for me. She's never been out of the country. I want to show her more of the world, open her eyes to all those things she is missing out on."

"Sounds good," I replied in absence of anything else to say. I was confused, but out of respect for my father, I didn't question him further on it.

"I'm going to want to show her around Jordan. I want you to help me with that," my dad said.

"Me?" I asked, surprised.

"Yes, you. As I've established, I am not a spring chicken anymore." My dad laughed. "I don't exactly enjoy the night life. She is still somewhat young. She will want to get a taste of it. You can show her a good time for me."

"But, Dad…," I objected, "I don't speak any English."

"I am aware," my dad said, sounding amused.

"Does this woman speak Arabic?"

"Unless she has talents beyond what I have discovered, I highly doubt it," my dad chortled.

"Then how are we going to talk?" I asked. There was a long pause in which I awaited my father's answer.

"You will figure it out" was all that my father would say on the matter. His tone suggested that he invited no further conversation. "Expect my arrival in a week's time. Farewell, my son."

"Dad! Wait!" I shouted quickly, hoping to stop him from hanging up the phone. I heard no click, and I heard no dial tone, which indicated to me that I had successfully stopped him. "Just out of curiosity, what is this woman's name?"

"Her name is Evanna. Goodbye for now," he answered. And this time, I did hear the sound of a click and the long beep of a dial tone. I slowly put the phone back on the receiver.

"Evanna," I said to the open air. "Pretty name!" I stared at the phone for a while, replaying the conversation with my dad in my mind. Well, if nothing else, I thought, this should be very interesting…

* * * * *

My father was nothing if not a punctual man. He said he would be in Jordan in a week, and that was precisely when he arrived. I was waiting for him and his mysterious woman companion, Evanna, in Queen Alia International Airport. Tourists were often struck by how spacious the airport was. More than that, they were amazed by how many businesses were located there. For instance, there were supermarkets as well as many international restaurants inside the airport. Oftentimes, tourists' first taste of local cuisine was in that very airport. I sat in the terminal, nervously awaiting my father. When I could put up with sitting no longer, I started to pace back and forth.

After what seemed like an eternity, I finally saw my father walking toward me. As promised, he was accompanied by a woman. I was so excited that I ran to him, barely acknowledging or even noticing his companion. It was only after I had hugged my father tightly that I really noticed the woman smiling next to him. Her hair was blond. Her brown eyes lit up happily, taking in all the sights around her. I surprised her by turning to her and giving her a hug. Apparently, she did not yet understand that in our culture, we are freer to be physically demonstrative than those in her culture.

"Marhaban," I greeted in my language. "Motasharefatun bema'refatek." Naturally, she didn't understand what I was saying to her. But my father helpfully translated. (Hello. How are you?)

"Ohhhhhh. Helllllooo," she said to me enthusiastically. Once again, my dad translated. "It is definitely awesome to meet you. Your dad has talked so much about you." She smiled at me cheerily. I smiled back at her warmly, grasping her hands before turning my attention back to my father.

"How was your flight? Smooth, I hope?" I asked.

"Very pleasant, my son," he answered with a smile. "You look well. It's very good to see you!" he said as we started walking to the exit of the airport. "Now let's go home!" He turned to Evanna. "Believe it or not, Evanna, there are lots more interesting things to see in Jordan." Evanna laughed and I found that her laugh had a musical quality to it. Together the three of us departed from the airport.

* * * * *

"Dad, I forgot to tell you, I'm working tonight," I said as we sat on the couch talking.

"Oh?"

"Yes, so I won't be able to show Evanna the town tonight," I said, answering his unspoken question.

"Why not, son? I'm sure she would love to see you at work." He turned to Evanna, speaking in English. "Would you be interested in going to my son's job tonight?"

"His job? What's his job?" she asked.

"She wants to know what your job is, son," my father said in Arabic. I eyed him strangely. He knew the answer to her question. He also knew that I wouldn't be able to answer her question in a way that she would understand. I didn't know what my dad was up to, but I knew he had some kind of purpose. He always did. I thought for a moment as the two looked at me curiously. After a few moments, an idea occurred to me. I stood up and started moving rhythmically. I danced like a typical nightclub visitor would do.

"He dances!" Evanna shouted excitedly as if she had answered a question in some kind of game.

"Yes, he dances," my father confirmed.

"Dances," I repeated in English. As it turned out, it was my first spoken word in English. Then, I began to sing one of the Arabic songs I typically sang when I performed. She listened for a few moments.

"You sing?" she questioned.

"Yes, he sings at nightclubs. And he's very good!" my dad answered.

"Oh, wow! Well, I'd love to go!" Evanna shouted enthusiastically.

"She would love to go. So no problem," my dad replied jovially. "And I will be staying here tonight. I'm feeling very…" He paused as he seemed to search for the word. "Air sick," he finished. He said this without any outward impression of being unwell.

* * * * *

Evanna and I exited the house into the open air. I had decided that we would go a little early so I could introduce her to a few people before I had to perform. The night was a chilly one.

"Are we going to drive?" she asked as she noticed that we were walking past the car. Although it was the family car, I had never learned to drive. I stared at her blankly, which reminded her that I didn't speak English.

"Drive. *Vroom…vroom,*" she said while miming spinning a steering wheel. That was enough to give me an idea about what she was trying to say. I shook my head no and then pretended two of my fingers were a pair of legs walking.

"We're going to walk? Must not be far," she said almost to herself. I said nothing, merely smiled at her. As we walked, I noticed that she was shivering a little. Evanna hadn't prepared herself to walk in the chilly air, so she left without a coat. Being the gentleman that I was, I quickly took off my coat and offered it to her. She smiled at me and thanked me. Once again, the sky was clear. I pointed at the sky. She followed the direction my hand was pointing.

"The stars?" she asked, not taking her gaze away from the sky.

"Stars," I said in response with a smile. I had just learned another word in English!

"Yes, the stars are beautiful," she said, her teeth chattering as she clutched my coat closer to her. I wanted to tell her what the stars meant to me, but this was beyond my ability to communicate. We walked in silence, occasionally "speaking" through gestures. This was actually a fun game: trying to figure out what the other was attempting to say. Before we knew it, we arrived at our destination: Sharaf's Dance Club and Bar.

Unlike some of our neighboring Middle Eastern countries, alcohol is not forbidden in Jordan. But it is hardly a liberal country.

Sharaf Baleid was an old friend of mine. I had known him my entire life. He always had a charming way about him. People looking to open nightclubs or bars in Jordan find it very hard to get permits. Sharaf had no such problem. I believe this is because of his friendliness and his ability to get just about anyone to like him.

Evanna and I entered the dance club. Aside from the flashing blue, green, and red laser lights that permeated the dance club, it was dark. The dance club was filled with Arabic music and people dancing. It was an interesting mixture of American tourists and Jordanian residents.

"Adam!" Sharaf called from his position at the bar. I smiled brightly, grabbed Evanna's hand, and proceeded to dance my way over to the bar. She was looking about, taking in her surroundings in awe. She had undoubtedly erroneously assumed that no place like this existed in Muslim cultures.

"You're early, man," Sharaf said in our native tongue, surprised. I typically made it to my shift exactly on time, not a minute early, not a minute late. As the lights flashed just brightly enough, he caught a glimpse of Evanna, whose hand I was still holding.

"And you brought a friend!" he said with delight.

"She's an American woman. My dad brought her from the US to show her the culture," I answered. Sharaf turned to her, taking her in.

"You are his father's wife?" Sharaf asked Evanna in English. Sharaf's English was far superior to mine. It had to be. A big part of his business was dealing with American tourists who came here to sample the local culture. In a lot of cases, they also wanted to get drunk in a Jordanian bar. It was well-known that Sharaf's was the place to do both.

"No," Evanna laughed. "Just a friend of his."

"I seeeee…," Sharaf replied, still trying to figure out the mystery of this woman.

"So his father brought you for him?" he asked, pointing a finger in my general direction. I would only know later exactly what their conversation was about.

"Not quite." Evanna blushed. "Just to see the world."

Sharaf did not seem any less confused. After a few moments of trying to wrap his mind around exactly what was going on, he gave up.

"I don't get it at all," Sharaf mused. "But you know what?" He paused dramatically. "I have no need to! Any friend of Adam's is a friend of mine!" He reached over the bar to give Evanna a big hug. "Would you like a drink?"

"Sure! Do you have a martini?" she asked.

"Of course! Even if I did not, I would find a way to make it for you," Sharaf replied with a courteous grin.

"Great!" She started fumbling inside her purse, looking for money. "How much is it?" she asked.

"Oh no, no. Your money is no good here. All your drinks are on the house!" he said with a sweeping dramatic gesture. Evanna looked overwhelmed and just thanked him, seemingly hundreds of times. "Of course! I like you, friend of Adam's," he confessed. "You two should come over for breakfast tomorrow morning! Your father included. It's been ages since last I saw him."

"Sounds wonderful," Evanna replied. "You're being so nice to me..."

"American women are deserving of all the kindness in the world," Sharaf flirted. "You can come over, meet my wife, and play with my children. My children will love you. They love playing with Americans! And because you are a girl, they may take it easy on you." Sharaf paused. "Might! We will have to see..."

Just then, Sharaf made a sweeping, theatrical motion to look at his watch. He turned to me. "You are up, my friend." I hesitated to move away, which my longtime friend was quick to pick up on. "Oh, don't worry, my friend. She will be well taken care of." I smiled, somewhat reassured. As I started to walk toward the stage to begin playing my music, he called out to me, "Who knows? She may even still be here when you get back!"

I briefly turned back to him and gave him a somewhat exasperated look. Evanna sat down and watched as I made my way to the stage. I got myself set up quickly, and I began to sing and play the piano.

There is no more effective a universal language than music. In America people go to the opera, and most will not understand a word that is sung. They simply feel the soaring emotions that touch their soul. Evanna couldn't understand the words of my songs. But like at an opera, she could feel the sentiments being conveyed and became overcome with emotions. Occasionally, the lights would brighten up just long enough for me to catch glimpses of her. What I saw on her face was something I had yet to see on a woman's face directed my way. It looked like sheer awe and adoration…

* * * * *

Hours later, I was dancing and singing on the streets of Amman with a laughing, mostly drunk Evanna at my side. She wasn't so drunk that I had to carry her, which was a good thing since I was in no way capable of doing this. Evanna hadn't been shy about taking advantage of the free drinks that Sharaf had offered. The American tourists that passed us glanced amusedly in our direction, but kept walking. For all I knew, in the United States, such a sight was a common thing. Evanna hummed along to the sound of my voice as I twirled her around. I was having more fun than I thought was possible to have with someone, without being able to actually talk to them.

Eventually, we made it home. Once inside we stood in the doorway looking at each other, smiling. In that moment, Evanna was having feelings that she knew there would be no way she could express to me in a way that I would understand. Except one way. She leaned in for a small kiss. The kiss surprised me, but I enjoyed the feel of her lips on mine. She pulled away, and we both smiled at each other.

"Good night," she said quietly. She danced away, up the stairs, humming as well she could, trying to remember one of the songs I had been singing. I watched her the whole way until she made it to the guest room and disappeared from view. I walked to my own bedroom. Without turning on the lights and using only my memory plus what little moonlight was shining through the window, I made my way to my bed. I lay down, wrapping myself in the blankets. I felt the room spinning a little bit as I lay there, smiling. I couldn't remember the last time I was this happy.

CHAPTER 2

At this point, there was no question in my mind that Evanna was falling for me. However, she was falling for the culture of Jordan even faster. According to her, the people of Jordan were much simpler and easier to be around than people in America. In Jordan, there was no such thing as "none of your business." In Jordan, everybody knows everything about everybody. Privacy does not exist there in the way it does in the United States. If you live in a large apartment building, it's like one large community. Not only do we know everything about each other, but we look out for each other.

Evanna would tell me that in America all she ever did was work, work and more work. In Jordan, we have more to our lives than work. We socialize more than we work. Typically we will work from eight in the morning until two in the afternoon. The rest of the time is split between family and friends. For us, Thursday through Saturday is the weekend. It isn't uncommon for a friend to call you up at one in the morning to tell you they are coming to visit.

Americans typically think that Middle Eastern countries are really religious and strict. Actually, that's not the case. Although you are supposed to visit a mosque five times a day, every day, this doesn't always happen. Friday is usually the big religious day on which everyone heads to the mosques or churches. Islam is the dominant religion in Jordan, but it is not the only one practiced. There are plenty of Christians. They live right alongside Muslims.

I'm not particularly religious. But in Jordan, you have to identify yourself as something. My father is Muslim, so therefore I am Muslim. What religion you are depends on where you happen to be born and who your parents are. If your parents are Christian, you will be Christian. And so on and so forth. However, I feel that some people do not understand that we are all worshipping the same God regardless of what religion one happens to be.

When Sharaf made his offer for Evanna and I to come over for breakfast the next day, he didn't mention that this was what I already had planned to do. In my culture, you take turns eating meals in your friends' and families' houses. Sometimes, I would go to Sharaf's house for five straight mornings. Then the next five mornings would be spent at my house. Hospitality and respect are very important in our culture. If a friend comes over, that friend gets fed.

There are a number of types of foods you can choose to eat for breakfast in Jordan. Falafel is frequently served for breakfast. This is deep fried, ground-up chickpeas and fava beans in the shape of balls. These balls are wrapped in pita bread and topped with anything from pickled vegetables to hot sauce, depending on what you're in the mood for. Breakfast is usually served with a hot bowl of *fuul,* which is boiled fava beans mashed with lemon juice, chopped chilies, and olive oil.

In Jordan, we generally eat far healthier than typical Americans do. When we slaughter an animal, according to Muslim law, it needs to be alive and healthy. The animal's throat needs to be cut by a very sharp knife, severing the carotid artery, jugular vein, and windpipe in one swipe. The blood must be completely drained from the animal. This makes it so there is no blood left in the meat. I can't eat meat from American grocery stores because the animal is handled differently and there is blood still in it.

In the beginning, I would take Evanna to McDonald's or Burger King in an attempt to make her feel more comfortable. She would object to this every time. She said she had eaten that type of stuff all her life. She wanted to change, and she wanted to eat healthier. Her favorite places to get food were the shawarma stands that populated my country. Shawarma sandwiches usually were made with lamb meat, but occasionally you could find places that served them with chicken. Plenty of Americans who come to Jordan end up regretting that they don't have the shawarma sandwiches in the States.

When Evanna and I would go shopping, shop owners would frequently refuse to allow her to pay. She would ask why, and they would tell her it was because she was American. Evanna often found herself dumbfounded and overwhelmed by this. She felt they were being more respectful than she deserved.

"Why are people so nice to me?" she would ask me. "In America, I am nothing, just a girl who works at Subway. Nobody cares. Here they treat me like a big celebrity." Increasingly, she was feeling like she really didn't want to return to the United States.

During the three months that Evanna and my father were on vacation in Jordan, Evanna and I spent a lot of time together. She started to teach me English. She turned out to be my first English teacher.

"He's getting good," my father commented at one point. "Almost ready to come to the United States." He had a teasing tone.

* * * * *

Evanna and I were both aware that her vacation was coming to an end soon. Any day I wasn't working, we would go out to restaurants, night clubs or just go on the long evening walks that I loved so much. Over time, my English was improving. Eventually, I was even able to articulate the intense joy I experienced from looking up at the night sky.

Near the end of her three-month vacation, Evanna realized that she loved life in Jordan and she wanted to stay. She had lost interest in going back to live in the United States, with its faster pace of life. Besides, she said that in the United States, she felt as though she was largely ignored by others and seen as a "nobody." In Jordan, she felt as though she was treated like a princess.

Without talking to me first, Evanna decided to speak to my father. Later, I was informed about how that talk went.

"Can I talk to you?" Evanna asked my father, who was reading a book at the time. My father glanced at her through his reading glasses. He put the book down and took off his glasses.

"Of course, Evanna. What would you like to discuss?" he asked kindly.

"I have an idea that I want to talk to your son about…," she said tentatively. My father's eyebrows rose as he looked at her. He was clearly curious, but waited for her to continue talking. "I don't want to go back to America," Evanna said, glancing more toward the ground than at my father.

"And why is that?" my father asked.

"I love it here. I think I'd be very happy here," she answered.

"And what does this desire have to do with my son?" he asked.

"I want to suggest that Adam and I get married," she said quietly.

My father couldn't keep the surprise off his face. He was stunned into silence. For a moment, all that could be heard in the room was the sound of a ticking clock. He let out a long sigh and stood up from his chair. He began to pace, still not quite breaking the silence, as he struggled to come up with a response. He finally turned to her.

"I don't know how to say this without being unkind…," my father started.

"Just say what you think," Evanna patiently responded.

"I think it's a bad idea," he said.

"Why?" Evanna asked, a look of hurt coming across her face.

"You are a good woman. I think highly of you. But you are not right for my son," he said with some difficulty.

"I see," Evanna said in response as she groped around for a chair to sit in. She felt a bit like she had been kicked in the stomach.

"You are at least ten years older than him. And because of your medical situation, you are not capable of having kids. I want my son to have kids, to experience the joy of being a father and all the wonders that come with that," he said, his voice filled with compassion. He hated saying these words, but he felt he must tell the truth about how he felt. "I want only the best for my son. I hope you can understand that."

There was another long silence, during which only the ticking clock could be heard. Evanna was gazing off into space, deep in thought.

"I didn't bring you here for this," he added.

"Then why did you bring me here? I thought this was what you wanted. You seemed to be setting us up to be lovers...," Evanna asked, confused.

My father considered her for a long time, almost questioning whether to give her an honest answer or not.

"No, I wasn't looking for you two to be lovers." My father shook his head.

"Then why?" Evanna asked.

"I brought you here so you can see Jordan," my father started. "And I was hoping he would learn from you, that you being here would inspire him to learn English. I've made no secret that I want him with me in America," he remarked. There was another long painful pause that eventually was broken by Evanna.

"I still want to do it. I love your son, and I want to stay here," Evanna said, her voice sounding hoarse and demonstrating a hint of the physical effort it took to say those words.

"You will do as your heart tells you. Everybody does. And maybe everyone should go by what their heart says. But you have asked for my opinion, and I have given it. I think it's a mistake," my father responded.

My father returned to his chair, put on his glasses, and returned to reading his book. The message was unmistakable. As far as he was concerned, there was nothing else that needed to be said.

* * * * *

I was in my bedroom, putting clothes away, when I heard a knock at my open door. I turned to see Evanna standing at my door. I smiled and quickly made my way toward her. I gave her a big hug and a kiss on the cheek.

"How are you?" I asked.

"I'm good. There's something I want to talk to you about...," she began.

"What's up?" I asked.

"Can we sit?" she asked, pointing to the bed. I did as she asked, looking at her curiously. "I love Jordan," she began.

"And Jordan loves you," I said happily.

"I don't want to leave," she said.

"You plan to stay?" I asked.

"I wish to," Evanna said simply.

"Where would you go? Where would you stay?" I asked, somewhat befuddled.

"Well, it was my hope that I would stay here with you. I hoped I wouldn't go anywhere," she said, biting her lip nervously. "I'd stay here and be your wife." The words stunned me, and I felt my heart beat speed up. I tried to speak, but only air came out. Every moment I said nothing only increased her tension.

"I would love you to be my wife," I said quietly. "But it isn't my desire to stay here forever." I paused. "Eventually, I'd like to join my family in the United States."

"We can do that," Evanna said hurriedly.

"But you don't wish to go back!"

"I wish to be wherever you are," Evanna replied.

"So this idea of marriage isn't just a way to stay in Jordan?" I asked cautiously.

"No. I love life in Jordan. But even more, I love life with you," she said with a bright smile. "I want to be wherever you are going."

I smiled at her and gave her a small kiss on the lips.

"One day I want to go to the United States to be a musician, a well-known one who makes a lot of money. You think I can do that?" I asked.

"I think you can do anything," she answered. "I think you're good enough to do very well there. In America the opportunities are limitless. The sky's the limit."

"You really think so?"

"I do," she responded. "In America, the stars will truly not be able to shine brighter than our future together." My smile brightened even more. I kissed her again, this time more passionately. She broke away, looking conflicted. "There is one problem…"

"What's that?" I asked, suddenly concerned.

"I told your father what I intended. He disapproves," she continued with a glimmer of a tear in her eyes. She hoped that my father's disagreement wouldn't stop me from doing this. I nodded at her and looked away for a moment.

"I will talk to him…"

* * * * *

"Father…," I said as I entered the study.

My father was sitting at the desk, writing in a notebook. He looked up, his face expressionless. "I trust you have talked to Evanna" was all he said.

"I have," I answered. "I would like to understand your objections. She didn't tell me much."

He let out a long sigh before putting his pen down and standing up. He approached me slowly. "I don't know if she told you about her medical condition. If she hasn't told you, I won't. That's not for me to share. What I will tell you is she isn't capable of having children," he said as he put his hands on my shoulder.

"I don't care," I replied genuinely with a shrug.

"That may be how you feel now, but feelings change. In the future, you might find that you intensely desire children. You can't with this woman. She's older than you, and she can't have children. She is a fine woman but not good enough for you," my father said.

"I disagree. I love her, Dad," I spoke quietly, respectfully.

"You love her? How can you be so sure of that after so little time?" my father asked.

"I feel it. I feel it in my soul," I responded. "I feel like this is right, like this is destiny."

"You are only fooling yourself, son," my father responded, shaking his head.

"I want to marry her, Father," I stated with vigor.

"I have lived long enough to know you won't listen to me." He laughed. It wasn't a joyful laugh. "You will do as you want regardless of what I say." He started to make his way to the exit of the study as I watched him go. "This is a mistake, son. I fear you will see it for yourself one day, at great cost," he finished sadly before leaving the study.

I was left there alone to contemplate his words.

* * * * *

My father kept to himself for most of the rest of his vacation. He didn't speak much to either Evanna or me as we planned our wedding. I was worried that my choice to marry Evanna would adversely and permanently affect my relationship with my father.

A Muslim wedding celebration can go on for a full week and can be very expensive. My family was neither poor nor superrich. Evanna and I decided to cut the wedding celebration to a single day. We decided to have the festivities in a local hotel. This decision was more about the availability of the people we wanted to attend than it was about the money. Three hundred of our friends and family were invited. Most of the family that I had in Jordan agreed to attend. The ones that resided in the United States declined to do so.

* * * * *

We booked a suite for the party at the Holiday Inn in Amman. The band we hired was somewhat inexpensive, thanks to the connections that I had built in my performing career. I was tempted to be the entertainment myself, but Evanna objected. It was my day to enjoy, not to work. There was singing and dancing and plenty of amazingly good food.

Jordanian weddings have taken on some western traditions, including brides wearing white dresses. Evanna looked especially lovely, dancing around and laughing in her beautiful white dress. From a distance, I smiled as I watched her dancing with pure joy. I was interrupted from this deep concentration by a hand on my shoulder. I turned to see my longtime friend Sharaf.

"You are a married man now." He chuckled at me. "How does it feel?"

"Wonderful! Terrifying!" I laughed.

"Sounds about right." Sharaf laughed. "You did well for yourself, my friend. She is a good woman!"

"You're right," I replied, beaming with pride as I watched Evanna cheerfully dance to the Arabic music.

"I envy you," Sharaf said.

"Oh?" I asked, curiously.

"You're at the beginning of the journey. Soon will come kids and a new exciting family," Sharaf said with a hint of wistfulness. "I miss the days when my family was new."

"Right. A new beginning," I echoed, declining to mention that there would be no biological children in this marriage. In Muslim law, adoption was legal. But the child was not truly considered to be your child in the Islamic view. The child kept the name of his or her biological parents. If I stayed with Evanna for the rest of my life, there wasn't really a chance to pass on the Noor name. I didn't worry so much about this as I did have brothers that could potentially carry the burden of keeping the name going.

I found myself standing next to Sharaf in silence, just watching the celebration around us. I glanced at him and noticed his eyes were a bit watery. There is nothing like a wedding to stir up the emotions. The feeling that life was moving on. That time was passing by. It was quite possible that this would be one of the last times everyone that was in attendance would be in the same room together.

As I looked around the room, taking in the faces of my family and friends, I found myself seeing a face that surprised me. It was the elder visage of my father. He was dancing around with some of his nieces and nephews, while they laughed in delight. On impulse and instinct, I found myself drifting in his direction. When he noticed me approaching, he reached out and gave me a big hug.

"Father! I didn't think you'd be here," I said, my voice filled with emotion.

"Of course! How could I miss the wedding of my eldest son?" he announced, beaming with pride.

"So you're not mad at me?" I asked.

"Mad? No!" he said simply as he pulled away from the hug.

"So you don't think this is a mistake any longer?" I asked.

"My opinion hasn't changed," he said gravely. "But if this is what you think will make you happy, then I support you. I hope I am proven wrong. Life is too short. We have to grab any chance at happiness." He paused and looked down at his nieces and nephews. All were urging that he join them again in dancing. "Now if you'll excuse me, my audience awaits! I believe you know the feeling," he said with a teasing gleam in his eye. Without a further word, he danced away, delighting in the sounds of happy children.

I looked from him back into the crowd, hoping to catch a glimpse of my wife. I finally did so, and I smiled. Life was good. Life was promising.

* * * * *

I enjoyed married life very much. The first year of our marriage was spent in Jordan. Evanna loved going out. But she might have loved it too much! It seemed as though we might have been going out every night. When I was working, she would come and watch me perform my music. When I wasn't, we would go to the clubs, go out to eat, or (not often enough) just take the long walks that I loved so much, just admiring the beautiful night sky and dreaming about our bright future.

As time went on, it became apparent that I was spending too much money. Evanna continued to want to go out every night. I couldn't quite afford to do so. Of course, I didn't tell her that, wanting to keep her happy. I started to think that it would be easier to keep up with the spending habits of my wife if we were living in the United States. My dad had continued to urge me to join him in America. I remembered that my dad had warned me that the years had a tendency to disappear.

After a year of marriage, I made a decision. I came to the conclusion that now was as good a time as any to finally make the leap and fulfill my dream of coming to the United States. I was going to be like many Jordanian men before me who had successfully become well-known Arabic performers in America.

CHAPTER 3

I was finally coming to the United States, joining my father, who had already been here for ten years! So in 1999, I arrived at JFK airport, ready to start my brand-new life. Our first stop in New York was to visit one of my brothers. Although my father lived in Massachusetts, he traveled to New York to accompany my brother to greet me. When I saw my father, I gave him a big hug as he welcomed me to the United States.

If there was any lingering anger at my decision to marry Evanna, he showed no sign of it. Upon our arrival, he was very nice to both of us. He was very excited to finally see me in the United States! I hadn't seen him this animated in years. He acted like our tour guide, showing us all over Manhattan and other parts of the city.

All my life, I had seen pictures of the Statue of Liberty. But as is typically the case, seeing the pictures did not do the statue true justice. Seeing the statue in person, I was overwhelmed with emotion. Standing next to my brother, father, and wife as we looked up at the Statue of Liberty, tears of joy flooded my eyes.

I'm really here, I told myself. But this fact didn't quite click into place until I looked at the giant statue with the green tint. Land of the free, home of the brave, where anyone could make themselves into something. I had no doubt that I would make myself into something big, that I would be the famous musician in America that I so yearned to be, the place where I believed my dreams were finally going to come true. My wife took my hand and gave it a gentle squeeze. It didn't feel like real life. It felt very much like I was living in a movie. Within five years, thanks to being married to Evanna, I would become an American citizen. I was utterly overwhelmed with emotion as tears continued to stream down my cheeks, moistening my new shirt.

* * * * *

My sister lived in New York, so my wife, my brother, and I went to visit her. I was hungry to see more of New York. I greeted my sister, whom I hadn't seen in a very long time, with a big hug. She gave my wife an equally big hug, happy to meet the woman she had heard so much about.

"It's nice to finally meet you," my sister said as she continued to embrace my wife.

"Likewise," Evanna said cheerfully.

We decided to travel into Manhattan, taking the subway. I was excitedly looking around, trying to take in all the sounds and sights of my new country. My eventual state of residence, Massachusetts, would turn out to be very different from New York. But at this time, I didn't know that. We walked in the streets of Manhattan, watching the countless people walking about and cars driving by, hearing the honking of the various cars and the sound of running engines. Smoke rose from the ground, seemingly from nowhere. Every now and again, you would hear loud music being played. It was overwhelming! All the activity going on around me!

I made several attempts to greet various strangers. But for the most part, they gave me a look and kept on walking. At first, I felt a little snubbed. But eventually I grew to accept that this was just how New Yorkers (and indeed Americans) were at times. They weren't as friendly as people in Jordan tended to be.

The stores were awe-inspiring because of how massive and spacious they were compared to the stores in Jordan. I hadn't been there long, but I was in love. I was in love with the United States.

I remember going to the Central Park Zoo for the first time. We spent an entire day walking around and seeing animals that I had not seen before. Elephants! How massive! Lions! Most impressive with their attractive golden mane! I found myself imagining, while eying the big cat as it licked its paw, that if it were to get out, that it would hunt me down with ease and enjoy eating me. Being so close to it was a scary and thrilling experience.

* * * * *

Eventually, I joined my father in Massachusetts. My wife and I lived with my dad for a while before eventually getting our own apartment in Meriden. I immediately jumped into action, trying to jumpstart my music career. I went to various auditions in Massachusetts but wasn't really making much headway. Massachusetts wasn't really where I wanted to perform in the end anyway. I wanted to perform in the big cities of Manhattan or Las Vegas, the big famous cities where other popular singers from Jordan eventually ended up.

I came to realize that the money I had was not going to last me and my wife forever. My dad was a generous man who would certainly help me. But I didn't want to be a burden to him. I had to get a job while I waited for my music career to take off. A temporary job might even help me achieve my goals by enabling me to save enough money to invest in my career.

I applied to a bunch of places around the Meriden area and beyond. I went to interview after interview, only to be told no. Eventually, I got a call from a local gas station. I was dressed in dress slacks, a white shirt, and a tie as I entered the spacious gas station. I fidgeted with my tie as I walked up to the cashier, a cute young girl.

"Excuse me. My name is Adam Noor. I'm here to speak to your boss. I have an interview today," I said somewhat nervously.

"Oh!" the cashier said with a chirpy, cheerful-sounding voice. "He's expecting you. Go on back." She pointed at a swinging door. I reluctantly made my way through the doors. I saw an office beyond the doors with an older white man sitting at his desk. He looked up when he noticed me coming through.

"Mr. Noor's son?" he asked. I nodded in agreement and surprise. He came out of the office to shake my hand. "I'm Mr. Peterson. I know your father quite well. He's the only reason I'm talking to you today," he said sternly.

"Yes, my father's a good man," I replied.

"Yes, he is. Come take a seat with me," the older man said as he started walking back toward the office. "I won't lie. Your lack of experience working here in this country makes me concerned," he said as he indicated for me to take a seat in front of his desk.

"Yes, sir. I just got here. All my working experience is out of this country," I answered honestly.

"And you were some sort of singer in Jordan?" he asked, sounding curious.

"Yes. I sing and perform," I answered. "If you like, I could sing for you." My voice raised a bit.

"No. That's okay." He chuckled. "Singing will not be a part of your job description here." He paused. "So tell me, Mr. Noor, why should I hire you?"

"Well, I am a very hardworking man. I'll be your hardest worker," I said. "And I'm very"—I paused, searching for the word—"punctual."

"Those are very important things," Mr. Peterson retorted. "Listen, I have great respect for your father. But I'm just not sure this will work out…"

"Please give me a chance," I chimed in urgently. "I just need a chance to make money, to achieve my dreams. I want to be a successful musician here in the US."

Mr. Peterson eyed me for a while. A long unbearable while passed before I heard him speak again.

"I may regret this," he mused, "but when you are that famous musician, I hope you won't forget me." He laughed and stuck out his hand.

"Forget you? No way!" I said happily.

"Welcome to the team. I trust you can start Monday?" Mr. Peterson asked.

"Of course! Of course. I'll be here Monday." I gave Mr. Peterson a big hug and quickly left, not giving him an opportunity to change his mind. *My first job in America*, I thought as I left the building, beaming with pride.

* * * * *

They loved me at the gas station. I would work any hours they asked of me, and I would do whatever tasks they needed to have done, without complaining. It wasn't long before I was racking up "employee of the month" awards. People were constantly calling out, and I was repeatedly agreeing to come in. There were weeks in which I was working seventy to eighty hours at multiple gas stations within the same company. I was practically glued to my phone, waiting for a call from them. This was back in the day before cell phones were the norm. All I had was a landline. It was like I was a teenager in love, waiting for a call from whomever I was in love with at that time. I was easily Mr. Peterson's favorite employee. He definitely did not regret hiring me. If there was a common trait among Noor men, it was a strong, hard work ethic. My coworkers thought of me as a freak of nature because I was always cheerful, and I never seemed to get tired. I got the impression that some of these coworkers were also making fun of me for my poor English. But this never bothered me, and I never said anything about it. I was finally in America, earning money. Given where I had come from, I appreciated this job more than my American counterparts did.

When I wasn't working I was either practicing my music, going to auditions, or going on road trips to see more of my new home country.

On one such occasion, I went to New Hampshire with Larry, a friend I had made at work. Larry was a forty-year-old man who wanted to show me his cabin on Mount Adams. He told me that he would go there once a year. When he did, he left his cell phone, TV, and computers behind. Larry was an avid hunter, and for his weekend jaunts to New Hampshire, he would rely on his skills to survive. Larry's philosophy was that all people should have this kind of experience during their lives. With mankind becoming more and more dependent on technology, it was good to get back to the basics every once in a while.

This trip was my first real encounter with snow. In Jordan, it snows but not like it does in the northeastern part of the US. In Jordan, it's like a dusting. It isn't the multiple feet of snow that can come down in America. I loved the sight of snow as it fell, and I loved seeing snow before it had a chance to be plowed or shoveled. I occasionally heard Americans complaining about the cold and snow, but it honestly never bothered me. I love summertime. But the cold, snowy season always makes me feel more alive. I also learned that I loved autumn in New England. Watching the leaves change colors from summertime green to the kaleidoscope of fall colors is a beautiful experience.

Larry and I stayed in the cabin, drinking hot chocolate, sitting by the fire, and talking for hours. We talked about anything and everything. I started to see what my friend was talking about regarding people being lost in devices and technology and forgetting the simple pleasures of connecting with another human being. At one point, while we were playing a card game called Go Fish, Larry looked up at me pensively.

"So there's a rumor going around…," he began.

"A rumor?" I asked, quizzically.

"People are saying that you are quite the singer," Larry said.

"They're saying that?" I asked, surprised that anyone knew I sang.

"Mr. Peterson mentioned it," Larry offered.

"Oh yes. He knows about that. Yes, I want to be a musician here," I answered.

"The acoustics here are excellent," Larry remarked.

"I doubt it," I shot back.

"Okay, maybe not. But you should let me hear what you got," he said.

"You want me to sing for you?" I asked, flattered and a little nervous.

"Why not? We got time to kill," Larry said.

I sat and thought about this before deciding to stand up. Then I sang one of my favorite Arabic songs. In a flash, my voice filled the space. Many would describe my singing voice as soft and filled with emotion. When I was done, I nervously looked at him.

"You, my friend, are going places," he said, sounding impressed.

"You think so?" I asked giddily.

"Absolutely! With a voice like that, you can't lose." He paused. "Too bad they don't have an Arabic American Idol TV show," he finished jokingly.

"You think people would watch that?" I asked, almost as if I was seriously thinking of creating such a show.

"Have you seen the marvelous shows on television?" Larry said, his voice dripping with sarcasm. "Americans will watch anything!"

After three days in the wilderness, it was quite a shock to return to reality, a world dominated by cell phones and computers. When I got home, I made a resolution to occasionally take a trip like the one I had just taken with my friend, to get back to basics.

* * * * *

"Your dad called," Evanna announced as I entered the house after my shift at the gas station. I was still dressed in my work clothes when I came home, carrying some mail in my hand.

"What about?" I asked absentmindedly.

"He didn't say. But he wanted us to go over there when you got out of work," she said with a shrug. Since coming to America, I really hadn't spent much time with my father. I saw him every day for only about a half hour. Like me, he worked a lot. *Too much*, I thought.

"So I suppose he wants us to come over now?" I asked, sounding amused.

"I suppose," Evanna giggled and gave me a peck on the cheek.

* * * * *

Evanna and I didn't live far from my dad, so we decided to walk. The air was crisp and cold. We walked close together for warmth. Her arm was wrapped firmly in mine, and her hand was close to my chest. It made walking a bit awkward, but it felt cozy. The heavy coats, scarves, and gloves seemed like no match for the cold. I didn't mind the cold, but Evanna hated it. Despite the years she had lived in New England, she could never adjust to the cold.

As we drew closer to my dad's house, I noticed an unfamiliar car in the driveway. I assumed it belonged to one of his friends. My dad must have spotted us, because as we approached his home, he opened the door and walked outside. He wasn't wearing a jacket but seemed unaffected by the cold.

"Hey, Dad. You have some friends over?" I asked, pointing my elbow toward the car.

"No, son. No friends. Just you two. More than enough company for an old man like me," my dad answered with a twinkle in his eyes. As we walked closer to the car, I noticed that it seemed only a few years old.

"Whose car?" I asked.

"Oh! The car. You noticed that!" my dad said jovially.

"Is it yours?" I asked. "Didn't think you were looking to get a new one."

"No, son. I realized I never gave you a real wedding present. So here it is," my father said, beaming at me.

"You're giving me a car?" I gasped, my eyes raised in disbelief.

"Yes, son, I am," he said, grinning from ear to ear.

"This is my car?" I asked again, not really believing what I was hearing.

"Yes," my dad responded, sounding a bit exasperated.

I looked it over, processing that this car was mine, considering all the ways it would make my life easier, especially during my hunt for musical opportunities. There was just one problem.

"Guess I'm going to need to learn how to drive."

* * * * *

My father didn't feel comfortable with the idea of teaching me to drive. So I enlisted the help of my friend, Larry. He was more than happy to help me out. As we sat in my car, I was both very excited and extremely nervous. Larry was quick to pick up on this.

"Relax. You'll do fine," he said. But he was only mildly effective with his reassurances. With my foot on the break, I slowly pulled the shift into drive. "Now, ease off the break a little bit…," he instructed.

I did so…and the car started to move. But this made me nervous, and I quickly slammed my foot back on the break, resulting in a huge jerking motion of the car. Now Larry looked a little nervous.

"Sorry," I said, smiling at him sheepishly.

"It's okay," Larry responded, a little less calmly. "Try again. Remember, just one smooth motion." I once again let my foot off the break, and we moved a bit further. But once again, I panicked, clamping down on the break, a bit softer this time. The jolt wasn't quite as strong when we came to a stop. I repeated this pattern again and again until we were in the road.

Larry shook his head. "Congrats. You are now driving on the road, and we aren't dead," he said, sounding amused.

"Am I doing well?" I asked.

"About as good as my sixteen-year-old son did," he said dryly.

"Is that good?" I asked, uncertain.

"You could use some improvement…"

* * * * *

Before long, I was driving like a pro, and my life became much easier. I no longer needed to get rides to work from my wife or anyone else. And going to auditions was far less challenging. As a result, I went to many more of them. I wasn't getting any breaks, but I was enjoying playing for people. This felt like progress, a reason for hope. My ultimate goal was to perform in Manhattan. While I was waiting for my break, I was doing a good job saving the money that my wife and I would need to enable us to eventually move there.

Now since I was spending most of my time going to auditions and working, there began to be tension in my marriage. Evanna started feeling angry at me for working so much. I kept telling her that it was for the greater good, that eventually I'd achieve my dreams and all the hours I was putting in would pay off. At times she seemed to understand. But this didn't stop her from getting mad at me and starting fights over it.

The tension rapidly progressed to such intensity that I began to go to a bar after work instead of going straight home. When I would arrive home several hours later, inebriated, Evanna would become even more enraged.

But one such outing proved to be nearly life-changing. I invited Larry to join me at a bar, making him a co-conspirator in avoiding my wife. The bar was dark and dank, filled with smoke, and populated by grumpy older men.

"You doing anything this Tuesday?" Larry asked me as he sucked down his beer.

"Not scheduled to work. Doesn't mean I won't. Why?" I asked curiously.

"I have a friend I want you to meet," Larry answered cryptically.

"If it's a girl, I'm already married," I said as a gulped down more of my beer. This was at least my third drink. "At least I am now...," I finished with a bitter tinge.

"It's not a girl." Larry laughed. "Just someone I think you'd enjoy meeting. Wouldn't kill you to not be available to work for once either."

I looked at Larry questioningly. I was tempted to ask him more questions, but I knew I wouldn't get any more answers.

"Sure. Fine. Tuesday it is," I said somewhat indifferently. Larry clapped me on the shoulder and took another big swig of his drink. We spent most of the rest of the time in that bar in total silence.

* * * * *

Tuesday came, and I found myself in Larry's car driving up to a huge house. It was practically a mansion. Whoever Larry's friend was, he had a lot of money. I was in awe of the extravagance. As I was looking around, I noticed a lot of musical instruments around the living room. I also noticed a beautiful deck and an Olympic-sized pool. Suddenly, I felt the sharp pain of Larry elbowing me in the side. When I looked up, I noticed a grey haired man in front of me. Clearly, I had been in some sort of daze.

"Hi," I said to the man who was smiling at me somewhat stiffly. "Sorry, I was just amazed..."

"Frankie Soprano. I had that reaction too when I was told I could buy this place," the man chuckled as he offered me his hand. "So you're a friend of Larry's?"

"Yes. I work with him…," I answered distractedly. "You play music?" I pointed to the instruments that littered the place.

"I used to play. Not anymore. I'm a full-time agent now. Turns out it's much more lucrative," the man said cheerfully.

"I'm sorry…an agent?" I asked, having never heard the word before.

"I help musicians with their careers," Mr. Soprano answered. "I understand you are a musician. That's what Larry tells me anyway." He paused for a moment. My jaw dropped a little as I listened. "Tells me that you have quite the voice," he finished, walking farther away from me.

"Larry is kind" was all I could say, finding myself in shock.

"I understand that you don't wish to work at a gas station for the rest of your life, that you came to this country to do more. I can probably help you with that." Mr. Soprano smiled.

"I would appreciate that, sir," I answered enthusiastically.

"Just one favor," he requested. "Sing something for me. I want to get an idea of your talent." Then he folded his arms, waiting.

My mind quickly went through the catalogue of songs in my head. Once I made my choice, I boldly dived in headfirst. I was feeling good. As I sang, my voice seemingly filled the entirety of Mr. Soprano's big house. All throughout my audition, his arms remained folded and his facial expression never wavered from neutral. In fact, I had no clue about whether or not he liked what he was hearing. When I was done, I found that my heart was beating about a million times per second. Still, he didn't say anything for a while.

Then abruptly, he asserted, "You, sir…are excellent. Larry, I should give you a finder's fee for bringing this man to me."

"I wouldn't refuse that," Larry enthusiastically replied.

"Should…but I probably won't," Mr. Soprano retorted. Larry merely shrugged, not seeming to be all that surprised. Mr. Soprano turned to me and once again shook my hand. "You and I are going to make some serious money together!"

"You think so?" I asked as a rush of adrenaline coursed through my veins. I was trying very hard to remain cool and not jump out of my skin.

"I know so! You like this house? Because it won't be long before you're living in one just like it."

"Yes, I love this house!" I crooned.

"Think you can take a little time off this weekend? I'm planning a trip to New Jersey to visit with some of my clients, and you should come along," Mr. Soprano exclaimed.

"Sure! I'm sure I can get time off!" I replied.

"Excellent!" Mr. Soprano clapped his hands together. "Do you drink? Because frankly this is a time to celebrate!" he said and started making his way over to his mini bar. He poured me a drink and I gratefully accepted, having absolutely no clue about what it was. The three of us toasted. As our glasses clinked, I excitedly wondered if this was finally the beginning. Could my dream finally be coming true?

* * * * *

I drove to New Jersey with Mr. Soprano. Getting the time off was easier than I thought it was going to be. Mr. Peterson had been aware of my desire to eventually move on with my singing career. And he didn't stand in the way of my major opportunity. We met up with five relatively well-known professional Arabic musicians in a local recording studio. While I didn't know any of them personally, I was familiar with one of them who was from Jordan. Abdulla Ghani acted like he was the leading musician of the group.

"You're from Jordan? Really? Miss that place. Whereabouts?" Abdulla asked me.

"Amman," I answered.

"Nice, man. I knew a lot of people there. I wasn't far away. I'm from Al Karak."

"I played in some night clubs there," I said with a raised eyebrow.

"Me too," Abdulla responded with a wide smile. "So what's your thing?"

"I play almost everything, but I'm mainly a singer," I answered.

"All right. We should start with that. Are you familiar with 'Quds Al Atika'?"

"Of course!" I replied excitedly. I began to sing, and the rest of the musicians played their instruments of choice. We played for four or five hours, but it seemed like only minutes. It felt like I was finally making it in America.

* * * * *

After we were done jamming, we decided to have dinner at a famous establishment in New Jersey named Club Aladdin. This was where all the top Arabic performers played. Upon entering, I was immediately in awe of the atmosphere. It was like a little piece of home. Flashing strobe lights and Arabic music filling the space. It was alive with activity and young people dancing. The seven of us (Mr. Soprano, the five musicians, and me) sat at a rather large booth, eating and laughing together.

As I sat there, I thought, *These men could really become my friends.*

"Do you know how much a typical singer gets paid to sing in this club?" Abdulla asked me.

"Nope," I answered with a shrug.

"Three thousand dollars…a night," Abdulla answered. I was impressed.

"That could be you. Easily," Mr. Soprano chimed in.

"You have the talent," Abdulla agreed.

"Where the heck have you been hiding all this time?" Mr. Soprano mused aloud.

"I haven't been hiding. I swear!" I answered. Mr. Soprano laughed, and I looked at him, confused.

"It's an American expression, Adam," he said, answering my unspoken question. "It means, why hasn't a talent such of yours already been discovered?" He paused. "Just my luck, I guess."

"Can you move to New Jersey? Would your wife be okay with that?" Abdulla asked me seriously.

"Absolutely! I'm sure she'd love it here," I said without hesitation. But truthfully, the mention of my wife's name at that moment inspired more dread.

"When can you move here?" Mr. Soprano asked.

"I'm not sure...," I answered uncertainly.

"Next week?"

"No, sir," I replied, somewhat alarmed. "I mean I would love to, but my mom is currently on vacation in Jordan for a month. I can't leave my dad right now," I answered.

"So one month then?" Mr. Soprano pushed.

"Yes. I should be able to do that," I said. Mr. Soprano smiled, seemingly satisfied. Thanks to my friend Larry, I seemed to have finally hit the big time.

* * * * *

The day my life changed forever began like any other day. There was no indication of that day being different from any other. Unlike in the movies, there were no ominous warning signs and no scary music playing in the background. It was just an ordinary, boring day. At breakfast, I was actually getting along better with Evanna than I had in quite some time. It was more like it used to be. In retrospect, that was kind of like a very cruel and heartless joke played on me by the fates.

It was August 8, 2000. It was a Tuesday night. I was one week away from no longer working at the gas station. My mom was set to return to the US from Jordan and I was set to depart for greener pastures in New Jersey. During the month that I waited for my mom to return, I went back to working eighty hours a week at the gas station. Although I was excited, I was also saddened by the prospect of leaving Mr. Peterson and Larry behind.

It was past midnight, in the very early hours of the morning, when Evanna called me at work to start an argument. The tone of our conversation had become conflictual, unlike the way it had briefly been the previous morning.

"I don't understand why you're still working so much," Evanna complained over the phone, her voice filled with irritation.

"We need the money," I protested.

"What for? Soon, you're going to be rolling in it. You don't need to be working this much," Evanna angrily replied.

"I want to," I responded, having not really thought through my words. "Evanna, it's only for one more week. Then everything is going to change."

At about this moment, a rather large man entered the store. He was muscular and tattooed. Upon seeing this man, he made no particular impression on me. The irony of glimpsing the man that would forever change my life was that I initially felt relief to see him walk through the door. As a customer, he was an excuse to stop talking to my wife. I told my wife to hold on and I put the phone receiver down. I greeted the customer in my typical friendly and welcoming way. He merely grunted.

"Newport 100s," he said, his voice cold and unfriendly. I reached above my head to get the cigarettes. Suddenly, a cascade of events began to unfold that would permanently change my life. I felt a sudden, sharp pain in my face. I felt myself falling backwards into the wall behind me. My head violently collided with the wall, and I felt horrendous pain in my back. When I looked up, I was stunned and alarmed to see that he was pointing a gun directly at my face. I was disoriented and totally confused. My heart beat a mile a minute, and I had to try very hard to concentrate and figure out what was going on.

"Give me your fucking money," the man said, his voice filled with cold, hard menace. In that moment, I didn't understand what was going on. My head throbbed, and my mind was cloudy.

"I SAID GIVE ME YOUR MONEY!" he yelled again louder and shoved the gun even closer to my face. At this point, he was so agitated that be began swearing at me, terrifying me even further. Panicked and not really thinking, I quickly reached into my pocket and handed my wallet to him. He threw my wallet against the floor, his face registering anger and disgust.

"I WANT WHAT'S IN THE DRAWER! DON'T GET CUTE WITH ME!"

"I…don't…know…how…," I stammered, my voice shaky and filled with fear.

"You don't know how?" he hissed, more quietly then before. This was somehow even more frightening. He pushed the gun up against my cheek. "Are you telling me you want to die right now? Is that it? You want to die?"

"No! I don't want to die!" I said, tears forming in my eyes. My voice was pleading and filled with fear.

"Then open the drawer now!" he barked. Then the man noticed a voice coming from the nearby phone that I had set down. It was the voice of my wife, worriedly calling my name. "Who the hell is that!" he asked me angrily. When I didn't immediately answer, he demanded again, "Who the hell is that!"

"My wife! It's my wife!" I yelled back, practically sobbing.

"Hang up the phone!" he commanded. I quickly complied. "Now open the drawer before I blow a hole in your head!"

I stood there, doing nothing, just staring at him. My heart now beat so loudly that it felt as though my eardrums were about to explode. My hands were sweating. I couldn't think. I was literally frozen with fear. I couldn't concentrate well enough to remember how to do something as simple as opening the drawer of the cash register and handing him the money. I did the only thing that came into my mind at that moment. I tried to run.

I moved quickly, trying to get to the door. Just as quickly, the man swung his gun into the back of my skull, causing me to fly to the floor. My head lit up with unbearable pain. This pain was so severe that the pain in the rest of my body as I collided violently with the floor barely registered.

"You stupid moron!" he yelled, kicking me in the stomach. The kick was so hard, the pain so intense that I was barely able to breathe for several seconds. The pain nearly caused to me to vomit, and I coughed loudly. "All you had to do was open the damn drawer!" he screamed, barely intelligible to me at that moment. He gave me another hard, painful kick to the stomach, sending spasms of pain throughout my abdomen. He tried to kick me again, but this time I grabbed his foot, trying to stop him. I tried with all my might to pull him to the floor. But he barely budged an inch. He violently yanked his foot away from my hands.

Then the man picked me up with seemingly no effort. He hurled me violently against the wall. I thought for sure that this was the end for me. That I was going to die here on the gas station floor. Everything I had done to try to achieve my dreams, for naught. My life up to that point was rendered completely moot and meaningless, ended by a single random violent encounter with a man whom I had never before seen.

The man stuck his foot against my neck. It became hard to breathe. I choked and fought futilely for air. I tried to get him off of me, but I was no match for his strength. He released the pressure from my neck after what seemed like an eternity. The sudden availability of air in my lungs was almost painful. I gasped and coughed and wheezed. He picked me up once more and slammed me against the wall, shoving the gun into my mouth. I tasted the metal of the gun and gagged.

"You got any kids?" he asked, with quiet menace. I couldn't talk with the gun shoved in my mouth, so I shook my head from side to side. "A wife. No kids. Just one person to miss you."

I wondered what was taking him so long. Why didn't he just pull the trigger and end my life right then and there? End it as I knew he was going to. In my mind, I begged for that last kindness from a man who showed me nothing but heartless cruelty. My heart and mind raced. My breathing was unbearable and shallow. Every part of my body ached. I just wanted it to be over. I just wanted him to end it. I barely noticed that he was tying me up against one of the shelves.

"Lie down on your stomach and kiss the floor," he demanded. I did as I was instructed without comment. I barely had the strength to keep myself upright any longer anyway. "Close your eyes," he said. And I did so. Only my arm stayed up, as it was tied by a rope to the shelf. Then, I heard footsteps moving away from me. I heard the sound of the drawer opening. And just as quickly as the man had arrived, he vanished. I just lay there, coughing and bleeding.

My mind went in and out of consciousness. The cold, hard darkness briefly claimed me…

* * * * *

How long has it been? Where am I?

My mind faded in, and I could see flashing lights that resembled the strobes I had so often seen in Arabic clubs. It wasn't those lights, however. My mind faded out and then back in. There were men standing over me.

Who are they? Where did they come from? Where am I?

My mind slowly faded to black again. It faded back in. I caught glimpses of my environment. I seemed to be at the gas station, but I did not know why. I was on the floor, but I did not know why.

Where am I? Who are these people?

"Sir. Do you know who you are?" I hear one of the voices speak to me, barely audible above the sound of my heartbeat.

"Adam," I answer, though I couldn't be sure I had spoken.

"Do you know where you are?" he asked.

"No…," I answer, confused. My mind goes fuzzy and black once more. I still barely hear the sounds of talking. I once again find the world coming back into view.

"Can you tell me about the guy that did this to you?" a man asked me.

"No…," I answer once again. I can barely remember anything that happened to me, never mind the man who did this to me. My mind once again fades to black.

* * * * *

"Are you comfortable enough to take him?" I hear a siren. Brief flashes of light. Random words. I can no longer make sense of any of it, sound and fury signifying nothing.

* * * * *

Where am I? How did I get here?

I could see darkness with streaking lights. I couldn't make sense of the images I see. Through the darkness, I glimpsed my father. He was driving, driving a car.

Why am I in a car? Where am I? How did I get here?

I heard myself laughing. I didn't know why. My father was trying to talk to me. I could see his lips move, but I couldn't hear what he was saying. All I could hear was the sound of ringing in my ears.

"Where am I? How did I get here?" I screamed. I did not know why.

I moved my head and looked out the window and saw nothing but a blur moving past the window.

"Where am I? How did I get here?" I cried. I did not know why. It was nighttime. I could see the stars. They seemed less brilliant then I remembered.

Where am I? How did I get here?

CHAPTER 4

My eyes opened. I was blinded by a bright, white light. I couldn't see anything beyond the light. My eyes felt a searing pain. They blinked. When they opened again, I was hoping I would see more. Still I saw nothing. Was I dead? Had I actually died?

"Am I in heaven?" my voice strained to ask.

"Afraid not, Mr. Noor," I heard a distant and elderly sounding voice say.

"Hell?" My eyes started to clear a little. I could make out traces of people moving about. More moments went by and my senses started to come alive. I heard the faint sounds of beeping and the chattering of voices all around me. My eyes gave me more and more detail until I could make out the man standing directly in front of me. He was wearing a white coat and sporting a graying beard. He was a stocky fellow, of short stature. Nevertheless, his bearing suggested confidence. Although I had yet to encounter one in America, I knew what he was. A doctor.

"Opinions vary on that," the man's voice started. I looked around and saw a bunch of people moving around in the background. "I, myself, don't quite see this place as such," he finished. I tried to get my bearings. I looked around and took in the hustle and bustle of activity. I was vaguely aware of my father standing next to me, holding my hand. "Do you know where you are?"

"Hospital," I croaked, my voice sounding hoarse. "First time in an American hospital."

"Do you know who you are?" he asked, drawing closer.

For some reason, that question seemed much more difficult to answer. I looked inward at myself. My mind seemed foggy, unclear. Thoughts seemed much more sluggish and slow. The question I was just asked took far too long for me to answer. Something was very different. I didn't know what, but I was disturbed by it.

"Adam," I answered hoarsely. But that was all I could really recall. I only vaguely understood who I actually was. I felt my heart start to pound faster, as my nervousness grew. The monitors hooked up to me made note of this fact.

"Do you know why you are here?" he asked.

I fought hard to remember how I got there, but it didn't come easy. I saw half-remembered images flashing about in my mind. I could not make sense of any of them. Then suddenly, like a movie being projected into my mind, I was back in the gas station arguing with my wife.

* * * * *

A rather large man entered the store. He was muscular and tattooed. Upon seeing this man, he made no particular impression on me. I initially felt relief to see him walk through the door. As a customer, he was an excuse to stop talking to my wife.

* * * * *

"I was working," I began. The doctor and my father stood by, patiently waiting for me to say more.

* * * * *

I felt a sudden, sharp pain in my face. I felt myself falling backward into the wall behind me. My head violently collided with the wall, and I felt horrendous pain in my back.

"Give me your fucking money," the man said, his voice filled with cold, hard menace. I didn't understand what was going on. My head throbbed, and my mind was cloudy. "I SAID GIVE ME YOUR MONEY!" he yelled again louder and shoved the gun even closer to my face. Panicked and not really thinking, I quickly reached into my pocket and handed my wallet to him. He threw the wallet against the floor, his face registering anger and complete and total disgust. "I WANT WHAT'S IN THE DRAWER. DON'T GET CUTE WITH ME.

* * * * *

"A man wanted to rob me...," I continued. "He beat me." My voice was filled with shame.

"Quite severely," the doctor responded, his voice filled with empathy.

"How are you feeling, son?" my father whispered.

"Terrible," I answered truthfully. Most of my body throbbed with moderate but bearable pain. The exceptions were my back and neck, which were on fire. "I feel different, fuzzy," I said, looking in the direction of the doctor.

"That could be the pain medication you're on," the doctor said with a shrug.

"I still feel pain..."

"Imagine how much worse that pain would feel without the meds," the doctor said, giving my leg a pat. "We've examined you, Mr. Noor. Your injuries are mostly superficial. Nothing broken or anything like that. Still we'd like to keep you here for a couple of days."

"My back, my neck—they really hurt...," I said, wincing in pain as I tried to move my head around.

"We'll schedule an MRI and take a look. But I think both should feel significantly better in a week's time," the doctor responded in a clipped tone. "If you'll excuse me, I have other patients to check in on. You'll see me later," the doctor said with a smile and started to walk away.

"Doctor!" I called after him urgently. He stopped, turned, and looked at me expectantly. "You sure I didn't die?"

"Pretty sure. The monitors you're hooked up to suggest your heart is beating. That's a good sign of your continued status amongst the living," the doctor said, his voice filled with good humor.

"I think I died," I said absentmindedly. "I feel like I died and left something behind when I returned." The doctor looked uncomfortable with that remark and, for a few moments, seemed to have no clue about what to say.

"You should get some rest," he responded after a few moments. Then he took off without further comment. After he left, my father started talking more to me, peppering me with questions and trying to reassure me I would be okay. I wasn't so sure. Suddenly, I felt a swelling of emotion building in me. I didn't know where it was coming from or why, but I slowly started to sob. Tears streamed out of my eyes as my dad looked on, helplessly trying to comfort me. I rolled away from him and cried. I cried for what seemed like hours. My dad never left my side.

* * * * *

I lost all sense of time. And I had a premonition that I would never really recover. Hours, then days, would escape without my notice. I faded in and out of consciousness. Mostly I just slept, waiting to leave, but not sure if I really wanted to do so.

One day, I got a visit from Mr. Peterson. I was happy to see him and initially touched, believing that his presence was merely about his concern for my well-being. Sadly, I was very wrong.

"Mr. Peterson." My eyes lit up happily upon seeing him. "I missed you, man," I enthusiastically called out.

"We've missed you at the store, Adam," he responded stiffly. "How are you feeling?"

"Got some pain," I answered quietly. "But I'll be back to work soon enough."

"That's actually why I came here," Mr. Peterson said gravely. "I wanted to tell you this in person and not by phone. I figured I owed you that much."

"Tell me what?" I asked, feeling apprehensive. As soon as I asked that question, Mr. Peterson let out a deep, drawn-out sigh. He didn't look happy. And by his expression, I could tell that I wasn't going to like whatever he had to say. My heart rate sped up.

"You're being let go, Adam," he said, his voice tinged with regret.

"Let go?" I asked, not understanding what he meant.

"My bosses have decided to fire you," Mr. Peterson clarified, while wincing.

"I'm being fired!" I yelled, my voice rising. I was engulfed by disbelief and shock.

"I'm afraid so," Mr. Peterson retorted, bowing his head and looking ashamed.

"What do you mean my son is fired? What did he do wrong?" my father demanded angrily.

"Corporate thinks that you and the robber were working together." Mr. Peterson sighed. "They think your plan was to split the money together."

"They think I was working with him?" I said, my anger increasing by the second. My heart was practically beating out of my chest. The anger was so intense that it made me forget the pain I was in. "Look at me!" I shouted. The volume of my voice attracted the attention of several people passing by my room. Mr. Peterson visibly stiffened. "Do I look like I was working with him?"

"Mr. Peterson, this is outrageous!" my dad yelled. "You've known me for many years. You should know that no son of mine would do any such thing." He was seething.

"I know that. Unfortunately, my bosses don't know you nearly as well," Mr. Peterson said regretfully.

"So he's fired? Just like that? No chance to defend himself?"

"It's policy," Mr. Peterson replied weakly.

"Policy," my dad parroted back in disgust.

"If a worker is suspected of this type of offense, they are fired on the spot."

"I did nothing wrong," I said, my eyes blazing with fury.

"I know you didn't," Mr. Peterson replied. "You're my best employee. Don't know how I'm going to run the store without you. This isn't my choice. My bosses have tied my hands."

"How convenient for you," I quietly said, my anger becoming more inward.

"My presence here is a courtesy. In all honesty, corporate would not approve of me coming," Mr. Peterson said quietly. "I wish you well, Adam." He finished, gave a general nod in my dad's direction, and started walking away. I wasn't going to allow him to walk away without letting my feelings be crystal clear. As he left, I yelled at him, spitting vitriol in his direction, even continuing several minutes after he was no longer in my sight. My dad hugged me.

"Don't worry. Things will be okay," my dad said. But his words did very little to comfort me. As I lay there, anger coursed through me with no place to go. I wondered if things could get any worse. As time would reveal, I was nowhere near finished discovering just how bad it would all get.

* * * * *

After a few days, I was released from the hospital. I don't know for sure how long I was there. Between the effects of the pain medications and the damage to my brain, I had lost track of time. Evanna was the one who drove me home. Our ride home was mostly spent in silence. She made a few attempts at small talk, but each attempt elicited no response from me. At this point in time, only one thought kept running through my foggy mind: "My life is over. My dreams are over."

I felt that all that was left in my life was for me to die. The pain had become increasingly harder to deal with, even with the prescription pain medication. It seemed that the medication they gave me at discharge wasn't as strong as whatever they had given me in the hospital. My back and neck hurt more than anything I had ever experienced. Each seemed to take turns being the most painful part of my body. The doctors, whose test results uncovered no new information, told me that the pain would eventually ease up as I healed, that in a couple of days I should largely be back to my old self. At least physically.

When Evanna and I entered our home, it felt as though it had been years since the last time I had been there. It didn't feel right to me, didn't feel like home to me anymore. I took in my surroundings solemnly as my wife watched me curiously.

"When are they going to let you go back to work? I'm sure they miss you," Evanna asked, somewhat awkwardly. My heartbeat seized when she brought up work. I had yet to tell her much of anything about the situation.

"I'm not going back."

"Because of what happened to you?" Evanna asked, seeming surprised. "You don't think you can handle it?"

"They fired me." As I spoke, my voice filled with shame.

"They fired you! For what?" Evanna asked in shocked disbelief.

"They think I planned the robbery with my attacker." I sighed.

"Did you?" Evanna asked reflexively without thinking.

"Of course, fucking not!" I exploded. "How could you ask me such a thing!"

"I'm sorry," Evanna stammered. "I didn't think you did. It just came out." She paused. "What are you going to do?"

"I don't know!" I shouted more viciously then I intended. "I'll figure something out." As I said this, my voice was softening. Evanna merely nodded, her face looking sad and upset. Without further word, I walked into the bedroom and lay down. I wouldn't leave the bed again for a long while.

* * * * *

For what felt like ages, I would only leave my bed to eat and to take pain medication. Otherwise, either I was lying there, staring off into space, or I was sleeping. I was vaguely aware of Evanna nagging me, saying that I needed to get out of bed and do something. I paid her no mind. Due to being fired for being a suspect in the robbery, I was not granted workers' compensation. To make matters worse, the health insurance that I had had as an employee of the gas station reported that they did not intend to pay for any of my medical bills. My debt due to my medical expenses increased by the day. In addition, my regular bills started to pile up as well. I was aware of this problem, but I honestly didn't give a damn. In response, Evanna tried to work more hours to make up for the lost income. However, she couldn't make nearly enough to make up for everything.

After a couple of days, when the pain did not subside as the doctors predicted it would, I had my dad drive me to Mid-State

Medical Center. I didn't like dealing with regular doctors. And it had become clear that I had more than just physical problems as a result of the accident. He felt I needed to see a psychologist of some type. I didn't fully understand the reasons at the time. But this was only the beginning of the doctor roulette game that I came to totally despise over the next decade of my life.

I left with a diagnosis of "acute stress syndrome." If you look that up, the diagnosis makes some sense: "A psychological condition arising in response to a terrifying or traumatic event."

This seemed to apply to my condition, so it made sense. Treatment of this particular issue is tricky. It can resolve itself spontaneously over time. Or it can evolve into full blown Post-Traumatic Stress Disorder. I had hopes that it would be the former. But as with everything else in my life, it proved not to be that simple.

* * * * *

Some part of me did care that my wife and I were starting to drown in our bills. But for the most part, not enough of me cared to do anything about it. Every now and again, I would be inspired to try to leave my bed for something other than eating and basic survival. I remember getting fully dressed for the first time in a long time. Prepared to go back out into the world, to try to land a job. I was fine until I stepped foot outside my house. The minute I was out on my porch, my heart rate skyrocketed. I grasped at my chest as I struggled to take farther steps. My breathing became shallow. Within a minute, I was on my knees.

"What the hell," I said out loud as I struggled to inhale a sufficient amount of air. I slowly turned away and started almost crawling back to my house. Once inside, I laid on the floor while trying to calm down and breathe. After a few minutes, I was back to normal, or rather my new normal, which wasn't the same as who I used to be. Not even close. I went back to my bedroom and went back to sleep.

* * * * *

I didn't attempt to leave my house alone again. Instead I started having my dad and mom go with me everywhere I went. A few times, I attempted to find work again. But in none of these cases did the interviews go well. They all pretty much ended the same.

"Mr. Peterson spoke very highly of you. Unfortunately, your tenure at your last job ended on a somewhat controversial note. So we don't think we can hire you at this time" was what all my potential employers said, even as the language they used varied. Being disrespected and falsely accused of something I didn't do not only got me fired from my previous job, it was holding me back from getting any other employment as well. In addition, this miscarriage of justice resulted in me being denied workers' compensation benefits, being denied receiving my health insurance benefits, and causing a host of financial problems for Evanna and me. This only increased my lack of motivation and reduced my will to do anything other than sleep.

* * * * *

After one of my failed attempts to land a job, I was out with my mom. I was making my way to my car when I heard a familiar voice call out.

"Adam!" I heard, and I turned in the direction of the voice. It was Larry, my best friend from the gas station.

"Larry," I said unenthusiastically.

"How've you been?" he asked as I gave him a half-hearted hug.

"Terrible," I said tightly.

"The place hasn't been the same without you. It's falling apart," Larry said lightly.

"Good," I said in a humorless tone.

"I've been getting calls from Mr. Soprano. He keeps asking me about you," Larry started. Indeed, Mr. Soprano had tried to call me more than a few times, but I hadn't responded. "You should give him a call."

"What for?" I asked irritably.

"He wants to know how you're doing. You should call him. Let him know what's going on. Maybe you can start up that music career you've been wanting," Larry suggested.

"What are you talking about?" I derisively laughed. "I can't sing anymore!"

"Why not?" Larry asked me, bewildered.

"Because I just can't! My life is over, Larry. My dreams are done! All I do with my time is lie in bed, waiting for death," I said, shaking my head.

"Maybe it doesn't need to be that way." Larry winced.

"It is that way," I stated firmly. "No amount of wishing will make it not so. I am dead, alive in appearance only. I wish that fucking robber had just pulled the trigger on me!" I shouted, my anger increasing. "They think I conspired with him?" I shook my head. "You know what I think?"

"No...," Larry answered hesitantly.

"I think the robber conspired with Mr. Peterson to destroy my life. They wanted me not to die but to suffer! They succeeded," I said, inches away from Larry's face. He appeared extremely uncomfortable.

"If it helps, Mr. Peterson feels really bad about letting you go," Larry said quietly.

"No, it doesn't help, Larry!" I shouted. "How do Mr. Peterson's bad feelings help me? Does it put food on my table? Does it pay the bills that are piling up? No!" I paused. "Because of the bullshit that's been spread about me, I can't get a job! Nobody will hire me. He has the luxury of feeling bad! Good for him! But it doesn't mean a damn thing to me," I vehemently yelled. Then I did a sudden about face and started walking back toward the car where my mom was waiting. Larry wasn't quite done trying, however. He followed me.

"Adam, if you need a little bit of money...," he started.

But I cut him off. "I don't need your charity!" I exploded with disgust.

He stopped in his tracks and just stood there, looking dejected. I got in my car and drove off, leaving my latest failed attempt to get a job and Larry behind.

* * * * *

After three weeks of complete misery, I thought I had finally managed to catch a break. The person who robbed me at the gas station was finally caught. When asked about whether I was working with him or not, the robber laughed. He was very amused about the notion that we had anything to do with each other. Just like that my name was cleared. This seemingly put an end to the workers' compensation lawyers and the insurance company lawyers having any rationale for denying me benefits. Within weeks, I was finally getting workers' compensation checks. But the insurance company was still refusing to pay my medical bills.

The money from workers' comp was not enough. It was certainly not enough to enable me to catch up on paying all the bills that had piled up. This mounting debt increased my feelings of worthlessness and uselessness. It felt as though I no longer had a purpose in life. My father continued to insist that one day I would find my purpose again. But I did not believe him. I couldn't predict my future, but I wasn't looking hopeful. My star had dimmed so much that it was barely still visible.

Despite my attacker being caught and arrested, I was not at peace with what had happened to me. Not sure I ever truly will be. There were times when I forgot that he had been arrested. In fact, several months after the arrest, I found myself asking my doctor if the attacker had ever been caught.

I thought the arrest would put an end to the countless number of doctors and lawyers I was being forced to meet. Sadly, I was mistaken. Still at issue was the year of unpaid medical bills, which the insurance company was trying not to pay. And the lawyer for the insurance company representing workers' compensation claimed that I should be able to work.

Oddly, the arrest of my attacker not only did not end the multitude of unwanted doctors' and lawyers' meetings, but it only served to increase their role in my life. My life had become an endless parade of doctors. It was hard to communicate with them. It took as much time to communicate with each doctor as it had taken the first time I tried to communicate with my lawyer. After a while, they seemed to give up even trying. The doctors acted like machines, doling out medications but never really attempting to talk to me.

The various medications that I now had to ingest caused a severe case of dry mouth. Even when I drank lots of water or juice, my mouth was always very dry. It became so extreme that my gums became damaged, weakening my teeth. I was afraid to eat because my teeth had become so weak. To help me with eating, my dad would buy me candy. He also hoped it would help with my worsening depression.

* * * * *

One day, I found myself lying in bed, attempting to sleep, tossing and turning, throwing my pillow up in the air.

Suddenly, I heard a loud noise. I nearly jumped out of bed. My heart was pounding. Evanna didn't seem to react. Then the door burst open, revealing my attacker. Angry, I ran at the attacker.

"How did you find me? How do you know where I live?" I yelled at him as I ran toward him. With one swift motion, he punched me in the face. I flew against the wall and fell to the ground. My wife still wasn't waking up.

"I know everything," my attacker said menacingly as he picked me up, choking me. I struggled for any breath I could manage. I tried to get him off me, but it was no use. He was too strong for me. He tied me to the bed.

"Please...just go. Please!" I begged.

He looked at my sleeping wife. "She's very pretty, too pretty for you," he said with a laugh. He walked slowly over to her. I tried with all my might to break free, but to no avail. I started yelling and shouting at him, but he didn't stop. He took a knife from his pocket.

He made his way slowly toward Evanna. All the while, I was screaming at him to stop. He put the knife to Evanna's throat…

* * * * *

I woke up screaming. Unlike in my dream, Evanna was quick to react. She jumped out of bed, completely startled.

"What's wrong?" Evanna asked me, terrified.

"He was going to kill you!" I shouted with tears in my eyes.

"Who was?" she asked me, confused.

"The one who robbed me. He found us. He was going to kill you…," I said, sweat drenching my entire body. The more I talked, the less sense I made. She eventually told me to just go back to sleep and tried comforting me. Hours later, I finally managed it.

* * * * *

It was late at night. I was lying next to my sleeping wife, tossing and turning. It was a bad pain day, and I couldn't get comfortable as my back throbbed. No amount of medication was helping me on this night. Suddenly, I heard a voice that startled me so much that I nearly fell out of bed.

Adam… It was a male voice. I looked around the room urgently, trying to locate where it was coming from. I saw nothing. I glanced at Evanna, who was still sound asleep. *Don't you recognize me, Adam?* the voice asked. And I indeed found the voice familiar.

"Who are you?" I asked quietly and out loud.

You know who I am, the voice answered and was followed by the sounds of laughter. *I'm the reason for your pitiful excuse of an existence.*

"The man who attacked me?" I asked aloud, with sudden startled realization.

Exactly, my old friend.

"We aren't friends," I said through gritted teeth.

How hurtful! You should have done as I asked. If you had, you wouldn't be as fucking pathetic as you are now. I didn't say anything to that. Merely nodded. *Probably should have killed you.*

"You should have," I replied sadly.

But this is much more fun, watching you suffer.

"Why didn't you fucking kill me?" I shouted with anger. At the sound of me screaming, Evanna jumped up, awake.

"What's wrong?" Evanna asked groggily, with fear in her voice.

"Nothing's wrong," I lied. "Just a bad dream. Go back to sleep," I insisted.

She didn't look entirely convinced, but she lay back down. Nightmares were almost a nightly thing now. So while she didn't entirely believe me, she accepted my answer. Within minutes, she was sleeping again. I grabbed a pillow and a blanket and went downstairs to the couch, hoping it would make a difference and that sleep would at last claim me.

* * * * *

"We need to talk."

There is no combination of words that is worse than these four. It doesn't matter what language or what culture you come from. These words do not portend anything good. When my wife said these four words to me one day, despite my barely caring about anything at this point in my life, my heart rate increased. I was going to try to blow her off, as I had done almost every day since I had left the hospital. But on this occasion, she was determined to outstubborn me. She blocked my attempt to go back upstairs to bed.

"What do you want to talk about?" I asked wearily.

"We are drowning," Evanna started urgently. "The bills are piling up. We're months behind on rent, electric bill—everything!"

"I know all this," I said with a shrug.

"So what are you going to about it?" Evanna demanded.

"Don't know what to do," I sighed.

"Well, we need to do something, or you and I are going to end up on the streets," Evanna cried. I was about to respond when I heard the voice again.

Adam…

"Who's there?" I asked, stepping away from the staircase and startling my wife.

"What are you talking about?" Evanna asked in a frightened tone of voice.

You're destined to live on the streets—you and your pretty wife, the robber said to me.

"The fucking robber won't leave me alone," I said angrily, looking back toward my wife. Evanna just looked at me, appearing very scared.

She is pretty. Maybe when you're on the street, I'll swoop in and save her, show her a good time. I heard my attacker laughing.

"Don't you dare fucking touch her!" I shouted at the top of my lungs.

What good are you? You can't take care of yourself. You can't take care of your wife. You are no man. PATHETIC!

"Shut the fuck up! Leave me alone!" I yelled.

Maybe I'll come finish the job.

"Go ahead and fucking do it! I don't give two shits anymore! Fucking kill me! Kill me!" I shouted to no one in particular. At this point, Evanna had had enough of watching me.

"Who the hell are you talking to? There's no one there!" Evanna yelled at me.

"He's here. And he won't leave me the hell alone! Why won't he just fucking kill me!" I shouted back at her. I continued to rant and rave at "nothing" as the voice continued speaking to me. Finally, since my wife was utterly clueless as to what to do, she just walked away, leaving me to my ranting. As I ranted, I noticed that my left shoulder had an odd stiffness to it. My heart was beating out my chest. My breathing became extremely labored. Every breath became torturous, like there was suddenly no air in the room.

Images flashed through my mind. I was back working in the gas station, arguing with Evanna on the phone. "No...," I said out loud as I fell to my knees.

A rather large man entered the store. He was muscular and tattooed. Upon seeing this man, he made no particular impression on me. I initially felt relief to see him walk through the door. As a customer, he was an excuse to stop talking to my wife.

I wanted to cry out. I wanted to warn myself to get ready to protect myself, but I had no influence over the images flooding my mind.

I tried to run. I moved quickly, trying to get to the door. Just as quickly, the man swung his gun on me, swiftly into the back of my skull, causing me to fly to the floor and my head to light up with unbearable pain. The rest of my body's pain as it collided violently with the floor barely registered with me as the throbbing pain in my head was felt above it all.

My heart was beating so fast it hurt. I gasped for air. My arm grew tingly. Finally, I mercifully went unconscious. I hit the floor with a sickening thud and fell into darkness.

* * * * *

Hours later, I woke up on the floor, lying in a small puddle of my drool. Things were increasingly getting out of hand. Scared out of my mind, I did as I always did when I really needed someone. I went to see my father. I knocked on my dad's door and waited. After a few moments, the door opened.

"Son! What are you doing here?" my dad said, his features lighting up with delight.

"Can I come in?" I asked, clearing my throat. I wasn't happy with the reason for my visit, but I viewed it as a necessity.

"Of course!" my father answered and moved aside to let me step in. I took a seat on the couch and sat there in silence for a while. "What brings you here?" he asked while handing me a drink.

"I was just wondering if I could borrow some money." I sighed.

"How much?"

"Fifteen hundred," I replied, wincing.

"That's a lot of money," my father responded, his eyebrow raised a little bit.

"I'm a little bit behind on bills," I answered quietly.

"I'm surprised you didn't come to me sooner."

"I was ashamed," I spoke quietly.

"There is no need for shame. I know your situation, and you are my son. Of course, I will help you," my father said kindly. "How are you doing otherwise?"

"Fine. Good," I lied.

"Son, ever since you were five and tried to blame the breaking of my favorite lamp on your brother, you have never been able to lie to me." My father laughed.

"You knew that was me?" I asked, laughing despite myself.

"Of course, I did! You can never fool me. One important skill about being a parent is knowing when yours kids are lying to you. So tell me the truth, Adam. How are you doing?"

"Badly," I sighed. "I'm doing badly." I found myself staring at the floor rather than looking at my dad. "I came back a shell, Dad. That's all I am. I'm nothing like I used to be. Something's changed."

"Like what?"

"Everything. Adam Noor died that day in the gas station. Your son is gone," I said, tears welling in my eyes.

"Son..."

"I can't think like I used to. I can't concentrate. I can't lift any-thing without feeling horrible pain in my back. No one will hire me. I'm useless. What good am I?" I asked, tears streaming down my eyes.

"There are plenty of ways in which you're good, plenty of ways in which you can still be of use," my father reassured me.

"I feel like one of those zombies from the movies that Larry always made me watch, except I don't like brains," I said with a heavy sigh. "I've been snapping at Evanna for no reason. I'm angry. All the time. Every single minute of every day, I'm angry. And I don't know why." I continued to talk for a while about my feelings, and my dad continued to listen without much comment. Every now and again he would interject with some effort to try to be positive. It made me feel better for a moment or two. But on the whole, I still felt nothing but down and worthless.

"Son, I'm buying a house with your mother soon. It's more than time that we took that step," he said after a while. I looked at him with interest, wondering how exactly what he was saying connected to what I had been talking about. "I can continue to shell out the money to keep you in your apartment for a while. I will help you that way if you wish. You are my son, and I love you. But I have a different idea. I would like you and your wife to and come live with us. Maybe we can make you more comfortable and take care of you better."

"I'd like that, Dad" was all I could think of in response. My dad stood up and sat next to me. He gave me a big hug.

"Am I going to be committed? Locked up?"

"No. I won't let that happen. You will be okay," he said to me quietly.

"How do you know?" I asked.

"Because in the end, you really have no choice but to be," he said, smiling at me. I sat there on the couch, holding my father. And in that moment, for the first time since I left the hospital, I felt like maybe he was right. Maybe I would be okay.

* * * * *

Months went by, and nothing really changed for me. I did not do much but sleep and eat. My dad had started to pay some of our bills. He agreed to do this until he succeeded in buying a house. He didn't know about the medical bills. I was keeping him from that burden for the time being. But they kept piling up. The voice of the robber and a few others were still in my head. I did my best to hide this from Evanna, as I knew the voices scared her.

* * * * *

When my dad officially bought his house, he invited me along to take a tour. It was a nice townhouse-style place with two bedrooms, a living room and a huge basement. My mom was with us the day my dad showed me around. He eventually showed me the room that would be mine. I sat there blankly, staring inside the room while my dad stared back at me, waiting for some type of response.

"Well?" he finally broke the silence.

"It's nice, Dad," I said quietly.

"But?" my dad retorted expectantly.

"I think I'd feel more comfortable in the basement," I said hesitantly.

"You want your room to be in the basement?" my dad asked incredulously.

"If it's not too much trouble, Dad. Please. I'd like the basement,"

"Evanna's going to be okay with that?" my dad asked. I hesitated. I hadn't thought about what she would desire.

"I'm sure she will," I answered.

"Very well. The basement it is, son," my dad replied with a shrug. "I'm sure I can use this bedroom for something." He paused thoughtfully. "Perhaps a study to get some writing done." He smiled broadly and walked away. I took one last look at what was now not going to be my room before closing the door and following my dad.

* * * * *

On the day I was supposed to move in with my dad, I was sitting on the couch, watching TV. My dad was coming in a little while to help me and my wife move. I had packed what I could, but Evanna did most of the rest. She came to me and sat down next to me as I watched TV, not really paying too much attention to what was on. She looked nervous, and I didn't quite know why.

"I'm not going with you," she spoke quietly.

"What are you talking about? You can't stay here…," I said, startled, my attention drawn to her.

"I'm not intending to stay here," she said.

"Then what are you doing?" I asked.

"I met someone."

"Met someone?" I asked, still not understanding.

"I've been seeing a man for the last month. I didn't mean for it to happen. It just did," Evanna said with evident struggle.

"You've been cheating on me?"

"Yes," Evanna said without elaborating. I believe most guys, learning that their significant other had been going behind their backs to sleep with someone else, would react with anger. They would yell, throw things, and possibly worse. What did I do? I just laughed. Hysterically. Somehow I think that reaction scared Evanna more than if I had gotten angry and started hitting her.

"These last few months with you have been so hard…," Evanna began, but I cut her off.

"You don't need to explain. If you wish to go, you can go. If you're not going to be here for me through this, then I don't need you," I said with no emotion in my voice. "I have my family. I have my dad. I don't need you."

Evanna seemed stunned by my cold words, so much so that she sat there, not speaking for several moments. I looked at her just sitting there, and I gestured for her to go.

"The faster you leave, the better" was all I said. I turned back to the TV and completely ignored her. She stood up, grabbed her purse, and started to head toward the door.

"Leave my stuff behind. I'll get them later," she said to me. And without another word, she left. Just as quickly as she had entered my life, she was now gone from it. I sat there on the couch, not caring. Not one bit.

CHAPTER 5

I wasn't sure what to expect from my dad when he heard the news about Evanna. He had never believed in my marriage to her. As it turns out, he didn't react much. He simply gave me a hug and told me I was better off. I agreed with him. Without her, I could just be left alone. My father hired movers to get my things. Per Evanna's instructions, I left her things behind. As I took a last look around the place, I was reminded of the initial hopeful and glorious experiences. Of course, now most of the memories were tainted and ruined. I was ready to leave it all behind. But that was not all I was ready to leave behind. A part of me wanted to leave my entire, hopeless life behind. Whenever I would express these thoughts to my father, he would quickly fill my head with encouraging sentiments and push me to keep going forth. His favorite thing to say to me was "You have no choice. You have to keep going forward."

The pain in my neck and back had not improved. Some days I thought it was getting worse. I visited doctor after doctor. Specialist after specialist. And they found nothing. I grew to despise MRI machines. I was scared of the machine because it looked and felt to me like a casket of death. As I lay in the tube, listening to the whirling and buzzing of the machinery, my anxiety always continually grew until it was so unbearable that I would have to demand to be let out. Also, I would start hearing the voices inside my head again, the robber taunting me, asking me if I was comfortable in my "little coffin."

Almost like the one I should have put you in..., the voice taunted me and laughed. It took all my might to resist responding to the taunting coming from inside my own head.

When I wasn't eating or visiting one of the many doctors, I was sleeping in the basement. That's all my life consisted of at this point. I had neither the will nor the desire to do anything else. Every once in a while, my dad would come down and try to get me to come upstairs, to do anything besides just lying there in the dark. He didn't think it was healthy for me to be so socially isolated and inactive. I didn't care. Every so often, I would find myself screaming and yelling at him, totally unconscious of anything I was actually saying to him. I was not even really aware of why I was yelling at him. He would just sit there, waiting patiently for me to stop yelling at him.

"Adam, I'm more than happy to have you living in my basement. I'm more than happy to take care of you. But please, show me a little respect," my dad would say.

"I'm sorry, Dad," I would say guiltily in reply.

"No need. I know what you're going through. But please remember, I created you," he said with laughter.

"Of course, Dad," I meekly replied. "Why did this happen to me?" I asked, tears forming in my eyes. "Why didn't I just die that day?"

"I don't know the answers to your questions. I wish I did. Fathers always want to know everything. What I do know is that what happened to you happened for a reason. God has a purpose for us all. We must believe that even if it's difficult to see what that purpose is. One day the reason for your suffering will become known."

* * * * *

After a few months, my father made a discovery that startled him. He was going through my mail and happened to notice unopened medical bills. When he took a look at them, his mouth fell open. He quickly came downstairs and woke me up.

"Have you taken a look at any of these?" he asked me, holding out the various bills.

"No," I answered groggily.

"These medical bills are piling up, and your insurance company is refusing to pay any of them. This isn't a joke. They will come after you," he spoke urgently. "I don't even have the money to help you here."

"So what can we do?" I asked, turning around in my bed, feeling spasms of pain as I did so.

"We're going to need to get a lawyer." He sighed.

"Seriously?"

"Seriously. This is getting out of hand, and we need to stop this from getting any worse. We need to get the insurance company to pay for these bills, or you're going to go bankrupt. I know you don't care about that now, but you might in the future."

"If you say so, okay," I simply said and then rolled over and returned to my slumber.

* * * * *

The attorney we chose was Daniel Shaw. He was an older man with curly graying hair. Despite his age, he appeared highly professional and confident. I liked him immediately. For the first time in what seemed like forever, I dressed in a presentable manner. It was the first time in months that I didn't look like I had crawled out of a sewer.

With great difficulty, I told the attorney about the events of my life over the last six months or so. This process was so emotionally painful that it seemed to take forever. Part of the trouble was that my English was not the best in the world. But far more significant was the fact that my mind was slowed down, disorganized, tortured by intrusive perceptions, and encased in a thick psychic fog that made it very hard to remember details. He listened with patience until I was done. When I was finished, I exhaled. I was sweating from the enormous effort I had to exert to explain everything.

"Mr. Noor, you are not going to need to worry about your medical bills anymore," he asserted after I was finished.

"Thank you, sir!" I said with relief.

"No problem. We're going to get your insurance company to pay for these bills, and I think we can probably get your former employer to start sending you checks as well," he added with a reassuring smile.

* * * * *

I was now fighting a battle on multiple fronts. I was trying to get the Workers' Compensation Bureau to pay for the wages I lost due to my injuries, fighting my former employer's health insurance company to pay for my medical bills, and battling the horrendous symptoms that were being created by my own mind. Throughout these ordeals, Attorney Shaw became a big part of my life. I looked forward to meeting with him because he always seemed to give me a temporary sense of hope. Having him in my life was like having another father. Unfortunately for him, I started to treat him as I had started treating my own father. (I think therapists call this transference.) Sometimes I would call him for no reason at all and start screaming at him. Why? I don't know! Maybe just as I felt about my own father, I was desperate for him to take care of me, to make it all better. He would patiently wait until I was done and tell me that things would be okay. This always calmed me…for a while.

* * * * *

Attorney Shaw and I had several meetings with a lawyer who was representing the insurance company for the Workers' Comp Bureau. In these meetings, it was recognized that the reports written by most of the doctors who had examined me expressed the opinion that I was disabled and unable to work. These doctors recommended to the insurance company that they settle the case. We had copies of reports from multiple psychiatrists who concurred with this opinion. For example, a report written by Dr. Finkelstein on May 23, 2001, communicated the following opinion:

Opinion

According to records reviewed, and as per history provided by Mr. Noor, he was the victim of an armed robbery on August 7th, 2000. In that event, a perpetrator entered the store where he was working, held a gun to him, threw him to the floor, and pressed his neck to the floor, and once again, threatened his life while holding a weapon to Mr. Noor's head. The nature of that incident and the variety of symptoms described by Mr. Noor are consistent with Post Traumatic Stress Disorder, which at this point, is chronic and quite severe. In addition, the patient appears to have developed a significant depressive underpinning to his illness along with distinct elements of paranoia.

It is eminently clear, based on Mr. Noor's mental status presentation and based on history provided by both himself and his father that he is unable to function reasonably in society at this time. His Post Traumatic Stress Disorder is a direct result of the psychic trauma sustained on the day of the incident and does not result from any physical injury. That is to say, Mr. Noor's psychopathology is directly related to the event of August 7th, 2000 and the abject fear and terror is occasioned, as opposed to any physical injuries he may have sustained during the incident.

In summary, Mr. Noor presents as a 32 year old man who, at this time, is completely disabled on a psychiatric basis from returning to any work situation of any kind. His psychiatric condition is total and, hopefully temporary in nature. It is directly and causally-related to the psychic trauma occasioned by the incident of August 7th, 2000.

Mr. Noor can barely leave his apartment, and it
is eminently clear that he is unable to function at
this time on any meaningful basis in society.

The lawyer for the insurance company seemed like a nice
enough man. He asked questions in a polite, kind way. After reading
over the reports from the various doctors and listening to me, he said
that he felt that the insurance company could not win the case. He
said that he would recommend that the insurance company should
settle. I was surprised that it appeared as though the case was going to
end so easily. Of course, things did not continue to progress this way.
The attorney was promptly fired for suggesting this course of action.

The next lawyer we met with was very different. I will never forget this man. He was a big, muscular guy named Attorney Lawson.
I suspected that he was a bodybuilder. It looked to me as though he
liked to show off his body. The instant I saw him, I knew he was
going to give me a hard time. He seemed to have no emotions. He
just wanted to do his job. He made it clear that this job was to make
sure that the insurance company would pay none of my medical bills.
At our first meeting, he looked at me like I was a bug on the wall that
he wanted to crush. He asked me questions in a very rude manner. At
the time, I felt that he must not have liked me because I was Muslim.

"I'm going to be blunt," Attorney Lawson bellowed with hostility, "your employment with your former employer ended under controversial circumstances. We feel that because of those circumstances,
the insurance company should not have to pay for the injuries that
you sustained as a result of the attack."

"There is no evidence that my client had anything to do with
the robbery," Attorney Shaw interjected.

"The company felt that they had sufficient evidence to fire him
for his collaboration with the assailant. That's good enough for me,"
the attorney responded.

"There is no evidence because I didn't do anything!" I shouted.
Attorney Shaw held out a hand, indicating he wanted me to keep
quiet. With great effort, I stopped talking.

"Furthermore, we feel that there is no real reason why your client can't be working. The insurance company does not feel that there are grounds to declare him disabled and thus he is ineligible to receive workers' compensation benefits," Attorney Lawson said almost robotically.

"I can't work! My back, my neck—" I started to yell, drawing an annoyed look from my lawyer. I was quickly cut off by the insurance company's attorney.

"I've heard all this before. Do you know how many such claims I hear in a year?" he asked with disgust. "The answer would shock you enough to send you to an early grave." He paused and stood up. "Everybody is trying to make money without doing a damn thing, claiming to have injuries that they do not. The percentage of legitimate disability claims is very low."

"Your predecessor felt our case was legitimate," my lawyer said pointedly.

"Hence why he is now my predecessor." The opposing attorney laughed.

"Several doctors and psychologists also back us up. They say that he is incapable of working, that he is both physically and mentally disabled," my lawyer said, holding up a bunch of medical reports to emphasize his point.

"We've had more than a few doctors say the exact opposite," the other attorney said quickly. "We've convinced the judge who is overseeing this case to order that your client get a second opinion."

"He's seen enough doctors to amass more than a few opinions already. How many opinions do you need?" Attorney Shaw asked, sounding angry.

"Until we are satisfied." Attorney Lawson smirked.

"And if my client doesn't go to these doctors?"

"Then the judge will decide the case in our favor, and this will be all over," Attorney Lawson retorted and then stood up. "If you'll excuse me, gentlemen, I have other clients." Rather briskly he left the room before we could even stand up.

"I don't want to go to any more doctors. I hate them. I just want to be left alone," I pleaded.

Attorney Shaw slowly raised himself out of his seat and replied, "You have no choice." At that moment, I almost confused my lawyer for my father. I would hear this sentence over and over again from people in my life that had more power over my life than I seemed to.

* * * * *

So began another round of the game of "doctor roulette," the insurance company sending me to doctor after doctor to "prove" that there was absolutely nothing wrong with me and that I should be able to return to work with no issues. I cannot even tell you how many doctors I ultimately went to see. I felt like a rat in a maze, playing some kind of game that I could barely understand.

My anger about the situation increased by the day. I took my anger out on both Attorney Shaw and my dad. At this point, they were the only two people that I really talked to. I did talk a little to my mom. My brothers and sisters were typically nice when they talked to me. But for the most part, they stayed away. There were two reasons that I could think of for their doing this. They either (1) were ashamed of my increasingly worsening physical and mental condition or (2) loved me so much that it hurt too much for them to see me.

I occasionally talked to the brother who lived in New York. He sent me money so that I didn't have to always rely on my dad. He wanted me to visit him, but I felt that I couldn't. I believed that I had to be home so that I could respond immediately if the insurance company ordered me to see another doctor. Aside from my immediate family and my attorney, there was no one else that I would ever talk to. I felt increasingly lonely and isolated. At the same time, I felt so miserable that I didn't have much desire for company.

I remember a particular lonely day in which I went upstairs and my dad started talking to me. In response, because I did not feel like talking to him, I just started yelling at him. I was screaming at the top of my lungs. I don't remember even one thing I said to him. I recall that I started walking away, and as I was doing so, I was overcome with sadness. I turned around and gave my father a big hug.

"I'm sorry," I said, crying.

"I know, son. Don't worry about it," he responded kindly.

"I know I shouldn't talk to you like that, that you hate it when I disrespect you like that," I sobbed.

"You're going through a lot."

"Thank you, Dad, for forgiving me," I said and squeezed him tighter.

"I could never be mad at you, and I never will be," he said. I let go and started to walk away from him. "There is one thing that worries me though." I stopped and turned toward him. "I won't live forever, son. When I go, no one else is going to take care of you. I'm very worried about that." I took in his words and nodded. I said nothing in reply, but I have never, for one day, forgotten what he said to me that day.

* * * * *

Sleeping in the basement during the summer wasn't bad. It stayed cool. But during the winter, it was cold. Very cold. I had layers upon layers of blankets. And they barely helped. The furnace was located in the basement. But it did very little to provide heat for the basement. It was an old furnace, and there was always a strong smell of diesel exhaust coming from it. In addition, with it getting dark earlier, and earlier during the winter, I found myself becoming even more depressed. How was this possible?

The basement had only one small window. I sometimes felt as though I hadn't seen the sun for months. It felt like a prison cell or, worse, like a coffin. I slept on a mattress on the floor. Sometimes I would go three or four days, barely waking up except to eat or take my medication. The doctors were ordering me to take so much medication that I felt like a walking pharmacy. And the voices in my head increased in frequency. It was now more than just the attacker talking to me. There were several distinct voices—some of them male, some of them female. All of them were negative and mean.

Just kill yourself, a female voice that I didn't recognize said to me.

"I want to," I said to myself while lying in bed. I didn't hate the idea of killing myself. I did, however, hate the idea of my father being the one to discover me.

Then why don't you? What are you waiting for? my attacker asked me.

"Couldn't do that to my dad," I replied sadly.

You'd be doing it for him, I heard a childlike voice say. It sounded like one of my sister's kids.

"What do you mean?" I asked.

You're nothing but a burden, a useless burden, draining his money and his energy like a parasite. You're sucking the life from him. He'll die sooner than his time because of the stress you put him through, the female voice replied.

"He doesn't seem stressed..."

But you know he is. End his suffering. End it because you love him, the female voice said with mock compassion. Tears started to form in my eyes at the thought of being the cause of my dad's suffering. I cried for hours, alone in the dark.

* * * * *

Every now and again, when I was trying to sleep, I'd feel my heart rate increase and my chest tightening. I had experienced this before, but this time it was different. This time, I was hoping it meant I was about to have a heart attack and die. No such luck. The symptoms usually went away within minutes.

One morning when I woke up, I couldn't see because I didn't have my contacts in. But I felt colder, and it seemed like I was all wet for some reason. I moved around and realized there was water all around me. Startled, I realized that what had once been metaphorical was now literal. I was literally swimming in shit.

CHAPTER 6

The sounds of my yelling filled the house. My dad was quick to react, running down the stairs. He was not happy to see the sight of his basement, filled with about an inch of water. Meanwhile, I didn't even as much as move. My dad angrily got out his phone and called his friend. It didn't seem like long before the two of them were down in the basement, discussing the situation. I still wasn't moving.

This is my life, I thought to myself. *I might as well enjoy it.* As it turned out, the pipes had frozen, resulting in water from the bathroom and the kitchen leaking into the basement. It would take a massive repair to fix. They cleared the water out of the basement. All the while, I just lay there.

"It's going to be a while before someone can fix this," my dad's friend said to me. "You sure you want to keep living down here?"

"I'm sure. I'm fine down here," I said in reply, not even really turning in his direction. The two of them spent some time trying to convince me otherwise. But after a while, they gave up. Once they were gone, I fell back to sleep. Eventually, my dad bought a machine from Home Depot to get the water out of the basement, and he showed me how to use it. He realized that I was going to be too stubborn to actually move out of the basement no matter how much he begged me too.

Why did I do this? I'm not sure. Maybe I was punishing myself. Maybe I was rebelling against a world that seemed to continually make my life miserable. Maybe I wanted to tell the world that it could do what it wanted to me, I would no longer change my plans to accommodate the universe's grand design. This action would allow me to symbolically retake ownership for some small part of my own destiny.

* * * * *

I wanted to stop seeing doctors, but nobody would let me. The doctors would all ask the same stupid questions over and over again.

"How old are you?"

"What's your name?"

"Where are you from?"

Is there any reason they couldn't ask the other doctors I also visited so I wouldn't have to waste time answering basic questions that I had already answered thousands of times before?

"Are you happy? Sad? Excited?"

"Look at this picture. Point out the one that best describes how you feel."

All this would be said in a clinical, detached, impersonal way. I doubt that any of them actually cared about me or about what I had been through. After a while, I grew fed up with being asked the same questions over and over. So I started flipping out on one particular young female doctor.

"Happy? How can I possibly be happy? My dreams are gone. I was going to be somebody! Adam Noor, famous Arabic singer! Now? I'm nothing! The highlight of my day is sleeping. How the fuck can I be happy? Sometimes I literally sleep in shit. Why must you all ask the same stupid fucking questions?" I snapped with vicious anger.

The look on her face was definitely priceless. It was a mixture of wanting to cry and being completely shocked. It was good to see that these doctors could exhibit actual emotions.

Every now and again, the insurance company doctors would have translators to help them understand me. It was usually some cute Arabian girl. These were the meetings I hated the most. I would feel shame and inferiority when I was in their presence. In addition, in most cases, even with my English not being the best, I knew these translators were not doing a very good job. I couldn't help but wonder how these doctors were supposed to help me if they could barely understand me. At times I thought they weren't trying to help me at all. They acted more like investigators out to prove I committed some crime instead of looking out for my well-being. They were just trying to prove that I was full of crap, that I had neither physical nor mental health problems. If only that theory were true, my life would have been a lot easier. Sadly, it wasn't.

* * * * *

At this point in my life, whenever I was awake, I wished to be dead. The medications made me tired and weak. Oftentimes I could barely stand or move. Most days, I wasn't even able to take showers or get to the bathroom. Sometimes when I needed to go, I went right where I was. Sometimes I was aware of what I was doing. Other times I was in such a deep sleep that I didn't even wake up. I was on antidepressants. These were not having the desired effect. If anything, they seemed to be worsening my depression. I was so miserable that I didn't see a point to being alive. I spent many waking hours thinking about ways to kill myself. I wanted to die. But most of the ways of killing yourself kind of suck.

Drown yourself, the voice of one of my sister's kids said to me. I pictured myself tying a cinder block to my ankle and chucking myself into a pool. The water was ice cold. At first, I would hold my breath. After a few minutes, I would try to breathe only to take in lungs full of water. My lungs would fill with pain. Soon the pool would fill with air bubbles. I would try to swim to the surface, desperate for air. But I wouldn't be able to get anywhere because of the weight tied to my ankle. Flailing around desperately, I would try to get the rope off my ankle…

"No," I sighed as I shook the imagery from my mind, and my heart started beating harder and faster.

Overdose. Take a bunch of your pain meds…, my attacker chimed in. Images of me swallowing a whole bottle of my pain medication flashed through my mind. I lay in bed waiting to pass out, never to awaken again. Then suddenly I felt a violently nauseous feeling in the pit of my stomach. I flung myself out of bed, looking for a safe place to vomit the contents of my stomach, only managing to find the floor.

"You do it wrong, and you just end up throwing up all over the place." I sighed, once again shaking the images from my mind.

Set yourself on fire? the kid suggested while laughing sadistically.

"Worse than drowning!" I shouted in disgust, not even dignifying this idea with imagining such a method.

Slitting your wrists is a popular way to go..., a female voice suggested. I imagined myself lying in the tub upstairs. The water was nice and warm. I turned on a radio that was playing my favorite song. I was hoping it would relax me as I grew anxious about what I had set out to do. I found myself thinking that the song would be the last thing I would ever hear. I slowly brought the razor to my wrists. I hesitated for a moment, staring at my wrists, my hands shaking. Then with one swift movement, I cut my wrists in a nice straight line. It hurt, but not as much as I thought it would. Then with less hesitation, I sliced the other one. I laid my hands back in the tub, tossing the razor blade as I did so. I closed my eyes, relaxing as the tub's water turned a dark red from all the blood mixing with the water.

Promising, I thought to myself. It seemed like the most pleasant way to go. Still I had a hard time imagining myself actually doing it. I wasn't a big fan of pain, and that was hardly a way I wanted my father to discover me.

* * * * *

In March of 2001, the results of an MRI (or coffin of death as I liked to call it) revealed the reason for my back pain. The MRI revealed a central disk herniation in my spine. A month later, Dr. Schultz, my orthopedic physician, concluded that this was indeed the cause of my neck, back and leg pain. The previous year of medical testing had completely missed this herniation. The doctors were not convinced that surgery was necessary. Dr. Schultz recommended I take Ultram, a non-narcotic used to treat severe pain. It didn't help the pain very much. It made me feel even more out it. Given my sleepiness up to now, I hadn't thought that was possible. As expected, the insurance company would claim that the herniation did not result from my attack the year before.

A month later, I felt no better. Dr. Schultz still did not think I should be considered a surgical candidate. As it would turn out, it would be another five years before surgery was approved by the insurance company. The doctor told me that I should lose weight and exercise to strengthen my back.

Two weeks later, a completely different doctor, Dr. Selden, was suggesting that there was no evidence of an orthopedic issue. He made this claim after doing a physical exam and yet another MRI. In his report, he said:

> I do not see any evidence of significant orthopedic pathology after having examined Mr. Noor today. There is definitely a large psychological overlay to his current complaints, given that he has such tenderness with even light palpation of the skin on his neck, back and legs. In my opinion, he does not require any further orthopedic treatment. I see no evidence of any orthopedic permanency related to the above injuries. Given that I cannot detect any evident orthopedic pathology, I would not place any restrictions on his activities.

Translation: the pain was all in my head, and there was no physical reason why I couldn't be working.

* * * * *

After spending many nights pondering the many different ways to kill myself, an answer came unintentionally from my brother in New York. He had been calling me at least a couple of times a week during this time, more than anybody else did.

"How are you?" my brother asked me.

"I've been better," I sighed.

"You get that money I sent you last week?" he asked.

"I did. Thank you, man." I paused. "It's so cold down here. I was thinking about moving my bed into the furnace room."

"Are you nuts!" my brother reacted with shock.

"What?" I asked, surprised.

"It's one of those old style furnaces, right?"

"Yes…"

"Adam, you sleep in there, and the fumes will slowly kill you. One morning, you simply won't wake up," he answered.

After talking a while longer, we hung up. I sat up in my bed and thought about his words. If I moved my bed into the furnace room, the fumes would slowly kill me. A painless death in my sleep—that was perfect! I moved my bed into the furnace room and attempted to go to sleep, hoping I would never wake up.

CHAPTER 7

September 11, 2001, was a day most people in this country will always remember. Despite my mental health issues, which usually caused me to be unaware of the passage of time or of what was going on around me, I am no exception. Most of my memory regarding this time in my life is foggy. But my memories of that day are as clear as day.

It was early in the morning, and I was making one of my rare appearances upstairs. I noticed my dad sitting in front of the TV, totally engrossed. He didn't seem to notice me at all. I walked slowly toward him, curious about what he was watching. He was flipping through channels. On every one of those channels was the Twin Towers. There was smoke emanating from the side of one of the buildings.

"What happened?" I asked, and my voice seemed to stun my dad.

"A plane crashed into one of the Twin Towers," he said absentmindedly.

"Wow. How'd that happen?" I asked in astonishment.

"Don't know. News isn't saying much yet," my dad said with a concerned tone in his voice as he continued watching. I sat down next to him and watched the buildings, waiting to find out what happened. We both thought it was some kind of accident. Right as we were watching, a plane hit the second tower. We watched with our jaws slack in shock. We just stared at the TV. My father started yelling and screaming. His channel changing became much more urgent. He switched from American channels to Arabic channels, all reporting the same event.

"Dad, what the hell is going on?" I asked, suddenly afraid.

"I don't know," my father replied with a mixture of fear and anger. "But this was no accident."

"Someone did this on purpose?" I gasped in utter disbelief. "Who would do such a thing? How could they?" I just didn't understand. I couldn't wrap my mind around it. There had to be thousands of people in those buildings, thousands of innocent people whose lives were now in danger.

"Terrorism—that's what this is," my dad said with a heavy sigh. Just as he said this, the news reporter on TV said the same thing. Before the second plane hit, there was speculation that this could be terrorism. But by the time the second plane hit, there was no more doubt. Someone had attacked America. Our eyes were glued to the TV, watching the news reports as they tried to make sense of what was going on. As we were watching, we suddenly saw a huge plume of smoke that seemed to envelop the second building. My father knew instantly what he had just seen. Before he had a chance to verbalize the horror, a reporter at the scene started talking:

"The second building that was hit by the plane has just completely collapsed. The entire building has collapsed as if a demolition team had set it off. Like what you would have seen if you had watched the demolitions of old building. It folded down on itself and it's not there anymore," Don Dahler reported.

"My God...," a random person could be heard saying.

"The whole side collapsed?" Peter Jennings asked, seemingly horrified.

"The whole building has collapsed," Don Dahler corrected.

"That's the southern tower you're talking about?" Peter Jennings frantically clarified.

"Exactly. The second building. The one we witnessed the second plane hitting..."

My dad and I stared at the TV in slack-jawed amazement, realizing that we were seeing thousands of people dying on live TV—men, woman, children. Realizing that there was no way that all the people had time to evacuate. People who just happened to be in that building. People whose lives had just been snuffed out.

My father cried, cried harder than I had ever seen him cry. It made me afraid. Who could do such a thing? Who could be cold-hearted enough to end the lives of so many innocent people?

We continued to flip through the channels, landing on CNN, which had a banner headline running under it reading: "America Under Attack!" But this was the strongest country in the world! I had always seen the United States as invulnerable. How could this happen here? Then, a more frightening thought came to mind. Was this the only place we were being attacked? Were planes crashing into the US elsewhere? Would our house soon be demolished? Unless you lived through these events, it would probably be hard to understand the fear that gripped the nation at this time. No one had any clue what was going on. Time flew by with our eyes glued to the TV, trying to soak in as much information as we could get. Suddenly, another major event was reported:

"Oh my God…It's hard to put it into words. Both towers of the World Trade Center, where thousands of people work, on this day, Tuesday, have been attacked and destroyed with thousands of people, either in them or in the immediate vicinity adjacent to them. There is simply no way to accurately describe the emotions that this evokes for people all over the world. Friends of the United States and enemies of the United States as well…," Peter Jennings said on the TV.

The second tower had collapsed. More people died. Perhaps thousands more. ABC reporter Peter Jennings's voice was quiet and low key. It wasn't long before my father was on his feet, reaching for his phone, trying desperately to reach my sister and brother who both lived in New York.

"They wouldn't have been in those building…," I said, trying to calm him.

"No. But who knows?" my dad said, panic-ridden. "Who knows what the hell is going on? He dialed numbers repeatedly and got no answer. He became more frantic. My heart rate was skyrocketing as I stood near him, just as desperate for him to get ahold of them.

My sister finally picked up the phone, and she was very upset. "Thank God!" my dad screamed. Tears were liberally falling out of his eyes. "I've never been so happy to hear your voice!" my dad exclaimed, still in anguish. I breathed a small sigh of relief while hugging him tightly. "I'll call you back!" my father bellowed. "I still have to hear from your brother." He hung up and quickly started dialing again. After another brief episode of panic, my brother ended up calling us, also in tears.

As we all now know, it was confirmed that this had been an act of terrorism. It was further confirmed, much to the eternal shame of many, that some of the men involved were Muslim. Ever since that day, many Americans have equated being Muslim with being a terrorist. Those committing acts in the name of Islam, killing thousands of innocent people, disgust me. And it disgusted my father. He was a gentle, amazing man who would never condone any act of violence. Islam and the Koran do not teach killing people. No religion does. Any group that preaches such beliefs is no religion at all and is not a worldview that anyone in my family, nor I, would ever be involved with.

"Everything is going to change now," my dad said with a heavy heart. "They will blame all of us for this."

"They can't blame all of us for this!" I said, shaking my head.

"Human nature is what it is," my father answered cryptically. I couldn't help but wonder how much worse the doctors and lawyers were going to treat me now. Most already treated me with disdain and disgust. How much worse would this attack on America, perpetrated by my own people, make it?

I remember wanting to go shopping to see if there were any differences in how we were treated. In the shopping mall, most people were just very quiet, walking around in a daze with an almost funeral-like silence permeating the building. Oddly enough, my life more or less returned to what had previously become my "normal." For me, this was hardly a good thing. My only interpersonal interactions were with doctors, lawyers, and occasionally, my own family. I didn't notice much of a difference in my life.

The president at the time was George W. Bush. He would become a divisive figure in America and abroad. I was no more a fan of him than anyone else that I knew. Although to be perfectly candid, for all intents and purposes, I pretty much slept through most of his presidency. All Americans were on his side when the attacks happened. Indeed the entire world was on his side. He went on television and condemned the terrorists and told them that this would not go unanswered.

On September 20, 2001, the president said: "I also want to speak tonight directly to Muslims, throughout the world. We respect your faith. It's practiced freely by many millions of Americans and by millions more in countries that America counts as friends. Its teachings are good and peaceful, and those who commit evil in the name of Allah blaspheme the name of Allah. The terrorists are traitors to their own faith, trying, in name, to hijack Islam itself. The enemy of America is not our many Muslim friends. It is not our many Arab friends. Our enemy is a radical network of terrorists and every government that supports them."

Compared to some the rhetoric we hear these days from politicians, this was a measured response. Today, we have politicians suggesting that we nuke the entire Middle East and politicians advocating banning Muslims from immigrating to this country. I believe that this rhetoric is highly irresponsible. Such comments are extremely unproductive. They only help extremists to recruit more terrorists. There are plenty of criticisms of what Bush did in the aftermath of 9/11, many of which I share. However, I will always respect him for having had the courage to say what he said on that day.

* * * * *

During the aftermath of the 9/11, all airports were shut down. Flights that were in the air were rerouted. Some were sent to Canada, and others landed in Great Britain. At the time that this terrible tragedy occurred, my mom was en route by plane from Jordan to the US. Her flight was sent to Britain. At that time, my father and I didn't know where she ended up. It was only after hours of stress and fear that we finally heard from her and learned that she was okay.

Every now and again, when I'm in a store or out in public, I will get funny looks from people. I know what they're thinking even if they don't say anything. They're wondering about me, wondering if maybe I'm a terrorist and if I were there to cause death and destruction. I've met plenty of wonderful people in America who do not instantly judge me and fear me. I've met just as many who do otherwise. What these people don't understand is that we were all attacked that day. When I'm out and about, I don't see white people or black people, Muslims or Christians. I see Americans. In my eyes, I'm not a Jordanian-Muslim immigrant. I'm an American citizen, just like everyone else here. And just like everyone else, I am haunted by the memories of what happened on that day.

CHAPTER 8

After briefly being aware of what was going on in the world, I returned to darkness. My life now consisted of doctor visits, conversations with lawyers and court appearances. I didn't feel like I was treated like a human being with feelings and value. I felt that I was being treated like an animal. Like cattle. The medications made it so I couldn't even stand up. Increasingly, I found myself wondering what the point of it all was. What kind of life was this?

Every night, I would go to bed near the furnace in hopes that the fumes would eventually kill me. Every morning I would wake up, still alive and disappointed. My nightmares became even more frequent and frightful. While awake, I had gone from hearing my attacker in my mind to hearing multiple voices. All of them created a constant stream of negativity.

When I was at one of my appointments, my mom would come downstairs and grab my dirty clothes to wash. When I would come home, I would find my clothes nicely folded and stacked in a safe place. A place away from where the leaks from the dirty kitchen and bathroom water fell. Oddly, I would find myself cutting up my clothes, not really sure why. Maybe I it was because I was bored and lonely. Maybe I felt that I did not deserve such nice clothes. Maybe I felt that if I looked too neat and clean on the outside, no one would realize that inside, I felt pain and deadness. I found myself having no desire to do anything or to see anyone. I remembered telling myself that the emergency room doctor had been wrong: I was in hell!

The basement gradually grew to reflect my worsening mental state. Dirty dishes and cups were strewn about. Fruit flies buzzing around the leftovers that I never quite got around to throwing away.

Occasionally, my sister from New York would visit. During her visits, I wouldn't see much of her. But I would find that my room had become far cleaner. I appreciated her and my family's efforts. But I didn't feel as though I deserved it. I felt I deserved to live in squalor. It was an outward reflection of who I had become. I felt that if everything was clean and tidy, it would be the equivalent of sweeping my pain under the rug. It would appear as if I was fine. But I wanted everyone to know that I felt far from fine.

* * * * *

On my birthday, while I was sleeping in the basement, I heard someone coming down the stairs. I looked up groggily and spotted my dad, who was carrying a chocolate cake with a single burning candle. He smiled as he walked towards me.

"I know you don't like celebrating your birthdays, but they are a reason to be happy," my dad said, answering my unspoken question.

"Thank you," I said quietly.

"The others wanted to be here. They couldn't quite make the trip," he said in a somewhat awkward way. Even in my worsening mental condition, I could read between the lines. They didn't want to come. They didn't want to see me like this. Their absence now felt no different from their absence all along. "You going to make a wish?" he asked me as I eyed the candle slowly burning wax onto my cake.

What do I wish for? Death? The end of talking to an endless array of doctors and lawyers? Wish that I hadn't been working the night I was attacked? There were so many things I could wish for. I couldn't decide. I'm not sure if I settled on any one thing when I finally blew the candle out.

"What'd you wish for?" my father asked.

"Can't tell you." I shrugged.

"Of course, not! Then it wouldn't come true," my father said in a chipper tone.

I didn't have the heart to tell him that I felt so demoralized that I had not really articulated a clear wish in my own head.

"I trust you don't mind if I take a few slices for your mom and I?" he asked.

And despite everything I was going through at the time, I laughed. I nodded "yes" with an amused smile. He cut him some pieces, kissed me on the forehead, and disappeared from view. I had some cake and then went back to sleep.

* * * * *

I was about ready to give up. Just let the insurance company win. I was tired of all the appointments with people who mostly didn't care one bit about making me better. I was convinced that even if they did care, they would be unable to do so. As far as I was concerned, I was permanently broken. I felt that I was part of some big game that I didn't understand. What I did understand was that the game wasn't about helping me. It wasn't about what was in my best interests. It was about doctors making money off of me and the insurance company saving their money. I believed that this was all that any of this was about. I wanted my life back. As crappy as my life seemed, I wanted my life to be mine. I did not want to be owned, controlled, or manipulated by lawyers, doctors, or the insurance company. My father, as always, would hear none of it.

"You have to keep going and fighting. You have to fight to get everything you believe you are entitled to," my dad said to me one day.

"This is never going to end. They're going to just keep sending me to doctors all over the place until I either give up or die," I said, frustrated.

"It will end. You have to trust your lawyer. He knows what he's doing," my father encouraged.

* * * * *

Near the end of 2002, I had grown weary of being a burden to my parents. I felt worthless and useless, and I was tired of it. They had done everything they could to take care of me. Despite my father never really showing it, I knew it was taking a toll on him. I felt that I offered nothing in return but grief and heartache. I loved both of them enough to not want to keep being an anchor around their necks.

My effort to kill myself by breathing the fumes of the old style furnace in my sleep did not seem to be working. I made a decision. It was time to hospitalize myself. A week before Christmas, I decided to check myself into the Institute of Living in Hartford, Connecticut. My parents were not happy with this decision. Despite everything, my father held out hope that I would still recover and one day be happy again. He held out hope that one day he would have his son back. I knew he was wrong. I knew deep down that the old Adam Noor would never be seen again.

* * * * *

When being hospitalized at the Institute of Living, you are allowed to bring clothes and general health-related stuff (toothbrushes, deodorant, etc.). Most of these items are controlled by the staff and kept locked up. Some people bring books or magazines with them. I elected to bring nothing but some clothes. I was packing a small bag of clothes when my father appeared by my side. He had a smile, but there was clearly sadness in his eyes.

"Are you sure about this, son?" he asked me sadly.

"It's what I need to do," I sighed as I looked at him.

"You can stay here as long as you want. I assure you I will never kick you out. You're my son and I love you."

"I know that, Dad," I said, trying to keep my expression neutral, fighting to keep from crying. "And I love you too." It was because I loved him that I was doing this in the first place. I zipped up my bag, threw it over my shoulder, and indicated that I was ready to go. He clapped me on the back and gave me a small hug. Without another word, we left the house.

* * * * *

It was called a hospital. But the experience of being in the Institute of Living was more like being in a prison. Entering the building, I was subjected to a security check. Not fun! The men who conducted the searches were big men, with permanent-seeming scowls on their faces. They were hard men who evidenced little to no emotion. I guess they had to be, dealing with the people they saw every day. Any sign of weakness might be very dangerous for them. I was strip-searched and had all my body cavities examined. It was a dehumanizing experience that I wouldn't wish on anyone. I had always been a prideful man and took the search to be even more evidence of how far I had truly fallen. Adam Noor, future famous musician, to Adam Noor, mental institution patient—hardly the American dream that I had once sought.

There were only two bright spots for me at this point. One: I was no longer a burden to my parents. Two: all the doctors that I had been required to travel to see at the behest of the insurance company were now inconvenienced and had to come to see me. In my little way, it felt as though I was now thumbing my nose at the insurance company and taking back a little control of my life.

Inside the hospital, we were watched every second of every day. If one had had thoughts about killing oneself, they would hardly have time to do so. We were constantly being checked on to make sure we were doing okay. It could be a doctor, an orderly, or a security officer checking in with you. Patients were hardly given a moment of peace. I felt that if a person was sane when they checked into the hospital, they would leave insane merely due to the constant pestering by the staff.

I observed the general population of the place and spent a good deal of time speculating about their various stories. How did they end up here? Who had they been before? Did any of them have hope to ever feel well again? I heard plenty of sad stories during my time there. This didn't help make me feel any better. If anything, I felt worse.

Medication was doled out at regularly scheduled times. We stood in lines that made it feel like we were just products on an assembly line. We were no longer human beings, but objects. One person after another was given medications. They had to gulp them down in front of the staff to make sure they were actually taken. No conversation. Just take your pill from the unsmiling staff member and move along. I had no idea what it was that I was taking, but it made me feel out of it and devoid of energy. Even more so than before.

I was put into a room with another person. In all my years, I had always had my own room. I believed that I could neither live with another person nor share a bathroom with anyone.

At the hospital, I was forced to do both, and it was probably the hardest adjustment I had to make. I could barely sleep at night with another person in the room. I feared that the other person might attack me if I fell asleep. I had no idea why he was there. For all I knew, he was institutionalized because he killed a bunch of people. I talked to no one and made no friends during my stay at the hospital. If someone approached me that wasn't a doctor, I brushed them off pretty quickly. I just wanted to be left alone.

* * * * *

"How are you feeling, Mr. Noor?" Of all the questions I had been asked by the various doctors I spoke to, this one seemed the most absurd. We were regularly subjected to counseling sessions with an assigned doctor. I was never under the impression that this doctor was any more interested in my well-being than any other doctor I had visited since this all began. He was merely doing his job and nothing else.

"Fine," I answered blandly.

"Do you feel like you're going to harm yourself?" the doctor asked. This was the only real question I was asked during those sessions. I was asked other questions, but this was the only one about which he cared about the answer.

"No" was always my response. For the record, if you ever find yourself on a locked psychiatric unit and get asked that question, no is the correct answer. I was in the Institute of Living voluntarily, but a yes answer to that question would have made it very difficult for me to leave.

* * * * *

Although I had the option of wearing clothes, I chose to wear the hospital robe and nothing else, literally nothing, not even flip-flops or shoes. I don't quite remember why I chose to act like this. If I had to guess, it was a means to make the insurance company doctors that visited me at the institute as uncomfortable as possible.

We were allowed smoke breaks every four hours. A bunch of us were taken outside and lined up right next to each other shoulder to shoulder inside a cage. The cage was just big enough to fit all of us with no extra room. We all just stood there taking drags from our cigarettes while being watched from above to make sure we weren't doing anything crazy.

Unexpectedly, I was even more miserable in this living situation than I had been at home. I didn't think that was even possible. I began seriously considering leaving. But leave for what? Going back to being required to travel to endless insurance company doctors that had no interest in helping me? To sleeping in the basement and being an endless burden on my parents? I didn't want to be in the hospital. But I was not happy about the thought of returning to what my life had been like before either. I felt trapped. With no real options.

* * * * *

One day, while I was staring off into space as I sat in the common room, I felt a tap on the shoulder. I turned to see a young-looking orderly looking down at me.

"You have visitors, Mr. Noor," he said to me gently.

Who could it possibly be? I stood up and followed the orderly until we got to the visitors' room. Upon entering, I was greeted by the sight of my mom and dad. I wasn't happy to see them. Nor was I unhappy to see them. I felt nothing at the sight of them. My dad and mom immediately gave me a big hug. They greeted me cheerily and asked how I was doing. My least favorite question these days.

"Son, you should really come home," my father said after a few moments of awkward small talk. The comment only made me sigh with sadness.

"Dad, I'm staying here for the rest of my life," I replied.

"You like it here?" my dad asked.

"Sure," I answered unconvincingly. "It's where I belong. I'm crazy. Broken. Can't be fixed."

"That's not true!" my dad yelled, finding himself surprised by his own angry outburst. "Time heals all wounds."

Except mine, I found myself thinking. I didn't say it out loud. I didn't want to argue with my father, nor did I wish to upset him. "I can't go back," I said quietly.

There was a very long and awkward pause before my father spoke again.

"I suppose I could move my study downstairs," my dad said. My eyebrows rose at that.

"You're thinking of turning my room into your study?" I asked, my voice sounding mildly perturbed.

"I might as well get some use out of it since you won't be coming home," my dad replied with an exaggerated shrug. He might have been feeling hurt and rejected by me for saying I liked it in the hospital. Maybe he was trying to provoke me into taking some type of action. I am not really sure.

He turned to my mother, who hadn't said anything since she arrived. "We should get going, my dear. We've taken up too much of our son's time," he said.

My dad turned back to me with a bright, cheerful smile. "It was good seeing you, son," he said. And without another word, they departed. I stared at them thoughtfully, only to be interrupted by the orderly who lead me out of the visitors' room.

* * * * *

99

About an hour after my parents left, I entered the doctor's office to begin another mind-numbing counseling session. These sessions had never been anything more than a waste of time. When I sat down in the chair, the doctor had not yet even looked at me.

"I understand your parents came to see you," the doctor said, still having not yet looked up at me. He was rifling through files and seemed to be writing reports.

"Yes," I said.

"How'd you feel about that?" the doctor asked me.

"I felt nothing." With that response, I finally drew the doctor's attention.

"Nothing?" he asked, surprised.

"Nothing at all," I confirmed.

"I see…," he reflexively responded. Then he launched into the typical question that led off every session: "How are you feeling?"

"The same as always, Doctor," I answered, sounding bored and weary. He resumed talking, and I actually quit listening. My mind wandered while he droned on. I was thinking about my dad. His seemingly idle comment about turning my room into his study poked at the back of my mind. I hadn't wanted to stay in the hospital. I was just as miserable here as I had been at home. More so actually. I had no privacy here. Something I desperately needed. I was watched on a constant basis. I never got much sleep, thanks to having a roommate that I spent time speculating might kill me or severely injury me at any moment. I wanted to die but not violently, not like that. What I was really more interested in was along the lines of going to sleep and never waking up, much like I had been attempting before I had come to the hospital. However, I remembered that the alternative was to be a constant drain on my parents and to deal with constant, stressful, and unenjoyable appointments with doctors and lawyers.

"Do you feel like you're going to harm yourself today?" he asked me after he was finished talking. I knew the "correct" answer to the question. However, in that moment, I was tempted to tell the truth, that I didn't want to harm myself but I wouldn't mind if someone else killed me nonviolently, that if someone came into that room right then and there and shot me, I wouldn't care in the slightest. My mind drifted back to the time I had spent in my basement. I found myself thinking about how it wasn't much, but it was still mine. I shared it with no one. In a way, it was my little kingdom. The dream of being a famous Arabic singer was long dead. I was nothing now, and it was likely that this would never change. However, if I did not go home and my dad converted my room into a study, my kingdom (the one place that was mine) would be gone. I decided to keep my mouth shut, knowing that if I answered the way I really felt, I would never be leaving this place.

"No," I said, and a small smile formed on my lips. "I wish to leave, Doctor."

"You wish to be checked out?" the doctor asked, surprised.

"Yes, sir," I said without a trace of hesitation.

"You are here on a voluntary basis, so that is your right. Still, I think you could benefit from further treatment from us. We can do that on an outpatient basis if you'd like," the doctor said.

"Sure," I said dismissively. What was one more doctor in my life?

Without resistance, I was released from the Institute of Living after only three days. My father came to pick me up and was especially cheerful in the car ride home. His "previous" son hadn't returned, but he was happy to have me in some form. I returned to the basement, my kingdom, and simply went to sleep.

Life went back to my version of normal: no better, no worse. But as time would eventually reveal, my time at the Institute of Living would not prove to have been a complete waste. As a result of my time there, I would meet the person that would be instrumental in improving my life. I was about to meet Dr. Rick, a man who would have a profound impact on me.

CHAPTER 9

Upon discharge from the Institute of Living, the insurance company's lawyer ordered me to see a psychologist three times a week. This enraged me. I wanted nothing to do with this. I was sick of doctors who were just trying to make money and who seemingly had no interest in helping me. They didn't care what or how I felt.

Dr. Richard Lautenbach was actually the manager of the Adult Day Treatment Program at the Institute of Living. This was an intensive group therapy program. I was referred to attend that program three days per week. My father and I canceled on him when we were originally supposed to show up for the program.

Months went by before my lawyer called and scheduled another appointment with Dr. Lautenbach. I still didn't want to go. Both my family and lawyer insisted that I needed to go. My lawyer was concerned that by refusing to go, I was jeopardizing my case.

Three months after I left the Institute of Living, I finally met with Doctor Lautenbach, whom I came to know as Dr. Rick. I went to his office with my family in tow. Expecting him to be no different from the many other doctors I had dealt with during the last three years of my life, I went in with a chip on my shoulder. The ironic thing is that I didn't like him at first. I didn't talk much during our first meeting. I just spent the entire time looking at my feet, with my dad and mom doing most of the talking.

"I feel it's important that I see your son one-on-one next time," I heard Dr. Rick say, though I barely cared at the time. After I was done with our first session, I called my lawyer and told him I didn't want to see this doctor anymore. Attorney Shaw, as usual, told me I had no choice. So I kept going to see him.

For the next few sessions, my father drove me and waited in the lobby. Dr. Rick, for his part, wasn't sure if he could really help me. He wasn't a trauma specialist for starters. Also, initially, he was having a difficult time understanding me. That was assuming I was even talking at all. He suggested a translator. Given my prior experience with them, I refused outright.

He tried to get me an Arabic psychiatrist who was actually from Jordan. I wasn't thrilled with the psychiatrist at all. Dr. Rick didn't understand the reason at the time, but I felt more shame in front of Arabic people. There is certainly a stigma attached to mental health issues in America. There is a lack of understanding about anxiety, depression, and other such issues. Those who do not suffer from one of these conditions simply do not "get it." If you're depressed, a person who doesn't suffer from depression will simply tell you to cheer up.

Anxious? Stop stressing out all the time. As bad as the stigma is in America regarding mental health issues, it is much worse in the Middle East. Because of this, I refused to be accepted into the Jordanian doctor's care. I wanted to see Dr. Rick or no one at all. Despite the fact that it seemed as though our sessions were initially unproductive, I liked seeing the man. He had a friendly way about him that I liked. From his own report he said:

> Getting reliable, accurate, complete information is difficult due to language difficulties. He speaks very broken English. His father speaks more fluently, but it is difficult to understand him as well. His mother speaks virtually no English.

He wasn't sure whether or not he was going to continue to see me. In his view, he just wasn't qualified enough to deal with my issues. Even though he felt overmatched, he ultimately decided to continue to be my psychologist. The alternative was no therapist at all, and that wasn't acceptable to him. He could see I needed help and couldn't, in good conscience, let me go without. Unlike most of the other doctors I had seen, he actually seemed to genuinely care about me and wanted to help me.

For quite some time, progress was minimal to nonexistent. It was a victory for me to even show up to my appointments. It was even more amazing when he was able to get me to say something even remotely useful. When he talked to me and I said nothing, he would try to put what he thought my thoughts, feelings, and experiences were into words and ask me if he was close to being correct. We did not understand each other very well at first. Despite progress being very slow, when I did go, I began to enjoy it. My basement was very cold and coming to his office was a pleasant experience because it was well heated.

It took about a month or two for me to start liking this doctor and for us to be able to do anything useful together. Gradually, I started to experience a benefit from going to see him. Somehow, he managed to understand me better than any of the other doctors even without an interpreter. I was amazed that he managed to understand anything I said to him. But little by little, I began to believe that he may have begun to understand some of how I was feeling and how horrible my life had become. As I saw the effort he was expending to attempt to communicate with me, it began to lift my spirits ever so slightly. He treated me like a person, not like an object to report on to the insurance company. Dr. Rick didn't push me like the other doctors. He gave me space to say what I wanted to say

As a result of meeting with Dr. Rick, I started to experience some improvement. Rather than dread appointments with him, I was excited about them. The appointments were one hour long, and that hour flew by. When it was over, I was sad that it was time to go home. My thinking started to change. I went from wanting to kill myself to having a bit of hope in my life. This took place despite nothing having changed in my life. I couldn't help but think that if I had started seeing Dr. Rick from the beginning, I would not have gotten so sick.

* * * * *

I have a vivid memory of one particularly pivotal session. I wasn't being very talkative. The voices in my head were being especially obnoxious on this day. I was very distracted, and my mind was somewhere else. Even after the therapy began to help me, there were times when I wouldn't talk much to Dr. Rick because of these voices.

"Adam," Dr. Rick said, "are you with me?"

I snapped to attention.

"Yes. I'm with you," I said quietly.

"You were saying something…," Dr. Rick prompted.

"I forgot," I said and let out a bit of an unpleasant chuckle.

"You seem distracted…"

I considered the doctor in front of me for several moments, wondering if I should tell him the full truth or not. Finally, I decided to trust him about this particular issue.

"I hear voices…," I started.

"Voices?"

"In my head…"

"I see…," Dr. Rick said, taking in this new information. "Do you recognize the voices?"

"Some of them. One of them is my attacker, the one who destroyed my life," I replied.

"What do these voices say? Do they tell you to do things?"

"No. They mostly just insult me." I laughed.

It was thanks to Dr. Rick that I started to recognize that the voices weren't real, that they weren't actually coming from any person or thing outside of myself. After this, they didn't scare me any less, but it did help.

* * * * *

A couple of months after I started seeing Dr. Rick, I was upstairs in my parents' house, cooking. It was the first time I had cooked anything for years.

My father had spent those years taking care of me, doing everything he could to help me. What he got in return was my yelling at him and treating him badly. But now, I seemed to be growing happier, and I wanted to do something for him. I knew he loved seafood. So I purchased salmon from the store and was cooking him a meal.

"Son?" I heard the gravely tones of my father from behind me. He sounded surprised. I turned to him with a warm smile.

"Hi, Dad."

"What are you doing?" he asked, trying to process what he was seeing right in front of him.

"I'm cooking you dinner," I replied, smiling brightly.

"Am I dreaming?" my father asked me, laughing while pinching himself.

"It's no dream, Dad," I said as I turned my attention back to my cooking.

He slowly approached me and gave me the biggest bear hug. He held me, seemingly forever. "Is it possible that I have my son back? After all this time?" he asked me with trepidation. "I've been waiting for this day." When my dad finished, he was nearly in tears.

"Me too," I said, my voice filled with emotion. When I was finished, we sat at the table. We ate together and chatted like father and son. It almost seemed like the good old days. Of course, it wouldn't last.

* * * * *

My father loved hanging out in the backyard. I was starting to get quite a bit better, and I started hanging out there with him, enjoying the warm weather together. It wasn't long before I noticed some people watching me. I assumed they were working for the insurance company. They weren't doing a very good job of hiding it. I wonder if it was their goal to make sure I saw them, a means of intimidation to make sure I didn't feel too comfortable. I wondered if they wanted me to know that they had their eyes on me. Whenever I went into my backyard or went walking, I would see the same car. Time after time. It wasn't a car that belonged to any of the neighbors. The occupants of the car were dressed in formal work clothes. They seemed to be watching me and writing things down on note pads.

At that point in time, I was far from being all the way back to being my old self again. But prior to these experiences, I had begun to start feeling much better. I had begun to be more active.

I brought this up with Dr. Rick. After asking a number of questions to understand as many of the details as possible, he shook his head with sadness and annoyance. He said that it was not uncommon for the insurance company for workers' compensation to hire people to watch those who had filed workers' comp claims. They were attempting to determine if my claim was fraudulent. He asked me to attempt to distract myself since focusing on these people might make me more anxious and distressed.

* * * * *

I was not well enough yet to drive myself. During all my trips to the various doctors, I was having a driver take me. The driver was hired by the insurance company. One day, as I opened the door to the car to go to an appointment with Dr. Rick, I noticed a very attractive Arabic woman in the driver's seat. My jaw dropped when I saw her. For the most part, she was dressed professionally. But she wore a low-cut shirt that displayed ample cleavage.

"You going to get in?" she asked with a seductive lilt to her voice.

"Of course…," I said and got into the car. While a part of me was enjoying looking at her, another part of me was eyeing her suspiciously. She started flirting with me and asking me questions about my life. At first, I enjoyed the attention. It had been a while since any woman had interacted with me in this manner. But at the same time, I couldn't help but be very wary of her motivations.

"You sure you're disabled?" she asked.

"Yes. Why?" I asked, feeling suddenly on edge.

"You seem okay to me." She shrugged. "And it's a shame…"

"A shame?" My eyebrows rose.

"I'd love to go out with you. Maybe grab some dinner?" she said in a shy manner or at least the appearance of shyness. "Maybe have some fun after…," she said, licking her lips. "You probably can't though, because of the condition…"

I stared at her, my aggravation growing by the second. I felt that my suspicion had been confirmed. I may have been damaged physically and mentally. But I was not a stupid man. The insurance company was throwing an attractive woman at me to attempt to seduce "the truth" out of me. I was almost going blind with white-hot anger. I couldn't help myself. I started yelling and swearing at her. She began looking scared. This was the first authentic behavior I had witnessed in her. The rest was just an act. When we arrived at Dr. Rick's office, I jumped out the car and looked back at the woman with pure rage.

"I don't want to see you again! I know you're working for them. Get the hell out of here and don't come back!" I yelled and slammed the door. I got away from the car as quickly as I possibly could.

* * * * *

I made my way to Dr. Rick's office as quickly as possible. The minute he saw me, I just started ranting and raving.

"I can't believe they would go this far!" I shouted while pacing back and forth.

"Whoa, whoa! Calm down. What are you talking about?" Dr. Rick asked with concern.

"The freaking insurance company hired an attractive Arabic woman in order to attempt to get me to 'confess' that I'm just fine!" I shouted with anger.

"You sure?" Dr. Rick asked, seeming astonished.

"They couldn't be any more freaking obvious about it!" I shouted and continued pacing. "They know that it would be the height of shame for an Arabic man to admit out loud to being disabled and not well enough to satisfy a willing Arabic woman. They thought they would shame me into claiming that I was not disabled in order to use these words against me in the court case. It was a dirty trick for them to use my own culture's attitudes to try to embarrass me into saying that I am not disabled! I want that woman gone! I am not going back with her. I refuse!" I shouted.

Dr. Rick managed to calm me down a little bit. He called the driver's company, and after some time, they agreed to send another person out to bring me home. This was only the beginning.

* * * * *

"The lawyers for the insurance company have called for an emergency court session," my lawyer said to me over the phone.

"An emergency court session? What for?" I asked, feeling kind of worried.

"They haven't said exactly. It's for this Friday," my lawyer replied.

"I can make it. I'm not busy," I said. "I'm not ever busy, unless I'm in court or in a doctor's office…"

* * * * *

I nervously sat in the court, waiting for the judge to arrive. I was fidgeting, twitching, and shaking my leg. Everything I do when I am nervous. My lawyer kept insisting that I try to relax, but it didn't help. I had no idea what this court appearance was all about. Our next regularly scheduled court appearance was not due to take place for a number of weeks.

"All rise!" the bailiff said. And the entire court room did as they were instructed. A door opened and an elderly judge swiftly made his way to the bench.

"You may be seated," the judge instructed. He glanced at the insurance company's lawyer. "Mr. Lawson, if you would be so kind. Please fill us in on what we are doing here today," he asked sternly.

"Certainly, Your Honor." Mr. Lawson stood. "We have conclusive proof that Mr. Noor is faking his injuries," he said, his voice dripping with disdain. I nearly exploded with anger upon hearing him say those words. I made a move to quickly stand up, but my lawyer held me down.

"Oh, do you now?" the judge said, his voice filled with a weary, tired sarcasm.

"You liar!" I shouted, earning me a dirty look from my lawyer.

"Mr. Noor, quiet down. There will be no outbursts in my court-room," the judge said, casting an angry look in my direction. "Well, Mr. Lawson, what evidence do you have for us today?"

Mr. Lawson signaled toward the back of the room. A TV with a VCR was brought up to the front of the courtroom by a very young-looking man. It was quickly plugged in and turned on. The TV displayed a shaky, slightly grainy video. It was clearly taken from within a car that was a great distance away. But there was no mis-taking that the person on the video was me. I stared at the video, stupefied. Eventually what I was doing on the video became clear. I was buying a phone card to talk to my mom. I recognized the clothes I was wearing and the store I had entered. That I was able to do this was a bit unusual for me, given my memory issues. I felt myself shak-ing with rage as I watched the video. When the video concluded, all that could be heard was static. The TV was quickly turned off.

"Mr. Lawson, what did I just watch?" the judge asked, seeming a little bewildered.

"He was able to go to the store and buy a phone card," Mr. Lawson said dramatically. "We obtained the footage from his driver on that day."

"And this proves that he has no significant health issues and that he should be able to work?" the judge asked, dumbfounded and with a bit of a chuckle.

"Your Honor, this is nonsense! This video proves nothing," my lawyer thundered and started talking in legalese that I didn't quite understand. He went on for a good five minutes. I was very proud of him and touched that he argued so passionately for me.

"Your Honor, there is more," Mr. Lawson continued.

"Present your evidence, Mr. Lawson," the judge said in an annoyed tone.

"In addition to this video, we have several pictures of the defen-dant walking to the mailbox, holding a bag. We conclude from these pictures that the defendant has no back issues and is perfectly fine. Therefore, he should be able to work and should not be eligible for disability."

The judge looked at the photos for several moments. I found myself wondering about this system of justice. I wondered how being able to carry a small bag was evidence of my being able to lift boxes of cans and other items as I had when I was working.

"Your Honor, we've been to several doctors who all say the same thing. Mr. Noor is not capable of working. He is mentally and physically disabled," my lawyer said as he stood up.

"Our doctors say the exact opposite," Mr. Lawson said with a shrug.

"What a shock! Doctors that you paid and are on your payroll agree with you!" my lawyer bristled, his voice dripping sarcasm. Mr. Lawson was about to make another comment when the judge had finally had enough.

"Thank you, gentlemen, but I've heard enough," the judge said briskly. "Mr. Lawson, if you had pictures and videos of Mr. Noor holding and carrying boulders, I might conclude that you were right. As it stands, this is proof of absolutely nothing. Mr. Noor being able to buy something from the store or walk to the mailbox, carrying a small bag does not prove that he is able to work," the judge declared. "Mr. Noor's status has yet to be ascertained, and it will not be determined today. We have a court date coming up in a few weeks, correct?"

"That's correct, Your Honor," my lawyer responded confidently.

"Very well. We will adjourn until then," the judge barked. Then he turned back to Mr. Lawson. "Mr. Lawson, if you attempt a stunt like this again and insist on wasting my time, I will find you in contempt. Is that understood?"

"Understood, Your Honor," Mr. Lawson responded, sounding chastened.

"We are adjourned," the judge said. And just as swiftly as he entered the room, he was gone. I found myself glaring at my lawyer, who was just sitting in silence at the table, shaking his head.

* * * * *

The fact that I was able to restrain myself from yelling at my lawyer immediately after this ordeal had ended was actually fairly impressive. Once we made our way through the crowd of people, he pushed me into an empty conference room. I didn't hold it in any longer.

"What the hell was that?" I shouted.

"Clearly one of your drivers took that video and sold it to the insurance company," my lawyer responded calmly.

"So I've been right! The insurance company has been spying on me!"

"It appears so," my lawyer said sheepishly.

"I'm getting sick of all this…," I said, my voice filled with frustration. "When is all this going to stop?"

"Hard to predict," my lawyer replied, shrugging his shoulders.

"I'm tired of doctors, lawyers, judges! I'm tired of it all!" I shouted angrily.

"I'll try not to take that personally," my lawyer said, attempting to make a joke. But it fell flat because I was hardly in a joking mood.

"I want to quit! I want to be done!" I yelled.

"Adam, listen to me. Eventually, we are going to win this case. The little stunt they pulled seriously weakened their standing with the judge. Everything is going to be fine. You'll see."

I just glared at him and eventually left the room without further comment.

* * * * *

So it was now confirmed that I was being spied on. They were watching me everywhere I went. Before this, I had been getting better. Now I was regressing. I was back to staying in the basement, mostly sleeping. I would start to get up, and the "helpful" voice would remind me that maybe it wasn't such a good idea.

You sure you want to get up? They are watching you. They probably have cameras in your room…, my attacker said to me as I started to try to sit up.

"That's ridiculous," I bellowed. "There's no camera in here."

How can you be so sure? Did you think they were going to be taking pictures and videos of you? Sending hot girls after you, trying to get you to confess? The insurance company is sneaky..., a female voice in my head added. I lay back down, unwilling to move.

* * * * *

All the progress I had started to make evaporated. I was back to not being able to leave my bed. I had stopped hanging out with my father and making dinners for him. No longer was I going to Dr. Rick despite the attempts of my lawyer and family to get me to see him. I believed I was going to remain in my bed for the rest of my life.

CHAPTER 10

I woke up. My heart was pounding hard. I was drenched in sweat. My chest was tight to the point of hurting. As I awoke, I was convinced that I was about to die. Before, I would have welcomed death. Now I wanted to try to live. This seemed like a cruel joke. I immediately called for an ambulance. Then I called my brother in New York.

"Tell Dad...I'm sorry," I began.

"For what?" my brother asked me, having no clue what I was referring to.

"I'm going to die..."

"What are you talking about?" he asked, his voice filled with alarm.

"I'm having a heart attack. I think I'm finally going to die. Let Dad know that I'm sorry...," I said with great effort as I found it increasingly difficult to breathe. In addition to my difficulty breathing, there was a tingling sensation that made me even more nervous. Things gradually faded out until darkness claimed me.

* * * * *

I woke up in another hospital with both my dad and mom at my side. It was explained to me that thanks to my dad, the paramedics located me and brought me to the hospital. A doctor was quick to join me to help explain my condition.

"Did I have a heart attack?" I asked.

"Mr. Noor, we looked at your heart seven ways to Sunday, and we didn't find any problems with your heart. So no, it wasn't a heart attack," the doctor said with a reassuring smile.

"Then what was it, Doctor?" my dad asked.

"We think you had a severe panic attack," the doctor replied. "Judging from your recent medical history, you've had a lot of anxiety and depression issues. The severity of the attack suggests the problem is getting worse. I'm not sure what you know or don't know about panic attacks, but basically it's your fear response going into overdrive…"

"Am I going to die?" I asked. I was scared to hear the answer.

"No, not from a panic attack. You can't die from a panic attack. It's just scary as hell as your body and mind are telling you that you are going to die. Theoretically, if you continue to have them and live under the stress you're currently living under, you could do damage to your heart and, after a period of time, die as a result of the heart damage. However, that would likely take decades to occur."

"What do you recommend?" my father asked.

"Not sure what I can recommend beyond what he's already doing. I would suggest going to your regular doctor. Maybe he will try adjusting or changing the medication. In addition, he could try working on techniques with his therapist to help him cope with his anxiety more effectively," the doctor responded.

"Thank you, Doctor," my dad replied, shaking his hand.

"When can I leave?" I asked.

"Honestly, there's no reason for you to stay. I can fill out the discharge papers now, and you can be on your way. Just give me, like, ten minutes," the doctor said and wandered away.

"More doctors. More medication," I sighed bitterly. My dad put a reassuring hand on my shoulder, and my mom gave me a hug.

* * * * *

By this time, most of the psychological gains that I had made were now reversed. I was back in the basement, sleeping almost all the time, much to my dad's sadness. He had really begun to be hopeful about having me back to being somebody who came even close to resembling my old self. I stopped going to Dr. Rick entirely.

Eventually, both my lawyer and my father reached out to him and Dr. Rick, seeing that the situation had become critical, started coming to my house to have sessions with me in my basement. The initial sessions resembled our first ones. A complete inability to communicate with each other. Eventually, thanks to his patience, I started warming up to him again and started talking more.

My family treated Dr. Rick as if he were a member of the family. This was something that occasionally made him uncomfortable. He wanted to be careful since he knew he was crossing a typical doctor-patient boundary. But he also felt that there were so many complicating factors (the severity of my illness, the language and culture differences, etc.) that the only way to be effective was to take a few risks. My dad always insisted that he stay for dinner after every session.

"I appreciate the offer, but I have to get home. My wife is making me dinner," Dr. Rick would usually say. Sometimes this would work. Other times, he would be coerced by my parents to have a little to eat. He had to walk a tightrope. He was trying to avoid going too far beyond the boundaries of what he felt he should be doing, while also not wanting to insult my family. It's a line that I did not appreciate back then. But I understand it more fully now.

His actions went beyond what he would normally do for a patient. But he recognized me as a wounded soul in need of help, and if this was what it took to get me that help, then so be it.

* * * * *

"Don't you feel I'm worthless? Useless?" I found myself asking Dr. Rick at one point while sitting on my bed.

"I don't feel that way at all. What is leading you to feel that way about yourself?" he asked me.

"I'm not working. I'm not doing anything, just wasting away. I feel like I should be working harder to get better."

"Adam," he remarked, "I've never met anyone with problems as severe as yours who works harder to get better, who pushes himself beyond his comfort zone. If I felt like you weren't working hard enough, I would tell you so."

He would tell me that he knew I desperately wanted to work and be healthy again. He said that he had hope that he could get me there. As previously mentioned, Dr. Rick was not a trauma specialist. As a result, he spent a lot of time reading and going to workshops in order to figure out how to help me. We tried relaxation techniques, which included breathing exercises, progressive muscle relaxation, relaxing imagery, etc. He tried to get me to talk about the incident while practicing these relaxation skills. He wanted to get me to a point where I could at least talk about what happened without having a severe anxiety reaction. Those attempts did not work. We tried something called Cognitive Behavioral Therapy. He coached me in strategies for altering the way I think when I'm in an anxiety provoking situation. An example of one of these situations was when encountering a person that resembled my attacker. This technique also did not seem to help me very much.

At one point, Dr. Rick was talking about a particular kind of therapy called Exposure Therapy. It's an attempt (after self-soothing and calming skills have been practiced) to expose a person to situations that gradually increase their similarity to the situations that cause them extreme anxiety. The hope is that this would desensitize the person to the situation well enough so that the situation would no longer cause major anxiety. He said it was a bit on the risky side and would only work if the person is not extremely overwhelmed. He didn't want to put me in a situation where I was overwhelmed emotionally. I would need to get to a certain level of stability before being able to try this. I have never really gotten to that point. I never really got to a point where I had mastered the coping skills well enough to keep me from being overwhelmed by my anxiety. After a number of months of this type of work, it was concluded that this approach was not having the desired result. As a consequence, Dr. Rick changed courses again.

He decided to attempt a more basic approach than what he was initially aiming for. I was not even leaving the house for anything. I became a permanent fixture in the basement, almost as permanent as the ceiling or floors. He started taking me outside for long walks, and he would start to ask me questions. "How are you feeling right now?

How's your anxiety?" He'd see someone that resembled my attacker, and he would stop and try to get me to do relaxation techniques before moving on.

Eventually, he would have me wander ahead of him so that I would begin to become more comfortable being outside without him being right next to me the whole time. This approach gradually began to work, and I was once again able to go out of my house without having a major panic attack. It was a modest victory, but a victory nonetheless.

CHAPTER 11

In 2004, I received the news that I was finally going to be able to become an American citizen. My ex-wife, Evanna, had written the Department of Immigration an impassioned letter, saying that I was an awesome guy and that I should be granted citizenship. In the letter, she said that the reason for the divorce was because she just couldn't live with me anymore, given my various mental health issues. Five years after arriving in this country, I was officially an American citizen. If I had not felt that my life was a living nightmare, I would have been far happier about the news. As it stood, I had decidedly mixed feelings. On the one hand, I was very proud to actually have achieved my dream of becoming an American citizen. It was an amazing feeling. But at the same time, I hadn't come to this country to become damaged and useless. My dream was to become a famous musician, not to become severely mentally damaged and have to live out my days living in a dark, dank basement, waiting to die.

"What do you think about trying to resurrect your musical career?" Dr. Rick asked.

"Music comes from deep within my heart. But my heart no longer has any feelings. I am emotionally numb. So I can no longer sing" came my reply.

It had been so long since I had even attempted to sing that my skills had probably atrophied. There had been a few attempts by Mr. Soprano to get me to sing. On occasion, he would invite me to a club in New York City. Each time, I would find myself unable to perform. The anxiety was too much for me to handle. It became very clear that

I would not even be able to attempt to become the singer I had once dreamed of being. Those days were done.

* * * * *

Despite feeling comfortable with Dr. Rick and making some progress, the insurance company was still sending me to other doctors for more evaluations. As I understood it, they were doing this for no reason other than to continue giving me a hard time. At one point, they sent me to see a doctor in New York. This psychologist was very mean to me. He asked me nothing but insulting questions. He didn't even pretend to be trying to help me. He did not seem to even be interested in ascertaining whether or not I was actually disabled. He seemed to have his mind made up before I even walked through the door. So it seems that I was sent hours away from my home, just to be insulted and have my time wasted. He repeatedly called me a liar. I'm not a violent man, but this person made me want to physically hurt him. I was convinced that the insurance company hired him just for this purpose, to get me to attack him, which would either be evidence that I was physically fine or get me arrested. I left that meeting extremely angry, and I did not cool down during the entire ride back home.

* * * * *

Then a new problem began to arise. My mouth was so dry as a side effect of the numerous medications I was taking that it had led to gum disease and weakened teeth. I had already been having a hard time eating. But now my teeth were starting to fall out. As usual, the insurance company was refusing to acknowledge responsibility for this. My lawyer sent me to see a dentist for an evaluation. The fear of losing my teeth made me temporarily forget about the other physical pain I was experiencing. All I wanted to do was save my teeth. Everything else in my life was messed up, and I didn't need any new problems.

The dentist was an elderly man. He seemed very nice. Very professional. I trusted him right away. In my endless trips to see doctors, I had yet to see a dentist. So I did not have the chip on my shoulder that I had regarding other doctors.

"Please, sir. Please help me," I remember saying to him. "I want to eat. I need to eat." He told me that he agreed with me. He thought the medications were causing my dry mouth, leading to my teeth weakening. He said he was going to write a report to the insurance company, stating this opinion and recommending that they should pay to fix my teeth and gums. I was very grateful to this dentist. Unfortunately, he turned out to the latest person lie to my face. He wrote a report saying the exact opposite of what he told me. He said that the medications were not responsible for my dental problems. Betrayed again! Why did he do this? I'll never know.

* * * * *

Finally, the insurance company relented regarding the issue of my back. They approved the surgery to fix my central disc herniation. It had taken nearly four years to agree to take care of my back.

I was excited when they initially announced the decision. I had hope that I was finally going to be out of pain. However, as the date neared, I became increasing apprehensive. I began to lose faith that the insurance company was really going to pay for my surgery. They had approved the surgery, which generally means they had agreed to pay for it. But I wasn't thinking logically.

They'll put you under the knife, but then they'll refuse to pay for it, the attacker said in my head.

You'll be on the hooks for thousands of dollars, said a female voice in my head.

Or worse..., I heard a little boy say.

"Worse?" I asked the open air.

They'll kill you..., the attacker suggested.

If you're dead, no more problem. Think of all the money they'll save! the woman's voice gleefully said to me.

Despite coming to understand that the voices weren't real, they still frightened me. And I was unable to simply dismiss what they were saying. I could not help but fear that they were right. I increasingly came to believe that the insurance company was going to pay the doctors to kill me so that their problem of the last couple of years would go away. Days before the surgery, I canceled. This annoyed my lawyer to no end. He thought that my having the surgery would help our case. I didn't care. I refused to have the surgery despite my ongoing physical pain.

* * * * *

My parents were becoming increasingly concerned about me continuing to live in the basement. They had seen me make progress, only to regress over and over again. They loved me too much to continue watching me wasting away in the basement. My mom got proactive. During a trip to Jordan in 2006, she noticed a woman who looked young and beautiful. She approached this woman and asked her for her name. Her name was Deena.

"Have you ever wanted to go to America?" my mother asked her.

"I've always wanted to go there," Deena said enthusiastically.

"I have a way you can go," my mother replied.

"How's that?" Deena asked, curiously.

"I have a son who needs a wife…"

* * * * *

When my mom returned from Jordan, the instant I woke up, she made a point of visiting me in the basement. I didn't often see her in the basement. So this made me curious.

"I've been talking to your father…," she began.

"Yes?" I asked, my heart starting to beat faster. I was anxious that she was about to tell me that they had gotten sick of me and it was time to kick me out.

"About your future," my mother responded vaguely.

"I have no future," I said reflexively.

"We disagree. I met a woman while I was in Jordan," my mother said. "And I think she would be good for you."

"Good for me for what?" I asked, a little annoyed.

"To be your wife," she said.

I couldn't help myself. I started laughing.

"You found a woman for me to marry?" I asked incredulously.

"Your dad and I agree that this would be a good thing" was all she said.

"Dad agrees with you?" I asked, astonished. I remembered how my dad was so against my prior marriage. Why would he think this was a good idea? Was it because it was a Muslim woman who could give me children? Even my completely screwed up mind realized that this didn't make any sense.

"This could be good for you. Give you a sense of purpose," my mother said. "Plus I could use some grandkids."

"Mom, you already have grandkids," I pointed out, shaking my head.

"What mother doesn't want more?" She laughed. "I bought you a phone. Her number is already programmed in. Give her a call. See how it goes," she said and gave me a pat on the leg. She handed me the phone and left the room, leaving me in the dark to ponder the situation.

* * * * *

Here's the thing about my father. He was head over heels in love with my mother, to the point where he could never disagree with a single thing she ever said. If she said the sky was purple, then as far as my dad was concerned, the sky was purple. They never fought because my dad never disagreed with her, at least not when talking directly to her. Sometimes he would quietly voice an opinion to me. But he was adamant that I should never tell my mother about his opinion. There were times when he seemed like a little boy who was afraid of his mother.

I remember being at a wedding in America before my assault. At that wedding, a man who had been married for fifty years was asked what the secret to a long marriage was.

"Yes, dear" was the response that came from him, much to the amusement of all the guests assembled. I believe that my dad took that advice to heart because that was how he acted when it came to my mother.

When she returned from Jordan with news that she had found a woman for me to marry, he did not say a word against her. But privately, he disagreed 100 percent with her regarding the notion that this was a good idea. When they were talking about it, he did not say so. As a result, my mom thought my dad genuinely believed that this was what they both thought was best for me. My dad never approached me to discuss the subject. He thought there was not a chance I would actually go for any such thing. My dad had faith in me to make good decisions, even in my terrible condition. Unfortunately for everyone involved, he overestimated me…

* * * * *

It was one in the morning and I was tossing and turning. I was having one of those stretches of time when I couldn't sleep at all. I found myself staring at the phone that my mother had given me. It was sitting on the night stand next to my mattress. I picked up the phone and noted the time. It was two in the morning. I had no idea what time it would be in Jordan. But I knew it would be later there. Was there ever a time when I knew the answer to that question? Maybe. If so, that knowledge was lost years ago when I was brutally beaten. Just like the rest of my life. I flipped open the phone and stared at it for a moment. Should I? Or Shouldn't I? I looked through the contacts. There was only one. Deena.

Hmmm. Pretty name, I thought. Oddly, I felt a strong sense of déjà vu. Don't know why.

"Do any of you have anything to say?" I asked the open air, waiting for the voices to chime in. They were curiously silent. They never responded to any of my requests. "No, of course, you don't." I sighed. I sat there for what seemed like an eternity just staring at the phone. "You know what? Screw it," I said and pushed the button. The phone rang. Each ring seemed to be drawn out for an eternity. I was worried that no one would answer, and I would have to leave a message. I didn't like answering machines, never knew what to say.

"Hello," a cute female voice finally answered.

"Hi," I said shyly. "I'm looking for Deena." My voice cracked a little bit. I was nervous. I hadn't felt this nervous talking to a woman since I was a little boy having crushes on the girls I went to school with.

"I'm Adam Noor," I answered, and I heard silence after that. "From America. You met my mother…"

"Oh yes! Adam! Wow! I'm so happy to hear from you!" she said excitedly. It had been a while since anyone had expressed excitement at hearing from me. It felt good.

"I didn't wake you, did I? I have no idea what time it is…"

"No! It's a little bit after nine in the morning," she replied, and I could hear the smile in her voice.

"Good! Very good!" I replied happily. "It's like two in the morning here."

"Two in the morning? You always up that late?"

"Sometimes," I replied vaguely. "What are you doing?"

"I just finished eating breakfast. I was going to go for a swim. I'd invite you along, but you're a little far away," she mused.

"Yes, a bit," I agreed. "Maybe someday not so far away."

"That'd be nice," she replied with a flirtatious tone. "Well, I'm about to go for that swim. Can I call you later?"

"Of course! Anytime," I replied happily. She said goodbye and hung up the phone. I found myself staring at the phone once more. This time, it was different. I was happily pondering the phone conversation I had just had. It stood in stark contrast to conversations I had been having for over five years now. I was experiencing a feeling I hadn't had in ages. I didn't think it was possible that I would ever feel again. I felt good. I felt happy. And I felt excited. Could this be the start of something good?

Chapter 12

For the first time in many years I had something to look forward to that didn't involve going to see Dr. Rick. Deena and I began calling each other at random times. I set the ringer on my phone to full blast so even if I was in the deepest drug-induced sleep, I would still awaken and get her phone call. As it turned out, she was quite the busy woman. She was going to school and working at a local day care center. Her dream was to come to America and teach special needs children. She was determined to do all that she could to eventually make her dream come true. In a lot of ways, she reminded me of myself. Or at least who I used to be.

"So I don't know if my mom told you, but she wants us to get married," I said out of the blue one night, hardly the most suave thing to do. But I had given up on being suave years ago.

"She mentioned it," Deena replied.

"You want to come to America, right?" I asked.

"I do!"

"Are you interesting in getting married?" I continued, not terribly romantically.

"I'm interested…," she answered quietly.

"But you don't really know me…"

"You sound like a wonderful man. Your mother says you are great," she purred.

"You can't go by what my mom says!" I said, laughing. "Mothers always think their sons are awesome. I'm sure Hitler's mother thought the world of her son."

"Are you Hitler?" she asked teasingly.

"Nope." I chuckled.

"Then you can't be so bad," Deena responded, giggling. "Are you interested in marrying me?"

"I don't know yet. I know nothing about you," I said thoughtfully. "I don't even know what you look like, though you sound beautiful."

"Thank you," she said. "I could always send you a picture…"

I thought long and hard about this, and neither one of us spoke.

"No…," I answered.

"No?" she asked, sounding surprised.

"Send me your feet," I said.

"My feet?"

"Yes. A picture of your feet," I said.

"For a second there, I thought you meant you wanted me to actually send my feet." She laughed.

"Not unless you are coming with them," I retorted.

"Good. Because I don't want to marry a serial killer," she said cheerily. "So you want me to send a picture of my feet, not the rest of me?"

"Just your feet. I really like feet," I responded.

"Okay," she said in a tone that suggested that she thought I was a little bit crazy. She really had no idea how right she was. I gave her my e-mail address. We said our goodbyes, and from that moment forward, I would continuously check my e-mail for pictures.

* * * * *

I finally got the pictures and her feet were indeed very lovely. Deena had to go to work, so she was unavailable to talk. As I lay there in the dark, attempting to sleep, I heard the phone ring. Without even looking at it, I quickly grabbed it and flipped it open.

"Deena?" I asked excitedly.

"Afraid not, brother" came the amused voice of one of my younger brothers who was currently residing in Jordan. In my culture, it is typically the eldest brother who would command the most respect. After one's father, it was the eldest son who ran the family. I was the eldest. But thanks to my condition after the attack, I no longer held that status. The favored son became Raafid Noor. I would have been surprised if I had any rank anymore.

"Raafid?" I asked.

"It's me, brother," Raafid answered.

"How'd you get this number?" I asked, surprised. The only person to know about this phone number, other than Deena, was my mother. Everyone else called me on a different number, if they called at all.

"Mother gave me the number. I'll forgive your lack of excitement to hear from me. I understand you were expecting someone else."

"A woman," I confirmed.

"I know all about that, brother. Mom has kept me in the loop," Raafid said. At the moment, I didn't quite understand what that meant. "Did you enjoy the pictures of Deena's feet?" he asked, amused.

"Very lovely," I responded, caught off guard. "How do you know about that?"

"Deena has been in contact with mom and me," Raafid said. "You going to marry her or not?"

"I don't know. She sounds lovely. But I am no good. Not anymore." I sighed sadly. "I don't know that I have anything to offer."

"Nonsense! I know about your situation. Perhaps marrying this woman could give you a sense of purpose. You just need a change…," he suggested.

"Mother said the same thing," I said absentmindedly.

"Our mother is wise," Raafid said.

"You really think this is a good idea?" I asked him.

"I wouldn't be involved if I didn't. It's your call though."

"I think…" I paused. "I think I would like to do this."

"Very good, brother," Raafid said, sounding pleased. "I will start making arrangements. I'll handle everything except for proposing to Deena. That part you will need to handle yourself." He laughed. "Farewell, brother. I will be in contact."

We hung up the phone, and I lay there, wondering if I was completely crazy to be planning to do this. Then I thought, *Mom,*

Dad, and Raafid all agree with this plan. If they all think it is a good idea, then it must be...

* * * * *

"I want to marry you," I said right off the moment Deena called me.

"You liked my feet?" she asked, laughing.

"I did very much," I replied honestly. "I want to marry you, but I feel like there's something you should know about me before we do..."

"Tell me," she said gently.

I didn't tell her the full extent of my problems. But I did tell her about what had happened to me all those years ago. I also gave her a rough idea of some of the problems I had been experiencing since then. Without providing all the details, I told her about living in the basement, feeling useless, and being an endless burden on my father. Despite his endless kindness, I knew that my condition was wearing on him. I knew it was making him older and even more tired.

"If you keep going on that way, you're going to kill yourself...," she said after I was finished.

"Yes, I will," I replied absentmindedly.

"You have some issues," she said seriously. "I'd love to help you, make you happy. I can make you happy, Adam."

"You believe you can make me better?" I asked.

"I do...," she replied.

"Then, Deena, will you marry me?" I asked quietly.

"Adam Noor, of course, I will marry you," she replied equally quietly but also happily.

* * * * *

Within days, we were getting married by phone. In my culture, to get married, all you need is permission from the family and someone to fill out the paperwork. At this point, I didn't know that she didn't yet have her family's permission to marry me. That's something that would come back and bite us both in the butt. But for now, we were happy. Raafid filled out the paperwork. And just like that, I was a married man for the second time in my life.

* * * * *

I came upstairs and saw my mom and dad watching TV in the living room. I slowly approached them with a proud smile on my face. My dad noticed me first, giving me a smile.

"Son?"

"I have news guys," I said, drawing the attention of my mother.

"Oh?" My father's eyebrows rose.

"I got married!"

"You…got married?" my dad said, sounding bewildered.

My mom was on her feet, making sounds of happiness. She came over and gave me a big bear hug. My dad barely moved.

"To the woman Mom found," I said, smiling broadly.

"How? When?" my dad replied, dumbfounded.

"Got married over the phone. Raafid took care of all the paperwork," I answered.

"He actually did it…," my father muttered to himself. I noticed the reaction but wasn't quite sure what to make of it at first. I was too distracted by my mother.

"I can't wait to play with my grandkids," she said, smiling.

"Son, can I have a word with you in private?" my dad said with a smile frozen on his face as he stood up. He pointedly spoke in English so my mom wouldn't understand him. "Maybe we can go downstairs and talk," he suggested.

"Sure, Dad," I replied hesitantly. He walked toward me, grabbed my arm, and started dragging me back toward the basement. "I'll be right back," he said in Arabic, briefly turning back to my mother. He barely let the basement door close before his attitude completely changed.

"Have you gone crazy?" he asked me with anger in his tone.

"What?" I asked, surprised.

"Have you lost your mind?"

"I don't..."

"Why did you marry that woman?" my dad demanded, exasperated.

"Mom told me you knew about this, that you agreed with her...," I replied.

"Of course, she did." My father shook his head. "I didn't really think you would do this..."

"So you don't agree..."

"No, I don't agree! Do you know anything about this woman?" he roared.

"She wants to be a schoolteacher," I answered.

"Anything else?" he asked.

"She has nice feet...," I answered sheepishly.

"So nothing else? Nothing about her family?" he implored.

"No...but...I assumed you guys did..."

"Son, you can't even take care of yourself. How are you going to be able to take care of a wife? If you have children, how are you going to be able to take care of them?" My dad's voice was filled with anguish and concern.

"I don't know..."

"You didn't think this through at all, did you? Of course, not." He sighed. "Why did you do this, son?"

"I thought I needed a change," I said with my lips quivering.

"I can't stop you from doing every stupid thought that enters your head," my dad grumbled. "You do what you want." My father waved a hand in disgust and walked away from me. I stared at the door sadly. More than anything else in the world, I hated disappointing my father.

* * * * *

"So how are you?" Dr. Rick asked me a couple of days later in his office. It had actually been about a month since I had seen him.

"Well...I got married...," I said, covering my face to hide my smile.

"You got married?" Dr. Rick exclaimed, astonishment in his voice.

"Yup. Two days ago," I answered proudly.

"Well...congratulations," he said, a little uncertain. "I wasn't aware you were seeing anyone..."

"My mother found her in Jordan. I started talking to her a couple of weeks ago. Married her by phone," I said.

I could tell he was bowled over. But he was a respectful and kind man, so he did his level best not to make it apparent.

"I see...and how did your family react to the news?" he asked.

"My mom was really happy. My dad less so. He thinks I made a mistake...," I answered regretfully.

"I can see why he would think that." Dr. Rick said.

"You think I'm completely crazy!" I laughed.

"Well..." Dr. Rick hesitated. "Let's just say that it's not what I think I would have done." He chuckled. "But this is your life and neither your father nor I control you. If this is what you think will make you happy, then more power to you. Congratulations!" Dr. Rick finished with a smile and a hearty handshake.

"So...you don't think it's a bad thing?" I asked.

"I have concerns, for sure," Dr. Rick replied honestly. "But my hope is that this will be a very good thing for you. Having companionship might do you some good. Endlessly staying alone in that basement isn't good for either your depression or your anxiety problems. In fact, isolation fosters depression." He paused. "So yeah, I would say I am concerned but optimistic for you. Is she coming here, or are you going back to Jordan?"

"I don't know yet," I replied quietly. "She wants to come to America, a dream I once had. I know from experience that the dream isn't all that it's cracked up to be," I added, my voice taking on a melancholic tone. "I don't know what I should do." I shook my head. "What do you think?"

"That's not a question I can answer for you. That's something that only you can decide. I can certainly argue the point both ways. For instance, maybe going back to Jordan and being immersed in your culture would do you some good. It may feel familiar and less of a challenge. Or maybe being in your culture will cause you to feel shame when you talk to others who do not understand why life is so difficult for you. It's something we should talk more about. But in the end, you will have to decide which feels like the best move," Dr. Rick said. "If she comes here, then I hope I get a chance to meet her..." He smiled.

"Dr. Rick, you're as close to being family to me as you can be, without being blood," I started. "If she were to come here, you'd be one of the first to meet her. After my mom and dad, of course..."

* * * * *

Months passed. The year ended (2006) and 2007 began. I was talking to my wife by phone on a regular basis, but I had yet to make a decision about whether I should go to Jordan or have her come to the United States. She never registered an opinion either way.

"I think it's time, brother," Raafid said to me during a phone conversation.

"I still don't know...," I said.

"Sounds like you're living no life there at all," he insisted.

"Not sure it matters where I am," I said quietly.

"Come to Jordan. You can live with me in Dad's old apartment, which used to be your old apartment, come to think of it. You, me, and your wife. I'll take care of you. It'll help you to heal, to get better. Within months, you'll be back to your old self again. No more panic attacks. No more depression. Just a happy life with your new wife," Raafid said with confidence.

"I'd like to believe that is possible...," I said sadly.

"Let me assure you, brother, it is possible. Your life will be so much better in Jordan with your people. It sure beats living in your dark, dank basement, where all you have to look forward to is death. That's what you've told me about your life, brother. You've told me endlessly that the only thing you have to look forward to there is death. I'm offering you much more," Raafid said with passion.

"I have so many problems that I don't think they'll just go away." I shook my head.

"I'll take care of you, brother. I promise you. Come to Jordan for a better life. Your beautiful wife is waiting for you," Raafid said.

I sat there in silence for what seemed like an eternity. I was aware that due to my mental health and physical problems, I was an endless burden to my mom and dad. I knew that if I stayed where I was, I would either kill myself or send my dad to an early grave. My life here was nothing more than doctors' visits, visits with my lawyers, and court appearances, with no end in sight. The insurance company seemed set on insulting me every chance they got while spying on me and making my problems worse. Maybe without the burden of all those factors, it was possible to really and truly heal. Maybe it was possible to regain my life and become the man I once was, the proud man with endless musical talent who was going to be something rather than the ashamed, sad, pathetic person I had become, a man that resembled who I used to be in name only. If there was any chance that I could recover myself, then I felt I needed to try to do so. What more did I have to lose? How much worse could it possibly get for me? There was nothing to lose. And maybe everything to gain. My brother was right. I needed to do this.

"All right, brother. It's time to meet my new wife…"

* * * * *

A few days later, I was packing my things. My brother had paid for my ticket and taken care of all the mundane details that I more than likely would not have been able to handle. For the first time in nearly seven years, I experienced excitement—excitement for a new start. I had no idea whether or not this was going to go well. But for the first time in longer than I could remember, I had hope that maybe I could be okay again, starting a new life with a beautiful woman.

"You're really doing this," I heard my dad's voice behind me. I turned to see him coming down the stairs.

"I am really doing this," I confirmed.

"Raafid does not know what he's getting himself into. No one could. He can barely take care of himself, let alone a mentally ill brother and his new wife," my dad said as he approached me.

"I know you think this is a mistake—" I began but was cut off.

"There is little point in telling you what you already know," my dad said, sounding slightly amused. "Are you sure this is the best move for you?"

"No," I said, and my father looked surprised to hear me say that. "But I feel like I must."

"May I ask why?"

"All that awaits me here is death. I have to hope that there can be a better life for me. Otherwise, there is no point," I speculated emotionally. "I want to believe I can be better again. I know I can't do that here. The guilt of what I'm doing to you, and Mom is too great for me to bear."

"Don't worry about us, son...," my dad implored.

"But I do. I don't know if I can be happy again. But I want you to be free of the burden of me," I said, tears dripping down my cheeks. My dad hugged me. "I know you disapprove..."

"My approval or disapproval is irrelevant. I only want what's best for you," my dad said, his voice sounding hoarse.

"I think it's this," I said.

"I hope so. Even when I've thought you were wrong, I've always rooted for you. I hope you're right, and this will help guide you back to yourself. I suppose only God knows the right answer. I've prayed for answers for you, but none have come. Maybe this is God's will," my dad said, still holding me.

"Perhaps, Father," I said.

"Allow me to drive you to the airport. I was here for you the first time you set foot in America. It's only fitting that I'm there when you leave," he said with a gleam in his eye.

"Of course, Father," I said and hugged him tighter. We stood in the basement, holding each other tight for what felt like an eternity. As I stood there, I pondered when or if I would ever see this man again, the man who had done so much for me, who showed me nothing but kindness even as I'm sure I often frustrated him. I once came to this country, seeking a better life. My hopes were now pinned on going back to Jordan and having a better life...

Chapter 13

Amman, Jordan, 2007

I hadn't flown in an airplane in nearly eight years. That was the last time I had seen my home country of Jordan. I was a mixture of emotions as I flew home to meet my new wife. I was excited to meet her and begin a new chapter in my life, a chapter that, hopefully, would be better than the last. But I was anxious at the same time, so anxious in fact that I had a panic attack while on the plane. It was a minor one, but even minor ones are extremely frightening. I was hoping that being home and no longer constantly being watched and stalked by the insurance company would help me finally recover from my various issues.

I arrived at Queen Alia International Airport in the early afternoon. I remember being very tired and moving very sluggishly. My state of mind now stood in sharp contrast to how I was the last time I was here, ready to depart for the United States. Back then I was full of optimism and energy. Now, despite being somewhat excited, I felt like a prematurely old man. For the first time in years, I was dressed in nice clothing, with a pair of sunglasses. I was styling! I thought I looked pretty good on the outside. The inside of me was a different matter entirely. As I walked among the people, I felt as though they could see through me, see the messed up, tired man that I really was.

Waiting at the airport were Raafid and my sister. My sister, who lived in New York, happened to be visiting Jordan. I approached them with a smile and gave them each a small hug. Suddenly, I realized that there was a woman with them that I didn't recognize, a very pretty young woman…*who was smiling at me*!

"Who's this?" I asked, followed by both of my siblings laughing at me. I looked back and forth at them with confusion. Why were they laughing at me?

"Adam Noor, allow me to introduce you to your wife," Raafid said dramatically as he gestured toward the smiling woman.

"Deena?" I said uncertainly with a smile on my face.

"Adam?" she said, her smile broadening.

"The one who sent me a picture of her feet?"

"That's me." Deena laughed.

I wanted to hug her. I wanted to kiss her. But I couldn't quite bring myself to do it. I was overwhelmed. I didn't know what to expect when I saw her. But I wasn't expecting her to be so beautiful. I felt my breathing grow shallow. My heart rate increased.

"Excuse me," I said with feigned cheerfulness. "I need to go find a bathroom. I'll be right back," I hurriedly said and then quickly took off.

I found the nearest bathroom, which happened to be a single stall, and quickly locked the door. I leaned up against the wall and slowly slid downward. I took off my glasses and wiped tears out of my eyes. Deena was a beautiful, charming woman. She had just married a crazy man with no future and no hopes. Deena could have had any man she wanted. Instead she was now stuck with me! What had I done?

I can't remember how long I was in that bathroom, sobbing and feeling horrendously guilty. It felt like hours, long enough for Raafid to come looking for me. I heard a knock at the door. I ignored it.

"Adam, are you in there?" Raafid said.

I let out a long sigh and, for what seemed like an eternity, didn't speak. Finally, "I'm in here," I said hoarsely.

"Good to hear you didn't die in there…," Raafid said lightly.

"Just taking longer than expected," I replied lamely.

Raafid made a noise of understanding that I somehow managed to hear through the door. "You should try some bran," Raafid remarked. "Man, you've been in America so long you've forgotten how to eat."

I chuckled at that. I stood up slowly, straightened myself out, and then quickly threw water on my face from the sink. I unlocked the door and opened it to see my brother patiently standing there. I gave him a small hug.

"Everything all right, brother?" he asked me.

"Sure," I said, unconvincingly.

"What's going on?" he inquired.

"I made a mistake," I said, walking away from the bathroom, my back turned toward him.

"A mistake?" Raafid asked.

"I made a mistake marrying, and I made a mistake coming here," I said, my voice tinged with panic.

"Why? Your new wife not pretty enough?" he asked incredulously.

"Too pretty," I said emphatically.

"Didn't think there was such a thing," Raafid replied, shrugging.

"I'm a crazy man!" I yelled, whirling around toward him and startling him. "She's gorgeous and can have any man in the world. And what she married is a broken-down, pathetic man. She deserves so much better than anything I have to offer," I said, looking down at my feet. "Why did I do this? Why didn't I listen to Dad?"

"You just have cold feet, brother. It's normal," Raafid said dismissively, trying to sound encouraging. "Any man would be a little nervous to meet his wife for the first time."

"It's more than that," I said quietly.

Raafid stared at me for several seconds, trying to think of what he could possibly say to me. The silence became very awkward.

"Look, we can't stay around the airport all day. Eventually they'll kick us out," Raafid said calmly. "Let's get your wife and go to dinner. I'm sure you're freaking out over nothing. It'll be fine. I promise," Raafid said, putting an arm around my shoulder.

I looked at him and said nothing. I was well aware that this was not a promise he was going to be able to keep.

Despite my brother pretending to play it cool, I knew this little scene had caused him to become a little wary. As my dad had said, he had no idea what he was getting himself into.

* * * * *

It should be obvious that the way Deena and I got married was unusual. I'm sure that there are plenty of people living in the United States who think that arranged marriages in the Middle East are common. It may very well have been in the past, but it isn't anymore. Our marriage was unusual by everyone's standards. It is not "normal" for anyone to get married after only talking on the phone for a few months. No guy chooses his mate based on their beautiful feet. Nobody in the entire world does what I did. Only me.

Typically in Jordan, when you find someone that you want to marry, you go to that girl's parents to ask for permission to do so. They either grant or deny you permission. If you're granted permission, the two families get together to hammer out some kind of financial agreement. Who will pay for what? Which family is responsible for this and that? And so on and so forth. Usually, this includes the head of each family, your father or the eldest son. After this, you are engaged for one to two years. Then if all is going well, you get married and have a big party with both families included.

This didn't happen with us. I was living in the United States, so it wasn't possible to go to Deena's father to ask permission in person. Nevertheless, as it turned out, her father was willing to give permission for us to be married as a long as we threw a party. A big celebration with both families. Even before I left the United States, I told Deena that I wanted no such thing. I wasn't aware of the specifics of her father's wishes, but of course, I was familiar with Muslim tradition. But I knew I wasn't capable of dealing with a big party and being social. My mental health issues insured that I would have serious issues at any such social gathering. Deena went along with this. But when her father learned that we did not plan to have the traditional big party, he was extremely angry. His tenuous approval of the union dissolved immediately. Deena fought her family at every turn. The tension between her and her family increased every day. Eventually, they basically swore her off.

"Who is this man? What's his background? What's his family like?"

These were the questions that she was asked. And she didn't know the answer to even one of them. The only thing she knew is that I lived in the United States, and that was good enough for her.

"If there are any problems and if he isn't the man you think he is, you will get no help from us," her father said emphatically. "Don't come crying to me for help because you will not get it." Effectively, they disowned her.

I was not aware of any of this. I was too distracted, being in my barely coherent fog of medications and sleep.

It was only because she was over eighteen that the wedding was able to take place at all without the permission of her family. Raafid, and obviously Deena, knew all this. Neither one filled me in on all the details until I was back in Jordan. Once I laid eyes on her and realized just how gorgeous she was, I feared that I would ruin her life. As soon as I was filled in on the details of what went on with her family, I was sure that I would be responsible for completely destroying her life.

* * * * *

From the airport, the four of us traveled to my sister's house. My sister's house was in a secure, gated community in Jordan called Deer Park. It wasn't very far from my dad's family house. It was a very fancy house located in an area in which the neighbors were mostly American. The American embassy was not far from where my sister lived.

Deena and I, along with Raafid and a bunch of other family members, had dinner at my sister's house. Many of those who were present that day had been at my wedding to Evanna many years earlier. I spent much of the time at dinner sitting next to Deena in silence. I would occasionally exchange awkward smiles with her. Now and then, others would ask me questions about America. I would give the briefest answer possible, sometimes no more than a single word. Most of them assumed that I was just jet-lagged from my journey. That was partially true. But more importantly, I didn't have anything pleasant to share about my time in the United States.

The good memories had long been tainted, and all that remained was a shadow of my former self. I spent much the time during dinner pondering how I screwed up, how my father was right and I should not have married the woman sitting next to me. It had nothing to do with her and everything to do with me. She was too good for me, and she had yet to realize that. I was painfully aware that it wouldn't be long before she realized I wasn't worth it.

* * * * *

After dinner mercifully ended, we went back to my old house. Raafid had moved into the house not long after I departed for America. He insisted that Deena and I stay there with him rather than find a hotel. My brother drove us there, and I spent the ride in silent contemplation. Deena was sitting next to me, holding my hand. I stared out the window, looking at the stars that I once enjoyed so much. I still enjoyed seeing them, but it felt like an emptier experience than it once had. I occasionally noticed Raafid sneaking glances in the mirror at us. He looked uncertain, concerned, perhaps wondering if he had done the right thing.

We pulled up to the house that I left nearly eight years ago, never really expecting to see it again. It didn't look that much different. I had a flash to a much younger version of myself: walking away from the house with Evanna the first night I ever met her, on my way to Sharaf's club, a happier time when life still held so much promise.

Quietly I exited the car, never letting go of Deena's hands. Her hands felt so warm and smooth. It had been ages since I had been graced with the opportunity to touch a woman's hands.

"This is home for you and your wife now, Adam," Raafid said as he gave me a hug. "I will take my leave of you two. Unlike you, brother, I am still a single man." He laughed. "I'll be back in the morning," he said. And then without another word, he left the house.

For a long time, I found myself looking around at the place. Raafid had redecorated a little. But on the whole, it looked the same. I was barely aware of Deena until she put her arms around me, hugging me from behind.

"What shall we do?" she whispered in my ear.

"I'm tired," I replied, barely audibly. "I would like to sleep now."

"I'll go with you," Deena said as she kissed my cheek. She led me up the stairs to our room. She had obviously been here before. Raafid must have shown her which room would be ours. I entered my old room with Deena. Raafid hadn't changed a thing. Whatever I had left behind was still in its original spot.

Apparently, he had taken up residence in one of the other bedrooms. I sat on the bed next to Deena. Her hands caressed me up my back to my shoulders.

"So tense," she said as she started to massage me.

"I can't remember the last time I wasn't tense," I said quietly. I felt awkward and uncertain as I sat there.

"We will have to change that," she flirted as she rubbed my shoulders harder.

Without saying a word, she removed my shirt. I turned to look at her, and in her eyes, I saw both admiration and desire. I knew that I would never truly earn what, without hesitation, she was giving me. I also knew exactly what she wanted and expected.

Wordlessly, I leaned in to kiss her. Our lips met. My hands touched her face. It had been so long. I honestly never expected to experience anything like this again. It wasn't long before our clothes were disappearing at a rapid rate as we kissed with increasing passion. Instinct overwhelmed my awkwardness and uncertainty. I enjoyed the warmth of her naked body underneath mine. My long-standing pain, both physical and spiritual, temporarily melted away in that moment. As we made love, I felt physical pleasure I hadn't in ages. But it was tinged with the knowledge that it would never really be this way again. This was as good as it was ever going to get.

CHAPTER 14

I awoke the next morning with the sun beaming through the windows and into my eyes. The bright sun was no longer something to which I was accustomed. I had become used to my basement, my kingdom, the dungeon of darkness and death. Maybe that was all behind me now. Maybe, just maybe, this hadn't all been a mistake. Maybe now I could truly and really heal. With this woman lying next to me at my side. My foggy, unorganized mind was still clearly damaged, and I still felt the physical pain in my neck and back that had characterized the last seven years of my life. But in this one moment, I felt spiritually at peace.

I stood up, the blankets falling off my body, and moved toward the window. I gazed out at the beautiful bright sky, feeling the warmth of the sun wash over my body. I turned and looked at my wife. The covers had partially fallen off her naked body, leaving her exposed. I stared in admiration, feeling that somehow I had luckily found a pot of gold at the end of the rainbow.

I was suddenly startled to hear a male voice say, *She's too pretty for you.* My heart rate skyrocketed. I looked quickly from side to side to locate the source of the voice. *She won't stay with you for long*, a female voice then added. This was when I realized that the voices had returned. I had hoped I had left them behind in the United States.

"No," I gasped, shaking my head.

Sooner or later she will know the truth, a little boy's voice said.

Then I heard the voice of my attacker, saying: *You are nobody, a loser, a crazy person. She gives you credit, and she admires you because you were in America. What she doesn't know is the damaged man you actually are. She doesn't know that I took your dignity, your livelihood.*

They fired you because they thought you conspired with me. I beat you nearly to death, and they thought you and I were friends!

Then I heard my attacker laughing maniacally. *And I didn't stop there. I took your voice, the one thing that made you special. You can no longer sing. You're nothing now. A nobody. Your wife will never love you. You are pathetic.*

"Maybe she'll love me for me," I argued with my attacker's voice. My hand clutched my chest as my heart beat harder and faster. It became difficult to breathe.

A woman requires a strong man, a man who can take care of her. You are weak and can't even take care of yourself. How long before your brother and your new wife abandon you, leaving you alone! Broken! Homeless! Pathetic!

"SHUT UUUUP!" I yelled at the top of my lungs, waking Deena, who jumped out of bed and was instantly at my side.

"Adam? What's wrong?" she asked worriedly as I fell to my knees. Tears filled my eyes.

"Nothing! Nothing!" I insisted, trying to get back on my feet and away from her. I was not very convincing. I finally managed to stand up, turning away from her. She continued to try to get me to face her, to figure out what was wrong. I closed my eyes and tried to ignore everything. My mind went somewhere else. I tried breathing, as Dr. Rick had once instructed me to do when my anxiety was at its highest. Slowly but surely, my heart rate slowed down. I opened my eyes, my breathing still labored. With one swift motion, I pounded my fist against the wall in anger. I was aware of my wife still trying to comfort me from behind. I turned to her, my eyes blazing with anger.

"Why did you do this?" I demanded.

"Do what?" she asked, confused and scared.

"Why did you marry me?" I clarified.

"Isn't that what you wanted?" she asked, her eyes filled with obvious hurt.

"Yes! But don't you realize that I am a crazy man? You made a mistake in marrying me. You should have known it!" I shouted.

"Look, Adam. Relax…," she said as I just glared at her. "You're just nervous." She sounded more than a little nervous herself. I didn't blame her. She quickly threw on a robe, covering her naked body. "I got you something…" She smiled at me and quickly left the room. Where she went, I do not know. But upon her return, she was carrying a blue stuffed dog. She handed it to me, and I took it. I stared down at it, pondering it for a few moments. Soon after this, I felt an anger building within me. I didn't know why. The anger wasn't about anything specific. I felt it swelling in me like a building tornado, bent on destroying anything in its path. I felt my hands tense around the stuffed dog, and with one quick motion, I tore the head off the dog's body. I threw both pieces away while Deena looked at me with horror. Tears filled her eyes. She couldn't believe what she was seeing.

"I am not just nervous! I am *nothing. A nobody!*" I shouted.

"That's not true," she said, her tone very upset.

"It is," I insisted.

"You're an American," she pointed out.

"That doesn't mean anything. That doesn't mean what people here think it means!" I shouted. "I was going to be someone! I was going to be famous in America! But that was a long time ago, and now I am *nothing*. The day I was attacked was the day my life ended. And yet because the fates have not punished me enough, I still draw breath!"

I was ranting and raving, no longer talking to anybody specific. I was not even aware of my wife's continued presence in the room.

"You married a nobody! A crazy person! I AM NOTHING!" I continued bellowing.

My wife started sobbing and quickly ran from the room. My heart rate, which had briefly been under control, spiraled once again as I went on ranting. I eventually found myself lying on the floor, coughing, still trying to rant. I was no longer breathing, just lying in a fetal position, shouting with what little breath I still had. My vision was becoming fuzzy. My arm started feeling numb. All I could hear was my heart pounding. Finally, darkness claimed me.

* * * * *

Later, when I woke up, I found Deena and apologized. This did not really help matters much. So I gave her a hug and a kiss and decided I needed to go for a walk. I couldn't stay in the house. Despite its spaciousness, it felt too confining, and I was on edge after my attack.

Much to my surprise there were still people kicking around the streets of Amman that recognized me from the days when I lived there. I would smile at them. But I was very curt. I did not feel comfortable talking to anyone, and I was embarrassed over my present life situation.

I thought returning to Jordan and being away from the insurance company would make things better for me. Unfortunately, it was now apparent that I had lived under those circumstances for far too long. I found myself suspicious of everyone I came across, thinking that the insurance company still had spies, even here in the streets of Jordan. My walk was not as relaxing as I had hoped it would be. I brushed off the various people trying to talk to me. Then I ran into a familiar face that seemed not to have aged even a day since we had last talked. Sharaf Baleid, my old friend, spotted me walking toward him. I pretended not see him, moving my gaze to the ground between my feet. He didn't let me get away with that for very long.

"Adam!" he called after me, running to give me a big hug. "I was hoping I'd run into you."

"You knew I was back?" I asked, surprised.

"Raafid filled me in," Sharaf answered, quickly letting go of the embrace. "Come! Come grab a drink with me!"

"I should get home…"

"Just a quick drink! We have much to catch up on," Sharaf insisted. I sighed and relented. I let him drag me where he wanted me to go.

* * * * *

Much to my surprise, he didn't drag me back to his own business. He dragged me to another bar. I was relieved because the place to which he brought me was less crowded than his nightclub. We sat at the bar, and he ordered two beers.

"So, Adam, what happened to Evanna?" Sharaf asked me after a few moments of silence.

"She left me," I said quietly and vaguely.

"Why?"

"She couldn't handle the person I'd become," I sighed.

"Because of your incident?" Sharaf asked, surprising me.

"You're better informed than you let on," I said.

"Your brother told me a little. Plus, I learned bits and pieces here and there from other sources," Sharaf said. "For the record, I'm sorry. I thought you two crazy kids would work out."

"It happens," I said dismissively, taking a swig of my beer.

"You lived in America for nearly eight years. Bet you're a rich man. You could probably buy my club." Sharaf laughed.

"You would think so. That's what I expected. But sadly, I only have a couple grand," I said.

"Seriously?" Sharaf said with surprise. "I thought you'd be opening a nightclub of your own if you ever returned, to drive me out of business," he finished lightly.

"Not so." I paused. "Your wife and kids. How are they?" I asked, partly because I wanted to know and partly because I wanted to head off any more questions about myself.

"Very good! Kids are getting too big. Got another one on the way," Sharaf said proudly with a warm smile. Despite myself, I found myself grinning and giving him a big hug.

"You're at the beginning of a new journey," I said, echoing the words he had spoken to me many years ago.

"To a new beginning!" he said, raising his beer before downing more of his drink.

"Hopefully one you will experience with your new wife," Sharaf declared, winking.

"I don't think so," I offered.

"Why not? You're not that old," he replied, clapping me on the shoulder.

"Age has nothing to do with it," I croaked with a quiet melancholy. Sharaf didn't comment on that.

"Listen, the boys miss you down at the club. Business has never been the same since you left," Sharaf exclaimed. I knew he was full of crap. He had always done quite well for himself with or without me. "It would be an honor if you came and sang for me, old friend," he exclaimed, finishing with his typical dramatic flair.

"I'm afraid not," I said.

"Why not?" Sharaf asked, sounding surprised by my answer.

"I can't sing anymore," I replied, meekly.

"Sure you can! It's like riding a bike…," Sharaf said, trying to bolster my mood.

"Singing is who I used to be. I'm no longer that person, and I can't be that person again," I said, my voice filled with sadness.

I stood up, Sharaf looking at me with a mixture of hurt and confusion. I couldn't stand it. It hurt my heart more than I could tolerate. It was one of the reasons I wasn't overly thrilled to run into him.

"Thanks for the drink," I said, dropping some money. He watched me go all the way out the door. I felt his eyes on me the entire time.

* * * * *

My brother had arrived home before I did and was greeted by my less-than-happy wife.

Deena told him the story of what had transpired that morning, and it only increased his wariness about me. What my father had already known and I had come to suspect was becoming apparent for all to see. My mental health issues were a phenomenon that Raafid was ill-equipped to deal with.

From that point forward, Deena and I would only occasionally get along. The rest of the time, we would be fighting. Suffice to say that the honeymoon was already over.

On the other hand, we still had plenty of sex. And the sex was good! Surprisingly, better than it had been with Evanna. The only time we truly and fully connected was when we were making love. I'm told that it is not that uncommon for some relationships to be held together mainly by the quality of the lovemaking.

It was my impression that Raafid had a bit of a mental health issue himself. From my point of view, he seemed to have some obsessive-compulsive symptoms. He liked to have things in their exact, specific spot. He would become very frustrated when things were not where he wanted them to be. Given my mental health issues, this caused us to frequently be in conflict. I could barely remember anything, never mind putting things in exact correct spots. As much as I tried to be cleaner and more organized than when I lived in the basement, I was only capable of doing so much. There was so much conflict in the house that it felt as though I had been married to both Deena and Raafid for forty years. I felt like I was in hell!

* * * * *

Time went by. Every day, it became more and more apparent that neither Raafid nor Deena could take care of me as well as my father had. Neither could get me to take a shower. Consequently, my hygiene deteriorated.

I began to have panic attacks with increasing frequency, resulting in frequent visits to doctors and hospitals. Finally, I ran out of money. So I told the doctors that the insurance company would send them money. As far as I understood, that was the truth. In the United States, the insurance company did send the doctors money for my medical bills. It was much later that I learned that they would not pay for doctors in another country. This caused me much more trouble. So the insurance company continued its tradition of screwing me even with me no longer being in the United States.

* * * * *

"I have something to tell you…," Deena began hesitantly as we were undressing for bed one night.

"What's that?" I asked, feeling my anxiety increase.

"You know how I've been sick recently? Throwing up a lot...," she continued and then stopped.

"Please get to the point," I said impatiently.

"It's not just a bug. I went to the doctor today, and they did some tests..."

I sighed with audible impatience but said nothing.

"I'm pregnant," she said, pausing for my reaction. Her look suggested she didn't quite know how to feel herself.

"You're what?" I asked, not being able to wrap my mind around the concept.

"I am with child," Deena said. "And yes, it's yours." She had a bit of a smirk on her face.

"I don't get it..."

"We are having a child together. You are going to be a father," Deena said, sounding more than a little impatient herself.

I can imagine how many other men would react to hearing that news, especially if they were married. I could imagine my longtime friend Sharaf jumping for joy upon the news of his latest. Most guys would feel a mixture of joy and terror. But I felt absolutely nothing. No emotions of any kind. As you can imagine, my complete lack of reaction resulted in yet another fight. Ready or not, my first child was coming...

CHAPTER 15

While I was ambivalent about the news that I was going to be a father, Raafid was panicky. He had no idea that taking me on would be such a stressful chore. The news that there was soon to be a new child that he was probably going to have to take some responsibility for did not fill him with joy. It filled him with fear. I knew that there was only one thing to do. I did not want to overburden Raafid, so we would need to strike out on our own. My pregnant wife and I left the house that very day with no clear idea about where we were going and without a dime in our pockets.

I had no choice but to try to get money so that we could afford a place to stay. I considered calling my dad. But just as quickly as the idea entered my head, I shook it away. I couldn't do it. I didn't want to burden him anymore. Instead I called Zahir, my brother in New York.

"Why not continue to live with Raafid?" my brother Zahir asked me, sounding worried.

"I don't want to talk about it…" I sighed. "Look, I have my pregnant wife and nowhere to go. I was hoping you could help me out."

"Of course, brother," he said quietly. "I'll wire money into the family account. Can you get to a bank?"

"I believe so," I answered after a few moments.

"It'll be there within an hour," he said.

"Thank you, brother," I said gratefully.

"And Adam…," he added.

"Yes?" I asked curiously.

"Congratulations on becoming a father."

"Thanks," I said, even though I didn't exactly feel like celebrating that news.

* * * * *

The nearest bank was a good twenty-minute walk from where we were. Back in the day, this was the kind of walk that I routinely used to take. Nowadays, it was a different story. I had to stop for frequent breaks. I just didn't have the energy or stamina that I once had. But I remained a proud person. I wasn't about to admit that to my new wife. So I led her to believe that I was stopping out of concern for her.

Zahir must have wired the money immediately since it was in the family account when we arrived at the bank. Next, we needed to find a hotel.

Thankfully, there was one nearby. Unfortunately, it was a shabby hotel. Even from the outside, it looked dirty and in disrepair. It reminded me of a hotel in one of the horror movies that my friend Larry used to make me watch. In addition, it wasn't in the safest area of town. On the whole, Amman is a nice city. But like any city, there are bad areas. I was hardly concerned about myself. I was feeling that dying would have been something of a blessing for me. However, I was worried about my wife, who was carrying my child. But I could not continue walking to find another hotel. I didn't have a choice. My legs felt like jelly, and at this point, it was amazing that I was even able to keep standing. Deena didn't say anything, but I knew she was quietly horrified. This was hardly what she signed up for.

The room was every bit as horrifying as the outside suggested, extremely dirty with unclean dishes and dirty blankets lying around. It reminded me a little bit of being back in the basement of my parents' home in the United States. I came to Jordan for an improved life, not for the same old, same old. But this was worse because I had someone that I was supposed to be taking care of in tow, with a part of me inside her. I felt like a loser, like a nothing. Looking at my wife, I felt nothing but shame.

Deena walked to a nearby store to get clean blankets and some food. I objected, of course, but weakly. While she was gone, I somehow managed to fall asleep in bed with no pillows. Upon entering the room, throwing the pillows away had been the first thing my wife had done.

I woke up covered in blankets with a pillow under my head. I had no idea how much time had passed. When I peeked my head up, I saw Deena cleaning. The room looked improved but still dirty.

"What time is it?" I asked groggily.

"Late," Deena answered quietly.

"You should lie down with me. You are tired," I said, half asleep. She looked like she wanted to protest but didn't. She crawled into my arms, and her body went limp. Something caught my eye in the corner of the room. When I turned my attention to that area, I saw nothing.

"Could have sworn I saw something move," I said aloud.

"A rat maybe? A cockroach?" Deena asked, sounding exhausted.

"I don't know…"

"Neither would surprise me," Deena said

"Nor me," I agreed. "Rest, *habibtaa*. You need it," I said, stroking her hair. Of course, right as I said that, we heard a couple in the next room start to argue. The argument seemed to get louder and louder. Suddenly, there was a loud, crashing sound. And then nothing. Silence. Long agonizing silence. We laid there, both listening, growing increasingly concerned that we might have just heard a murder. Then just like that that, the fighting started anew. I started laughing. I couldn't help myself. Deena looked up at me like I was nuts. After a moment or two, she too started laughing. Before long, despite the yelling never quite stopping, we were both fell asleep, both to our own world of dreams.

* * * * *

A rather large man entered the store. He was muscular and tattooed. I thought nothing of the man other than relief to see him. It was an excuse to stop talking to my wife. The irony of seeing the man that would forever change my life was that I was relieved to see him when he first walked through the door. I told my wife to hold on, and I put the phone receiver down. I greeted the customer in my friendly and welcoming way. He merely grunted.

"Newport 100s," he said, his voice cold and unfriendly. I reached above my head to get him the cigarettes, and that was when everything changed. I felt a sudden sharp pain in my face. I felt myself falling backward into the wall. My head violently collided with the wall, and I felt horrendous pain in my back. I looked up, stunned and surprised, and was suddenly staring at a gun directly in my face. I was disoriented and totally confused. My heart rate accelerated, and I tried very hard to concentrate and figure out what was going on.

"Give me your money," the man said, his voice filled with cold, hard menace.

* * * * *

I was startled awake by the sound of knocking. My breathing was labored, and I was sweating. The sheets and blankets were drenched in sweat. A dream. I was having a dream. The start of a nightmare. More knocking. Who would be knocking at my door? Who would possibly want me? Deena remained dead asleep. I quickly changed clothes and answered the door. I was surprised to see my mom standing at the door.

"Mother," I said, surprised.

"Son," she said gravely, Raafid standing behind her. "May we come in?"

"Of course," I said quietly and stepped aside. Both my mother and Raafid entered. My mother's gaze was drawn to Deena, who was sleeping.

"She looks peaceful," my mom said serenely, sitting on the edge of the bed to get a better look at her. "She is with child now. We mustn't disturb her sleep." She turned her gaze back toward Raafid and me.

"Mom, how did you find us?" I asked curiously.

"Zahir" was all that my mom said. I nodded with understanding. "Raafid and I have been talking. We wish for you to return home," my mom said.

I looked at her for a few moments, considering this.

"With respect, Mother, I cannot do that," I said quietly.

"Then why not?" my mom asked.

"I came here hoping to recover. But also because I could no longer stand to burden you and Dad. I thought being here would help me. But instead it just shifted that burden," I said, looking more at the floor than at my mom. "I can't do that to you guys, to any of you. I love you too much."

"You're sure I can't change your mind?" my mom said after a moment of silence.

"No," I said grimly.

"Brother..." Raafid started to speak up. But I stuck out a finger to silence him, and he did so. It was a brief hint of dominance, my old self briefly reasserting itself. Despite my brother taking on favored-son status, I was still the oldest. A little bit of that former pride remained within me.

"If you change your mind...," my mother said and then trailed off.

"I will call you."

My mother's attention turned back to Deena. She smiled down at her.

"So peaceful," she repeated. "Even sleeping, she still has the glow of motherhood."

She looked back at Raafid. "Come, Raafid. Let us go before we wake her."

She made her way to the door, and my brother followed her.

She turned back to me suddenly. "Almost forgot." She walked toward me, reaching into her pocket. I eyed her curiously as she walked. She took out a wad of cash and plopped it into my hands. "From your father," she said simply, kissing me on the cheek before they both left the room.

The words were like a bomb going off in my chest. I nearly cried. My father knew. Of course, he did. He somehow always knew. I stuck the money in the drawer and crawled back into bed with my sleeping wife.

CHAPTER 16

Between the leftover my money that my brother gave me and the money my mom handed me from my dad, we had enough to last us for a few days at the hotel. It gave us enough time to figure out our next move. I had no desire to stay in the hotel room but wasn't sure what our options were. I considered reaching out to my former friends, but I quickly brushed the thought aside. Most of my former friends were now big-time singers either in Jordan or in the US. I was nothing now and wasn't sure they would even remember me. I considered reaching out to Sharaf, knowing full well he still knew who I was. Pride, pure and stubborn pride, was what kept me from doing that.

Of course, Deena reached out to her family. But it was futile. After all, she had defied her family and gone along with all my wishes. She figured it was a lost cause, but she felt she had to try. During the process of trying to get help from her family, Deena received a call from her uncle. He was a rich guy who was thought of as an important man. During this conversation, her uncle told her to hand the phone to me. Somewhat apprehensively, I took the phone.

As soon as I took the phone, I could hear Deena's uncle bellowing, "You know, Adam, I told her not to marry you. I asked her what the benefit of marrying you was. I asked her what she knew about you. That you're from America? So what?" He continued, "I have businesses in America, and I have businesses in Jordan. Sure, they have a lot of rich people in America. But a lot of poor people as well. People are without homes. America has a lot of crazy people in it. What do you know about this guy?"

I continued to listen to him, wearily taking in everything he said.

"Well, now we know who you are. And guess who was right! She went against her entire family. For you?" He laughed. "And look where you guys are. Best of luck to you," he said and hung up the phone.

I sat there, holding the phone, listening to the dial tone. My heart hurt. I felt guilt and pain for what I had done to this woman. I knew why she married me.

There are many people who go to America, thinking that it will make them something, that it will make them cool. What do they say on the TV? Beautiful houses. Easy life. Nice cars. Very beautiful country. Without a doubt, America is a very beautiful country. She wanted the American Dream. She wanted to come to America to be something, to seek out the land of freedom and opportunity. Instead, she got me. Maybe the American dream does exist. Maybe that dream is possible, but not for everyone. It doesn't even necessarily depend on how hard you work. It may just come down to how lucky you happen to be. Before being brutally attacked on the job, I was perhaps the hardest worker around but, as it turned out, not the luckiest one. Far from it. What happened to me wasn't my fault. It wasn't because of something I did wrong. I was just in the wrong place at the wrong time. I looked at my wife, who looked at me curiously. My eyes were watery.

"We are on our own," I said simply and handed her the phone without turning to face her.

I found myself eyeing the package I had brought with me from America. It was a package that contained jewelry and a ring from my parents. I was supposed to present the contents of this package to Deena as a gift. But my foggy brain never quite allowed me to remember what I was supposed to do with it. As it turned out, that might have been a good thing. The jewelry my parents had given me was very valuable. I wasn't sure how much I could get for it, but I believed that I would get enough money to last for a while.

"Are you sure, Adam?" she asked me as I looked through the jewelry. "Your mom and dad wanted us to have this?"

"We don't have a choice," I said quietly.

"How about asking your family?"

"That is not an option," I insisted. I had made the decision to keep them out of things as much as I could, and I intended to stick to that. For better or worse.

I found an establishment nearby that was willing to buy the jewelry. I honestly don't remember how much we got for it. It was a decent chunk of change, and it was enough to keep us afloat for a couple of months.

We found a place to rent nearby. The landlord was a decent enough middle-aged bespectacled guy. He didn't require a down payment from us, just the first month's rent. The landlord gave me the benefit of the doubt because I was an American citizen and he believed that Americans were trustworthy and honorable. It reminded me of a time when I felt the same way.

Even the inexpensive apartments in Jordan were bigger than some expensive places in the US. A $1,800 apartment in America would be a broom closet compared to what you would get in Jordan for that kind of money. The apartment we landed didn't cost that much but was huge for what we would have gotten in the US.

A common misconception many Americans have relates to the value of the American dollar in Jordan. They believe that American money is more valuable than other forms of currency. That's just not so. At the writing of this book, the exchange rate on American money into the Jordanian dinar is seventy cents. To be clear, for Americans coming into Jordan, one American dollar will get them seventy cents in Jordanian money. This was shocking to many of the Americans I spoke to.

I didn't have the energy to go out and buy a bunch of furniture, and so I rented it. The people I rented from furnished the place for me.

"What happens when we run out of money?" Deena asked me. I gave her the only answer that was truly honest.

"I don't know…"

There were more than a few times when I thought of calling my father and asking for him to buy me a ticket to the United States. I could leave my wife behind and just go. But I couldn't do it.

I have never been a particularly religious guy. There are many people who go to the churches or the mosques just so they can show other people that they are doing so. They believe that just by showing up, it automatically makes them good people. I've known plenty of people that call themselves men or women of God, who are just vile human beings. I have never been that guy. I still had a keen sense of what was right and wrong. Believing in God and attending church does not make you a good person. I didn't feel any need to go to the mosque to put on that kind of show. My statement of who I was came from my actions and how I chose to conduct myself. I would see Deena sleeping, and any thought of leaving her to her own devices vanished. Even in my severely damaged mental, physical, and emotional state, I still fervently felt a need and duty to protect her and my unborn child. Deena had given up so much to be with me. She was now my responsibility. It was what I believe God expected of me.

My mom regularly visited our home. She wanted to check up on her unborn grandchild and to bring items that would enable me to take care of Deena and the baby after it was born. Several of my family members came and went during this time. A notable absence was my father, as he rarely left the United States. He was too busy with things going on in America. We talked on the phone occasionally. Despite disagreeing with many of my decisions, he was happy that he was going to be a grandfather once more.

As the money started dwindling, the tension between Deena and me increased. We started fighting every day. Sometimes the verbal altercations were related to my mental health issues. At other times, they would be related to her resentment toward me for convincing her to trade in her previous life for a "bill of goods." I tried to make her realize that most of that was not me. It was mainly the well-meaning work of my brother and mother. Granted, I wasn't totally truthful about just how far gone I was. But there was more than enough blame to go around. In marrying me, she was essentially responsible for jumping off a cliff before looking to make sure there was water down below.

We lasted a few months at our first apartment before we started to get behind in paying the rent. So we had to go. For the next several months, we would bounce from town to town, apartment to apartment. Each landlord would know I was an American and give me the benefit of the doubt without putting any money down. We would stay for a few months in each apartment. Eventually, we would fall behind in our rent payments, and we would leave.

We fought every day. We became enemies more than lovers. I tried to be the man she and my unborn child needed, but I couldn't be. I knew that I needed someone to take care of me and that I wasn't capable of taking care of a family.

Often I pondered, *Deena does not have mental health issues. Why did she make the unwise decision to marry me?*

I grew so tired that I couldn't take it anymore, and I broke my agreement with God. One day, I told Deena that she was divorced. In my culture, if the husband tells his wife that she is divorced, then you are divorced. That's it. Nothing more complicated than that. Just like that, Deena went back to her family. They were very gracious and kind in taking her back.

Deena is a very good woman. She had given up a lot to be with me. It was a mistake for her to marry me, and it was a mistake for me to marry her. She suffered a great deal because of me, and I felt and feel guilty about that every day. I was in pain, and I was making her feel my pain. It wasn't fair and I knew it wouldn't be fair to my child. I didn't want to inflict myself upon them and make them suffer more.

People without mental health problems do not understand that when you're in pain, emotional or otherwise, it's hard to be with someone. You feel that you must continually put up a front and behave as though you are okay. That gets exhausting. I can understand why some people might judge me harshly for divorcing Deena. But at the time, I thought of my action as being merciful.

Twenty days later, I was in court to get Deena back. In Muslim culture, you can divorce two times and still get back together. After the third time, you can't remarry unless there is another marriage in between. In court, I said that I had been angry and had made a mistake in divorcing my wife. I did not mention my mental health issues. As guilty as I had felt for keeping her around me, I felt even guiltier for abandoning her.

"Adam, I need you to come back to the United States," said Mr. Shaw over the phone.

"That's not going to happen," I snorted.

"If you don't come back, the court will drop your case, and the checks from the insurance company will stop. In addition, they will no longer be paying for your medications or doctors' visits," Mr. Shaw said, sounding a bit annoyed.

"I don't care about that," I said dismissively.

"I'm sure you don't now, but you will."

"Look, I am not going back the United States to be a toy for the insurance company. I am no longer interested in playing that game. I'm not going to see a thousand doctors. It's not going to happen."

"Not a thousand doctors. Just one more," Mr. Shaw said.

"What?" I asked, surprised.

"The insurance company has agreed to have you see just one more doctor to make a final determination about whether you are disabled or not. This is it, Adam. With this report, we can win this case," Mr. Shaw intoned passionately.

I said my goodbyes to him over the phone, promising nothing. I stood there by the phone, thinking about what to do.

"Deena," I called. And Deena slowly made her way into the room.

"Yes?" she asked.

"You are divorced," I said. And her mouth gaped open. This was divorce number 2.

Although I had no desire to return to the United States, I had to do it.

CHAPTER 17

United States, 2008

I returned to the United States with trepidation. At this point in time, I was more comfortable being in Jordan. My dad picked me up at the airport and gave me a big hug.

He took me home, and I went to the basement. The place looked about the same, but significantly cleaner.

"Guess you didn't turn this place into your study," I said dryly.

"No, son, I didn't," he chortled. "Does it feel good to be home?"

"It's good to see you," I said quietly. "But I have no feeling at all about being back here in the United States."

I wasn't there for long before I had a meeting scheduled to meet with my lawyer. As usual, my father went with me. Mr. Shaw looked a little rounder and a little grayer since the last time I saw him. That aside, nothing else had changed about him.

"One thing I may have failed to mention to you is that the doctor that the insurance company has decided will make the final report, Dr. Kenneth Selig, actually works for the insurance company," Mr. Shaw said. He waited for my angry reaction.

"He works for the insurance company?" I said incredulously.

"Yes, sir," Mr. Shaw confirmed.

"And this is the man that will be deciding my case?"

"It appears so," Mr. Shaw answered.

"So you brought me back to the United States so I could lose this case," I said with more than a hint of anger in my tone.

"No, I don't think that's accurate. Dr. Selig, in addition to being a doctor, is also an attorney. I've known him for many years, and I know that he is a good man. I feel like we still have a decent shot at winning this case," Mr. Shaw said confidently.

"A decent man? Says the lawyer," my dad said indignantly.

"You know what? I don't care anymore. I just want this over with," I replied. And I truly did not care anymore. Eight years of this nonsense was more than enough for me.

As time went by, I learned quite a bit about Dr. Selig's reputation. He was tough. Nine out of every ten cases that came before him were decided in a way that would make an insurance company happy. This man worked for and was paid by the insurance company! I felt that there was no way that this man was going to decide in my favor. I had lost eight years of my life to this case, and I no longer gave a damn.

* * * * *

So I went to see Dr. Selig. Surprisingly, I was relaxed that day. I was let into the office, and I saw an older man with a big beard, wearing simple clothes, not dressy, formal clothes like most doctors.

"Mr. Noor?" he inquired.

"That's me," I responded indifferently.

"I'm the guy who will be writing the report regarding the status of your workers' compensation case," he said, gesturing for me to sit down in a chair. I merely nodded at him. "To make it easier for you, we are going to wait for the woman who will be the translator to arrive."

I wasn't happy to be dealing with another translator who was most likely going to be Arabic. By this time, I had had plenty of experience with translators, most of it bad or useless.

"Look," I began with an air of impatience, "I know you work for the insurance company."

"That I do," Dr. Selig confirmed.

"I know you're going to give me a bad report. I want to tell you something. Do you know where I am from?" I asked.

"I know where you're from."

163

"Do you know that I am Muslim?" I asked. To be honest, I am not sure why I asked him this.

"I know that too," Dr. Selig said, seeming curious about where this conversation was going.

"Please. Just give me a bad report. I don't care. I don't care. I just want this to be over. Eight years of my life gone." I paused. "You can kill a man, and then he is dead," I sighed. "Or you can keep him alive and torture him daily. Make him die a thousand deaths. That's what has been done to me by the people you work for," I said, pounding my fist on the table.

He eyed me cautiously but did not respond. There was a knock at the door. He yelled for them to come in. A beautiful Arabic woman entered the room. This did not make me happy.

Dr. Selig started asking me questions. But his questions were not of the stupid, insulting, ridiculous type that I was accustomed to fielding from doctors. He seemed different. Not by any means like Dr. Rick but different from most doctors. In a good way.

One of my responses prompted a laugh from the translator. A big, loud, open-mouthed laugh. She made no attempt to conceal her reaction. It made me very uncomfortable. Dr. Selig was quick to pick up on this.

"I think we have no need for your further services today," Dr. Selig said to the translator. "You may go now. We will send you a check for your services today." He stood up, quickly ushering her out of the room.

Honestly, I was very impressed by that. I found myself with the overwhelming desire to hug him. I felt this despite knowing that he worked for the insurance company and still believing that he was likely to write a report that was not favorable to me. Dr. Selig won me over big time with this small gesture.

"Adam, I'm out of time. I'd like to see you again because I think I need a little bit more information before I can draw any valid conclusions about your case," Dr. Selig said after two hours. He was so easy to be with that I hadn't realized that so much time had passed.

* * * * *

About a month later, I was in his office again. This time I was even more relaxed. I just wanted to talk to him and forget that he was supposed to be my enemy. That he was going to write an unfavorable report to the insurance company. Hours flew by before he closed his notebook.

"I think I have all I need," Dr. Selig said. "I think everyone is going to be surprised about what is going to be in my report." This made me apprehensive. I had no idea what that meant.

"Can I ask you a question?"

"Sure," Dr. Selig answered in a friendly tone.

"Do you believe in God?" I asked.

"I very much do," he answered.

"Look, nobody is going to change your mind about what you're going to put in that report. I am Muslim. You are whatever you are." I paused. "Remember, God judges everyone—me, you, everyone. Please make this report between you and God. Forget about who you work for and write what you believe."

"Adam, don't worry. I am a doctor. In my mind, that means being honest. I don't work for you. I work for the insurance company. But I don't care. All I care about is the truth. I believe in my job, and I believe in God. I will write what I feel," he said.

These words eased my mind a little bit.

"Can I see you again?" I asked.

"Afraid not. This will be the last conversation we have," he said.

"Why?" I asked.

"I'm not sure I can explain that to you," he replied. "I'm not going to take you on as a patient, but I wish you good luck." He stood up and shook my hand. And that was that.

* * * * *

Without waiting for the final report, I went back to Jordan. As much as I missed my dad, I had no desire to remain in the United States.

Upon my return to Jordan, I was tempted to seek out Deena. But I opted not to. And although she knew I was back, she made no effort to reach out to me. I didn't want to burden her, and I thought my best move was to just leave her alone.

Many months later, I got a phone call from Deena's brother. He was at the hospital.

"Adam! Congratulations!" her brother yelled.

"Congratulations?"

"Your baby was just born. You're a father!" he exclaimed.

"What?" I asked, bewildered.

"You have a daughter," he said, sounding exuberant.

"Who...me?"

"Yes, you." He laughed. "You should come to the hospital and meet your daughter."

There was a long, awkward silence. I just stood there, trying to process what I was being told. I expected to feel joy or terror or something at this news. Instead, I felt nothing. No emotion. My total lack of emotion really bothered me. But I told her brother I would be there as quickly as I could.

* * * * *

Hospitals make me very tense. It wasn't always that way. But ever since my attack, being in a hospital has increased my anxiety tenfold. I went to the information desk to find out where my ex-wife and newborn daughter were. But my cloudy brain made it hard to communicate what I was trying to say. As I tried to talk, I thought they were going to direct me to the psych ward. I knew I was coming off on the crazy side.

Once I got the information I needed, I went in search of her room. It was on the third floor. Room 232. I had to get directions from multiple people along the way before I finally found the room. In the center of the room was Deena, looking tired and sweaty, holding a small human being in her arms!

It's hard to believe how small babies are when they are first born. So fragile. So helpless. They look easily damaged and broken. But I guess we humans are vulnerable to damage, regardless of our age.

Deena saw me and gave me a weary half-asleep smile. My mom and several of her family were already in the room. My mom came up to me and gave me a big hug.

"Congratulations. You're a father now," she said to me quietly.

"I don't believe it," I said. (I meant this literally.)

"Do you wish to hold her?" my mom asked.

"Oh no...," I started. "No," I repeated, scared—scared for a million varied reasons, most of which I can scarcely articulate. My mom gently took my daughter out of Deena's hands and brought her to me.

"Take your daughter," she commanded. I awkwardly held out my hands, and my mom slid her into my arms. I took her, terrified that I was going to drop her. I stared at my daughter in awe. She didn't open her eyes. Most newborns can't right away. In that moment, despite all my reservations, I fell in love.

"This is mine?" I asked, my voice filled with wonder.

"This is yours." My mom laughed.

"I can't believe it," I said (this time, meaning it figuratively).

"I think maybe you and her should get back together," my mom suggested, pointing at Deena. "Your beautiful daughter is good reason to do so."

I looked back at my daughter then at Deena. She was looking at me with droopy eyes that suggested that the minute everyone was out of the room, she was going to fall fast asleep and it was going to be a while before she would be awake again. I couldn't fault my mom's logic. I believed that this was what my father would have wanted and expected from me. I believed that this was what God would expect from me. I found myself staring at my daughter and feeling filled with a desire to protect her, to not let a single harmful thing ever happen to her. I looked back at my mother, who was looking at me expectantly.

"Okay," I said with a beaming smile. And just like that, for the third time, Deena and I were back together again.

CHAPTER 18

After a couple of days, Deena and I left the hospital. She came and stayed with me at my most recent place of residence. Raafid and my mom would visit with food and things for the baby. I was very appreciative of my family. Deena and I did not have much money, and caring for a new child is difficult even if you do have plenty of money.

I often looked at my daughter with a mixture of pride and guilt. I had pride about how beautiful and smart she was. But I also felt as though I had done a bad thing by bringing a child into this cold and heartless world. Moreover, I felt guilty that this beautiful girl had to have the misfortune of being born to me, a broken and weak man.

"Father, I feel like I can't handle this," I said to my dad over the phone one day.

"That's not an uncommon feeling among new fathers," my dad said with traces of his vintage humor in his voice.

"I feel like I don't know what I am doing, like I am not up to the job," I added.

"Adam, all new parents feel like that. Those are not unique feelings or fears."

"Did you feel that way?"

"Of course, I did!" my father roared.

"Really? You?" I exclaimed, astonished.

"You know, sometimes I get the impression that you think I'm some kind of superhero instead of the old frail man that I actually am." He chuckled.

"You're not old, Dad," I loudly asserted.

"In your eyes, I'm not old, because you refuse to think of me as such. But I assure you that I have become old," he said, being uncharacteristically serious. "There is no instruction manual out there on how to take care of or raise a kid. Sure, there are books. But none of them are worth the paper they are printed on. Every kid is unique and different. What might work with one will not work with another. We all wing it, every day. Anybody who tells you they know how to raise kids is absolutely full of crap. Nobody does," he finished.

"I'm not well, Father, not well in the head…"

"I know. But my sympathies shifted the minute your daughter was born. Well or not, you have a responsibility to that child. You will do just fine," my dad reassured me.

"How do you know?"

"Because as I said many times, you have no choice," he replied firmly. "And Adam…"

"Yes, Father?"

"I expect to see my grandchild soon, sometime before I die," he said, his voice filled again with humor.

* * * * *

After a few months, I got another call from my lawyer, Mr. Shaw. I was in no way thrilled to hear from him.

"The report is in," Mr. Shaw said.

"The report?"

"Yes. Dr. Selig's report."

"Oh, that report," I said with no emotion. I had forgotten all about that.

"It's good news!" Mr. Shaw said happily.

"Is it?" I said with surprise.

"Dr. Selig found in your favor. The insurance company is steaming mad. It's glorious!" Mr. Shaw laughed. "I need you to come back to America."

"Again?"

"Yes. Get back here. You're about to win your case!" he said and quickly hung up the phone so as not to hear an objection. I sighed. Deena heard me. I told her what the phone call was about. She just rolled her eyes and went into the other room. She knew what this meant. Divorce number 3.

* * * * *

Once again, I traveled back to America. How long was I going to be there, I had no idea. Preferably, just long enough to get my case settled, and then back to Jordan I would go. After seeing my dad once more, I quickly visited my lawyer's office to get my hands on Dr. Selig's report.

Highlights from Dr. Selig's report included the following:

> I interviewed Mr. Noor in my office for one hour on April 16th, 2008, and for one hour on May 15th, 2008. He is Jordanian but does speak English.
>
> Psychiatric Findings
>
> Mr. Noor is a twice divorced, Jordanian-born man who was working on August 7th, 2000, when he was assaulted and robbed; sustaining injuries to his back, head and neck along with psychological trauma. His physical injuries have been considerable and have been well documented. Indeed, Commissioner Delaney, after reviewing a variety of reports and one formal hearing, issued an opinion on May 14th, 2007, concluding that Mr. Noor had sustained compensable back and psychological trauma which arose out of and in the course of his employment. Commissioner Delany concluded that Dr. Schultz's recommendation for back surgery, including a decompression and fusion, constituted reasonable and necessary medical treatment as a result of the work incident on August 7th, 2000.

Mr. Noor has been in psychiatric treatment with a variety of providers from August 24th, 2000, to the present. Primary diagnosis has been Post-Traumatic Stress Disorder. He has also, at times, been diagnosed with Major Depressive Disorder, with psychotic symptoms. These symptoms, including hearing the voice of the assailant who robbed him, have also been described.

When I met with Mr. Noor, he was talkative and cooperative. He was very tearful and wore sunglasses, which he would not take off. His right leg was constantly shaking and he was quite agitated. He was irritable and sad about his life. He was very upset about being back in the United States and wanted very much to return to Jordan. He felt that in Jordan, "They treat me like a person. I can say what I want to say." He does not have a language problem (obviously) in Jordan.

He finds being back in the United States to be extremely unpleasant and highly re-traumatizing. His back hurts a great deal, but he would prefer to not undergo back surgery. He is very anxious that it may not help he fears that his family in the U.S. would be overburdened if they had to attempt to take care of him during his rehabilitation. His preference would be to return to Jordan, re-enter psychiatric treatment, and, at some point, when appropriate, have surgery in Jordan. He recognizes that, in order to accomplish this, he would need to settle his Workers' Compensation case, which he would like to do.

His mental state and symptoms were very similar when I saw him on May 15th, 2008. His hygiene was more impaired and he looked like a chronic mental patient. His leg was constantly shaking and he wore dark glasses, a dirty shirt and a dirty baseball cap. He was agitated and anxious and had a great deal of trouble focusing on any particular issues or concentrating. He emphasized that he wanted to settle his case and return to Jordan as he felt that he could not live anywhere else.

Summary and Recommendations

On the basis of the aforementioned evaluation, it is my opinion, within reasonable medical probability, that Mr. Noor has sustained a compensable psychiatric injury as a result of being assaulted and robbed while working on August 7th, 2000. Diagnoses are Post Traumatic Stress Disorder and Major Depressive Disorder, recurrent, severe, with psychotic features. He has remained totally disabled since the date of his injury and continues to be temporarily totally disabled. At this point, it is my opinion, within reasonable medical probability, that Mr. Noor has reached maximum medical improvement psychiatrically. Given that it is almost eight years since the date of injury and he has responded to numerous treatments, it is unlikely that he is going to improve more.

Mr. Noor will require ongoing psychiatric treatment for the rest of his life. This will include anti-depressant, anti-anxiety, and anti-psychotic medication, as well as intensive psychotherapy at least once a weak. He is competent at this time to make a decision regarding back surgery and I recommend against his having back surgery. It is my opinion that the best approach at this point psychiatrically would be for him to resolve his Workers' Compensation case, return to Jordan, and enter psychiatric treatment in Jordan. He feels less alienated in Jordan and there are fewer triggers of the August 2000 trauma.

Using the AMA guides to the Evaluation of Permanent Impairment, fifth edition, it is my opinion that Mr. Noor has sustained a marked impairment in activities of daily life, social functioning, concentration and adaptation. He has forty to fifty percent permanent partial impairment of the brain. This is one of the highest permanency ratings, which I have ever assessed, but I believe is warranted in this case given his lack of improvement and substantial impairment in his functional capacity. He has become apparently permanently and totally disabled, extremely isolated, and extremely psychiatrically impaired despite treatment.

* * * * *

In Mr. Shaw's office, I finished reading the report (much of which I didn't understand). I turned to Mr. Shaw with an atypical grin on his face.

"This sounds…good," I said uncertainly.

"Oh, it's very good. This is game over. We win!" Mr. Shaw said, grinning from ear to ear.

"Really?" I said in disbelief.

"Really. This case is a done deal!" Mr. Shaw said. "We should go out and celebrate!"

* * * * *

Although I was ecstatic about believing I had won the case, this was significant for me for another reason as well. I had come to believe that there were almost no trustworthy people in the world. That most people, especially those involved with a business of any kind, were only interested in helping themselves. People would lie, cheat and do any manner of things that were wrong, just to make more money.

As previously mentioned, Dr. Selig is Jewish and I am Muslim. Given the animosity between these 2 groups of people, I fully expected that Dr. Selig had more motivation than most people to allege that I was not disabled. I figured that if he gave the insurance company a report that favored them, the insurance company would continue to employ him to do these types of evaluations. I also figured that he would come into the meetings with pre-conceived negative ideas about Muslims in general.

Dr. Selig's report not only gave me a chance to win the workers' compensation case, but it also restored a little bit of my faith in humanity. I reasoned that if a Jewish man (who has power over a Muslim man and has financial incentive to harm that man) can be honorable toward a Muslim man, maybe there is hope for the Jews and Muslims of the world to find a way past their collective grievances.

* * * * *

Of course, just like every other step along the way, this next step would not prove to be that easy. The insurance company was hopping mad about Dr. Selig's report. They didn't want to accept the report of their own doctor! The one they hired to do the job. So they fought the report like they fought everything else that didn't happen to go their way. Once again, I tried to live in the United States while waiting for the end of the workers' compensation case. As time passed, I became more and more deflated by the tactics of the insurance company.

"You should bring your wife and daughter here," my dad would insist.

"No, Father," I said sadly.

"Why not?" my dad asked, sounding hurt.

"I know what that would mean for you. That would mean that you would end up taking care of my daughter, my wife, and of course, me. I refuse to do that to you any longer," I replied forcefully.

This wouldn't stop him from continuing to argue the point.

While they were challenging the validity of Dr. Selig's report, the insurance company quickly returned to its effort to spy on me. I had had enough of their shenanigans. Once again, I decided to leave it all behind and return to Jordan.

CHAPTER 19

I returned to Jordan with the intent of living alone. Once again, I did not seek out Deena as I assumed she would have no interest in talking to me. As far as I was aware, there was no way to reunite with her at this juncture because we had now divorced three separate times.

While looking for a place to live, I happened upon some relatively cheap apartments. The owner of the building was an older man. When I knocked on his door, he didn't seem thrilled to see me.

"Hi. I'm Adam Noor from the United States," I said, counting on that fact earning me instant credit with him. "I'd like to rent one of your apartments."

"You are from the United States?" he asked skeptically.

"Yes, sir," I replied.

"You look like a homeless bum," he snorted. "You're full of crap, young man."

"I assure you, I'm not," I said, sounding offended.

"Do you have any proof that you are?" he asked.

I dug through my knapsack, the only possession I had. Finding my passport, I quickly handed it to him. His mouth dropped open in shock.

"Never seen someone from the United States look so bad," he said, shaking his head. "How long have you lived in the United States?"

"Ten years," I answered.

"This isn't fake?" he questioned.

"It's not fake."

"What's your story?"

"My story is long. I could write a book." I sighed.

"Let's hear it," he insisted.

I proceeded to tell him the whole story. I did it with great difficulty, as I was having trouble concentrating. I'm not sure he understood half of it.

"That's some story," he said when I was done.

I nodded my head and said nothing for a moment, just feeling tired and exhausted. "I'd like to rent an apartment," I repeated, hoping that everything I had said to him had been enough to get past whatever skepticism he had about me.

"Not going to be any trouble, are you?" he asked.

"No trouble. Too tired to cause trouble," I said with a half smile.

"See that you don't," he said and then led me inside.

The apartment was on the bottom floor, for which I was thankful. When he opened the door and showed me where I would be living, it looked more like a prison cell than a place where a person should live. I didn't care. There were scarcely any windows, just like my basement back in America. I was fine with it. It seemed like this was a place where I would be left alone with my demons. This was what I had been looking for.

"Do you have any furniture?" the old man asked.

"No," I said.

"Not even a bed or anything?" he asked, sounding concerned.

"All I have on me is in this bag," I said, indicating the knapsack that was slung over my shoulder.

"So your plan is to sleep on the floor?" He laughed.

"I've slept on worse," I answered.

He gave me an odd look, a look that suggested there was no way that particular statement could possibly be true. But he didn't say what he was thinking.

"You know what? I believe I have something for you...," he said and quickly exited the room. He came back with a dirty worn-out mattress and a pillow. "It's not much," he paused. "But better than the floor."

"Thank you," I said, feeling tired and weary but grateful. He added that if I needed anything else, I should let him know. The moment he was gone, I reclined on the mattress and instantly fell into a deep sleep.

* * * * *

Back in the United States, the courts, the insurance company, and Dr. Selig were fighting over the validity of the psychological report. I honestly didn't care about the outcome. I was just tired of the whole thing. I cut myself off from the rest of the world for a time.

A few months went by. In my self-imposed isolation, I had only this older man for company. In the beginning, he visited me a few times per week. He gave me food or furniture and sometimes engaged in some other act of kindness. But in time, he began showing up at my door so often that it annoyed me. Generally, I wanted to be left alone. Unfortunately, he ended up on the receiving end of my diseased mind. Like my father, my lawyer, and everyone else who had been close to me, we ended up getting into numerous verbal altercations.

"You know what!" he screamed at me during one of these interactions. "Being in the United States helped me to buy this building. What do you have to show for being there?"

This question stung me worse than a slap in the face. I knew the expectations of my people. Sharaf had assumed that I would be able to buy his club with the riches I had earned while in the United States. But despite my time in America, I could barely afford a sandwich. I was so deeply ashamed and embarrassed about this that I told him to leave and never come back.

Later that day, he came back to apologize and to invite me to dinner. I accepted.

During our meal, he said, "I spent most of my life in the United States, and I loved it there. It is due to my time in the United States that I have all that I have today. I feel badly for you, so I'm going to treat you like one of my sons."

"I feel guilty," I replied.

"Why?" he asked.

"I've abandoned my wife and daughter. I should be with them," I said sadly. "But when I am with them, I feel guilty for inflicting myself on them."

"You never should have gotten married," he said.

"I know," I sighed.

"In your situation, you need to be worrying about you. No one else," he said.

I agreed with him and added that this was one of the reasons why I was now in my self-imposed exile from all those that I cared about.

* * * * *

My landlord was very kind. He really did treat me like a son. On one occasion, I ran out of my medication, resulting in one of the worst panic attacks I had ever experienced. When he found me lying on the ground, he did his best to comfort me and calm me down. But nothing that anyone did helped that much. I either had to ride it out, go to the hospital, or take medication. He took me to the pharmacy and got me medication.

After more time passed, I began to feel suspicious about my landlord's motivations and about the manner in which he was helping me. I had trusted too many people and been let down far too many times to take his help at face value. Was he gay? Did he want to sleep with me? I no longer believed that good people actually existed in the world. I came to believe that everyone had an angle. I started to feel very uncomfortable around him.

I became so uncomfortable that I called an old friend. Prior to this, I had declined to reach out to former friends out of shame and pride. But I told him what was going on, and he agreed to help me out for a little while. He showed up with garbage bags to pack my things.

My landlord became extremely angry when he found out I was leaving. He offered to let me live there for free. I declined. I felt certain that although my rent might be free, there would be some kind of price attached. Whatever the price, it was too high.

* * * * *

Another few months went by in a blink. Mostly I slept. Even though he was not pressuring me to leave, I was aware that I couldn't stay with my friend forever. I also knew that I couldn't continue to jump from apartment to apartment, not paying rent. One day, there would be no more places to live, and I would find myself living on the streets of Jordan.

At this point, I turned my phone back on, and I decided to call my dad.

"Tell you what, son," he began. "I will pay for you to get an apartment, and I will pay your rent—on one condition." Then he went silent.

"What's the condition?" I asked.

"You get back with Deena," he replied.

"She's probably married to someone else by now," I said with a heavy sigh.

"She isn't."

"How do you know?" I asked, surprised.

"Your mother has been in constant contact with her," my dad said.

"Of course, she has," I said with mild irritation.

"Take her back, and I will pay your rent," my dad said sternly.

"I can't, Dad. We've been divorced three times. The courts won't allow it."

"That is where your problems are actually an advantage for a change. If you tell them about your mental health problems, they will tell you that your divorce did not count, and you can have your wife back," my father replied.

"B-b-b-b-but they are better off without me," I stuttered.

"No daughter or son is better off without their father," my dad interjected forcefully.

"In this case—" I began but was interrupted.

"In this case, nothing. If you want my help, then you need to return to your wife and daughter. You shouldn't have gotten married, and you shouldn't have had a kid, but you did. I don't care what your problems are. No son of mine will ignore his responsibilities," he said. There was clearly a great deal of anger behind his words. There was nothing else I could say. I agreed to his conditions.

* * * * *

As it turned out, my father was right about the courts. Ordinarily, you were allowed to divorce and reconcile twice. After the third time, you were done. Unless there was another marriage to another man in between. When I told them about my mental health problems, the judge told me that my divorce didn't count in the eyes of God. It was explained to me that I was considered to have blacked out and been unable to know what I was really doing. By that same logic, perhaps I shouldn't have been allowed to marry in the first place. But that was neither here nor there. Essentially, this was a free pass to divorce Deena as many times as I wanted to. Despite my efforts to leave them alone, thanks to my dad, we were once again together. For better or for worse.

CHAPTER 20

Deena and I found an apartment. As promised, my dad began paying the rent. A year or so went by relatively uneventfully. Nothing had really changed. But my mental condition was taking its toll on Deana. She had once been a proud and beautiful woman. Having previously worked for a cosmetic company, she had always dressed nicely and worn makeup. Now having had to care for a child and having to deal with me on a continual basis, she had begun to look very tired. She had let herself go. No more meticulously well-thought-out outfits nor matching makeup. Deena looked like a homeless person, just like I did. Despite her attire, she was still a very beautiful woman.

During this stretch of time, I would typically make a brief visit or two to the United States to deal with the insurance case then quickly return to Jordan. I often wondered why I even bothered with this, as it seemed like the case would just go on and on forever. Periodically, my lawyer would call to give me an update on the case. I would barely listen.

* *

During my absence from the United States, my father was busy having my old room in the basement renovated. He cleaned it up and turned it into a small apartment. He even had new windows installed. The crew he hired charged him $15,000 to do this work. My dad wanted my wife, my daughter, and me to come to the United States and stay in this apartment.

"I want to play with my grandchild," he said with cheeriness in his voice. I never really answered him. I kept putting him off. I didn't want to say no, but I also didn't want to be a burden on my father.

At some point in 2010, I started to suspect that Deena was pregnant again. I'm not sure what made me suspect this, but I became very worried. Just a feeling.

"I think you're pregnant," I said to Deena.

"No...no, I'm not," Deena replied.

"I think you are." I snorted. "We need to go to a doctor."

"No, we don't," Deena insisted.

This initially calm conversation soon turned into an argument. We fought all night.

* * * * *

I won the argument, so we went to the nearest doctor's office. I was very nervous. My thinking was that we didn't need another child. I loved my daughter, but I realized that I was not capable of being a good father to her. My mental health problems pretty much guaranteed that. I did my best. But my efforts never felt like enough. For this, I felt endlessly guilty. It weighed on my mind each and every day. Adding another child would increase my guilt exponentially, not to mention adding to our financial burden.

"Good morning," a very professional young secretary said to me.

"If you bring us good news, I swear I'm going to bring you a very nice gift," I said to the woman. Next to me, Deena was rolling her eyes at me.

"Yes...I hope I will be able to give you good news," she said with a smile.

Undoubtedly, she was thinking that good news would have been an announcement that Deena was indeed pregnant. In fact, I meant the opposite.

We got the test done and waited for what seemed like hours without saying a word to each other. I was begging God to give us a negative result.

"Adam Noor?" I heard the secretary call.

"Yes?" I said, standing up fast.

"The doctor has news for you," she said. She indicated for me to go into the other room to see the doctor. Upon seeing the doctor, she smiled broadly.

"Congratulations!" she said to me.

"Why?" I asked.

"Your wife is pregnant!" the doctor shouted excitedly.

Deena stayed silent, keeping her emotions in check, waiting for my explosion.

"No," I said quietly.

"No?" The doctor asked, confused.

"No. You are a liar," I said, shaking my head. Deena was looking at the ground, not saying a word. She began slowly moving away from me.

"What do you mean?" the doctor asked, her face looking very concerned.

"I don't need this," I snarled. "I don't need this!" I repeated this but louder.

The doctor was watching me, looking a little scared. And then I started shouting very loudly.

"Sir!" the doctor yelled. "I'm going to need you to calm down, or I'm going to have get the police involved!"

"I don't need this," I reiterated, much quieter, my voice filled with pain.

"What the hell is wrong with you?" the doctor inquired, taking a glance in Deena's direction to see if there might be answers forthcoming. There weren't. Deena said nothing, just looked embarrassed.

"I tell you that your wife is pregnant, and this is how you react?"

"You don't understand…," I started to say, tears in my eyes.

"I sure don't," the doctor said, disgusted. She turned to Deena. "I'd like to see you next week for more tests, to make sure everything's running smoothly."

"That's fine," Deena responded quietly. The doctor gave one more disgusted look in my direction and then left us.

I glanced at the secretary as I was leaving. "When I see your face, I know I'm going to get bad news," I said angrily.

"Excuse me?" she said in a surprised manner. "Your wife is pregnant…"

I proceeded to swear at her while she just looked at me, appearing both scared and confused. We left the office. As soon as we got in the car, I started yelling at Deena.

"Why did you do this? Why!"

"We did this…," she pointed out quietly.

"I'm a crazy man. We're going to bring another life into this world and make them crazy!" I shouted. "We don't have any money! We have nothing! Are you stupid? Can you give me one good reason to have another kid?"

My heart was beating out of my chest. My breathing became labored, shallower. I continued shouting while Deena just stared at me with tears in her eyes. This continued until my anxiety overwhelmed me, and I ended up in the hospital.

* * * * *

Looking back at this incident, I am not proud of my behavior. I did not consider another child to be good news. Part of me was happy. But most of me was scared out of my mind. We were living in a crappy situation without much hope of it getting any better. It seemed like my insurance case was never going to end, and if it did, I highly doubted that it would be in my favor. I had felt guilty about bringing our daughter into a world so fraught with turmoil. Now that we were bringing another child into this world, I felt much worse.

Deena and I didn't talk for a while after this. When we did talk, it was a fight. Eventually, I realized that I didn't have any option but to accept the fact that I was going to be a father again. There was soon going to be another person in the world that would eventually resent me for not being good enough for them.

* * * * *

In the beginning of 2011, I got a call from Mr. Shaw. He sounded excited, but I didn't especially care what he had to say. Sometimes, the only reason I even answered the phone to talk to him was because I was lonely and wanted to hear the voice of anyone not involved with my day-to-day life.

"The case is over," Mr. Shaw said excitedly.

"What are you talking about?" I asked, startled. "I've heard this before…"

"It's for real this time. The insurance company and I have come to an agreement," Mr. Shaw said. "I need you back home."

"For how much?" I asked.

"I'm not sure at this time. Meet me in my office in a couple of days, and we will discuss it," he said and hung up the phone. After a few moments, I followed suit.

I went into the bedroom, where Deena was lying down, and said, "My lawyer just called. He said that he reached an agreement with the insurance company and my case is done. I need to go back."

"Am I divorced?" Deena asked.

"No. I won't be there that long…"

* * * * *

I went back to my parents' home in the United States. I slept in the basement, which was still being worked on. A few days after I arrived, I complied with Mr. Shaw's instructions and showed up at his office.

"How was your trip?" Mr. Shaw asked me enthusiastically.

"Fine," I said tonelessly.

"Okay, so here's the deal. The insurance company is going to give you $100,000," he said with a smile.

"Really? One hundred thousand dollars?" I repeated with amazement.

"In addition to that, they will give you weekly payments and an annuity," he added.

"Okay," I said, smiling.

"A lot of money," Mr. Shaw said, grinning.

At this point in my life, this amount did sound like a good amount of money. But I didn't know what an annuity was, and I didn't ask. I was told that if I accepted this deal, the annuity would pay me a $12,000 check once per year. In addition, I would receive monthly checks for $1,300. This was just $1,000 more than the amount they had already been paying me.

"Take two weeks and think about this," Mr. Shaw said.

* * * * *

It took only a few days for me to decide. I went to the courthouse, feeling anxious about whether or not I was making the best decision. But I had decided to take the deal. I knew that if I said no, there was a chance that I would be tied up in court for another ten years. I couldn't afford that. My wife and children needed me to have this issue settled. With another child coming, it was even more urgent to get that money. I went before the judge and just said yes to all his questions. When he was done, I signed the agreement. As time would tell, I was totally oblivious to all the ways that this agreement would complicate my life.

* * * * *

Before I signed the contract, aside from discussing it with my lawyer, I hadn't talked to anyone else about it. I should have. When my dad learned about the details of the settlement, he was furious!

"What'd they give you? A hundred thousand dollars? They should have given you at least a million!" my dad exclaimed.

"I don't know...," I said.

"You're going to suffer now because you didn't make a good decision." He sighed, shaking his head.

"Dad, it's a big insurance company. It's all they think I'm worth," I said sadly.

"Who's going to take care of you after I die? You're going to suffer. Your kids are going to suffer."

* * * * *

Next, I met with Dr. Rick. I had not seen him for a long time. It was good to see him again. Time had not really seemed to age him very much since the last time I had seen him. I handed him the settlement agreement.

"Can you look this over and tell me if I made a good deal?" I asked him.

"I can," he said. "But at this point, it doesn't matter what I think. The deal has been finalized."

"Just read it," I insisted.

He did as I asked. While reading the document, a look of confusion and intense concentration never left his face.

When he was done, he looked up at me and said, "Adam…I'm an educated man, and I can't make heads or tails of this thing…"

"It's in English…," I said.

"It's written in legal gobbledygook," he said. "Legalese! If I really took my time with this thing, I might eventually understand it. But I don't understand it now, and I suspect you don't either. I can only hope your lawyer explained it to you better than I can."

* * * * *

To give you an idea of what I'm talking about, here's a sample of what the settlement said:

AWARD BY STIPULATION FOR FULL AND FINAL SETTLEMENT.

It is claimant's contention that on or about July 1st, 2000 and August 7th, 2000 and for the entire course of employment with the employer-respondent from December 14th, 1999 to

August 7th, 2000, as a result of repetitive trauma or otherwise, while at work for the employer-respondent, he injured his low back, neck, teeth, right shoulder, and left arm; that as a result of this accident he sustained numerous injuries, including but not limited to the following; tooth pain; infection in gums; periodontal disease; dental caries; dry mouth; xerostomia; deep periodontal pocketing; heavy sub gingival calculus; mucositis; sucular inflammation and suppuration; chronic neck pain; neck sprain/strain; radicular pain into right shoulder; tenderness along the anterolateral aspect of the right shoulder decreased lordosis in cervical spine; low back sprain/strain; chronic back pain; back spasm; central disc herniation of the nucleus puposus at L4-5; radicular pain down right leg; tightness and stiffness of the back muscles; lumbar lordosis; loss of normal T2 signal at the nucleus pulpous at L4-5; tear of the annulus fibrosis and L5 radiculupathy; small left posterior vertebral body hemangioma at L2-3; acute low back pain; lumbosacral spine strain; burn on left arm; emotional problems; severe depression; post-traumatic stress disorder; insomnia; panic attacks; paranoia; auditory hallucinations; visual hallucinations; dissociative flashbacks; despondence suicidal thoughts/ideation; major depressive disorder, recurrent, severe, with psychotic features; social and emotional withdrawal; intense anger; tearfulness; hyper-vigilance; poor concentration; poor memory; extreme dysphoria; anaerobia; agoraphobia; poor hygiene; hopelessness; helplessness; nightmares; fragmented recall; restricted affect; condyloma; erectile dysfunction; urinary frequency; nervousness; intrusive thoughts; difficulty talking; intense fear; delusional beliefs.

The claimant further contends that as a result of said injury he suffers from a 50% permanent partial disability to the brain, a high degree of permanent partial disability to the jaw, teeth, neck and low back; and that the permanent disabilities may increase in the future; that he required medical, dental, psychiatric, psychological, pharmaceutical, surgical, and hospital treatment; that he has attempted to work at his former job, but is unable to do that type of work; that he has been disable totally and partially and may in the future incur such disability.

Alleging that said injuries arose out of and in the course of his employment, the claimant sought compensation for his disability past, present and future, both total partial, compensation for permanent injury and specific compensation and payment of all reasonable medical, surgical, hospital and incidental bills incurred or to be incurred in connection with the treatment of his condition.

The respondents admit the low back and psychiatric/psychological injuries of August 7th only. The respondents however, deny that any permanent physical injury resulted, deny that the claimant is now suffering or will in the future suffer any disability either total or partial; deny that the claimant will in the future require further medical, dental, psychiatric, psychological, pharmaceutical, surgical, or hospital care as a result of these injures and deny that the claimant has suffered any permanent partial disability as a

result of these injuries, but if any, deny the extent
as alleged by the claimant.

* * * * *

If you tell the average person that he or she is going to receive
a one-time payment of one hundred thousand dollars, plus twelve
thousand dollars every year, plus thirteen hundred dollars every
month, they would think that this was a good deal. They would be
wrong. The insurance company made my life a living hell for nearly
eleven years. They stole eleven years of my life. I was getting better
under the treatment of Dr. Rick. Not 100 percent better, as that
is impossible. But I was improving. Then the insurance company
started spying on me, taking videos of me, setting me up with female
drivers who were instructed to try to seduce "the truth" out of me.
They sent me to an endless parade of doctors, none of whose interest
was in my well-being, playing an extended game of "Gotcha!" with
me.

I was already mentally ill. I already had severe mental health
problems. But they piled on. Their responsibility should have been
to my well-being, to try to make me better. Instead they made things
worse. A lot worse. To this day, I still get the feeling that there are
people spying on me. Whether I am walking the streets or just relaxing in my home. I still get the feeling that there are people who are
out to get me. But as the saying goes, you're not paranoid if they
really are out to get you.

Frankly, in addition to owing me for the damage I received
while on the job, they owed me for the pain and suffering that they
caused over the eleven years of the workers' comp case. If not for
all they put me through, who knew where I would be now? Maybe
I'd be significantly better. But apparently, that's not how insurance
companies work. They work to make sure they don't have to pay you
a dime. They work to make your life miserable, simply hoping that
you will give up on trying to receive benefits. The money they gave
me did not make up for all the pain and suffering they caused me.
Ultimately, they hurt me more than the man who severely beat me.

One of the details I did not understand when I signed the agreement was that on the day I signed, the insurance company would drop me. That I would now be responsible for paying the costs of all my medical care. Doctor visits, psychologist visits, and the cost of my medications were now all my responsibility to pay.

In a nineteen-month period, the cost of my medications is $19,000. That's in Jordanian money. I receive the money from my settlement in American money. As I've explained before, an American dollar is only worth seventy cents compared to the Jordanian dollar. In Jordan, my one hundred thousand American dollars are only worth seventy thousand Jordanian dollars.

Prior to the settlement, the insurance company did not send any money to my doctors in Jordan. As a result, prior to the settlement, I racked up a debt of $60,000 in Jordan. Again, this was in Jordanian money. In order to pay off that debt, I used up a good chunk of my $100,000. But shouldn't the insurance company have paid all my injury-related medical expenses prior to the settlement? They would not do so. My having to pay these expenses drastically reduced the amount of money from the settlement that I would be able to use for living expenses for myself and my expanding family.

But there were additional reasons why this was a bad deal. Between the monthly payment and my annual payment, I pull in about $28,000 a year. The average person might say, "Twenty-eight thousand? Without working at all? Pretty good deal!" But what this average person wouldn't be understanding is that I am not capable of working. I am mentally and physically disabled. In addition, because of my medications, I sometimes spend most of my time sleeping. The medications usually sap the life out of me.

If you imagine some generic person making minimum wage, they will take home about $12,000 in a year. If that person is married and their spouse works a minimum-wage job as well, that's another $12,000 in take-home pay. If you add two kids to the mix, at the end of the year, they will likely get a tax return of $10,000. Add all that together, and the couple will net about $34,000 in a year. The poverty line in the state of Massachusetts for a family of four is currently at $30,000. According to these guidelines, I (but not the imaginary person that I was just discussing) am living in poverty. But the imaginary person has the potential to make more money. He/she can get a raise, work more hours, or leave their current job for a higher-paying one. None of these options are available to me. No matter what, unless I receive help, I am stuck with the same amount of money. There is no ability to improve my life by making more.

Even with the tax return, the imaginary family of four will struggle. My actual family of four will struggle even more. I get a monthly check of $1,300. Let's say the average two-bedroom apartment in Maryland is around $1,000 a month. At this point, I'm down to $300 left. And I haven't paid any bills yet. The electric bill is probably around $100 per month. Now I have around $200 to live off. This $200 would need to stretch enough for me to take care of my wife and two kids—food, clothing, school supplies, etc. That's if the only bills you are paying for are rent and electricity. This doesn't take into account cable and internet expenses or gas heat. When taking these other expenses into account, financially, you end up in the negative. And that's how you end up behind.

All this assumes that I'm living in the United States. But at this point, I had no desire to do this. Everywhere I went in the United States reminded me about what had happened to me and what I had lost. I had no desire to ever return to America. In Jordan, that US$1,300 will enable me to purchase the equivalent of $900 worth of goods. The $12,000 I get annually is more like $8,400 in Jordan.

* * * * *

Another important point: the settlement agreement should have been translated into Arabic! That settlement was my future, my life. I should have been helped to understand every single sentence that was in that agreement. Dr. Rick, a pretty smart guy, couldn't even understand several parts of that agreement. My lawyer should have made sure that I understood exactly what I was signing. He didn't. Once I realized that I had made a horrible, hideous mistake, I tried calling Mr. Shaw. He didn't answer. He never answered another phone call from me. This guy was my lawyer for eleven years. Eleven years! Once the settlement was signed, he was done with me. No further use for me. He seemed so kind and so caring. He seemed like he fought for me because he cared. Apparently, that wasn't the case. He was just another person who disappointed me and dropped out of my life the minute I was no longer valuable to him. You know what the best part of this whole thing is? He made $150,000 from the case. He got more money than me. I'm the one who is suffering. So explain to me how that is even remotely fair. This is the world we live in.

* * * * *

All this leads to the obvious question: why did I accept such a bad deal? Why didn't I hold out for more? While trying to understand this during my meetings with Dr. Rick, he tried to help me by using a metaphor of a man in the desert searching for water.

He comes across a man who offers him a glass of something to drink. What are you going to do? Refuse it? No, you're going to drink it—no questions asked. I was that man in the desert. I was desperate, desperate to provide for my family and to make my life better. I was tired of playing the game with the insurance company. I wanted it to be over. When I heard about the general outline of the settlement, it sounded good to me. It would to anyone until later when I learned about the actual details. As they say, the devil is in the details.

I tried calling other lawyers. I explained the situation and everything that I had gone through. Once we got to the fact that I had a signed settlement, that was the end of the conversation. Every single time. The damage was done.

And now, my family and I would have to live with it. I have had a great deal of time to think about this whole ordeal: employer firing me for no good reason, the workers compensation commission hiring a selfish insurance company to administer the workers compensation benefit, the selfish insurance company hiring the most heartless lawyers it could, the workers' compensation judge allowing the insurance company to treat me cruelly, and my lawyer not looking out for my best interest by not providing me with an Arabic translation of the legal agreement and not making me aware of how this bad agreement would not leave me with nearly enough money to live my life and pay for the treatment I needed. No cost of living increase over time. Not enough money to pay for my medications and treatment. Shame in my culture for not being able to pay for my treatment. No payment for transportation to my treatment. One signature, and everything was lost!

But it was all done according to the law. Every part of "the system" took advantage of my misfortune to get their own needs met. The last person whose interests were considered was me. I was the only one whose needs were not adequately met! So, according to "the system," it was all legal. If everyone was able to get their needs met but the victim, this essentially can be considered legal exploitation. This is how it is possible for a person to "win" a workers' compensation case that would be worth $1.33 million dollars over the course of a lifetime and end up homeless (a foreshadowing of my future).

CHAPTER 21

I returned to Jordan unhappy and defeated. At the same time, I was relieved to be done with it all. Despite accepting a bad deal, I had some hope for the future. I thought there was a chance that since I was no longer dealing with the stress of the insurance case and was no longer being spied on, I might get better. I tried to work a number of times. In each case, these attempts were met with failure. I couldn't take it. Sadly, my hope and temporary optimism would prove misplaced. Still, I was more relaxed than I had been for a long time.

One of my doctors in Jordan issued an opinion, writing that the settlement was in no way good enough to take care of my medical needs. He wrote the following:

> As to the Insurance Company, it is the sole winner in this case. The patient suffered a heavy blow due to his acceptance, while under great psychological pressure, their settlement conditions. The patient was mistreated physically, morally, psychologically and materially. I say and reiterate that his monthly and annual payments are frivolous and insufficient for the cost of his medicament. So how can the patient manage his living needs?

I decided to buy an apartment for me and my family. It wasn't very big. But for our purposes and our budget, it would do. I obtained a mortgage from a bank and used some of my settlement money as a down payment. The mortgage was roughly $600 a month in Jordanian money.

The day I was set to sign the mortgage, my wife went into labor. I drove her to the hospital, then left her to go back to the bank. As a result, I wasn't present for the births of either of my children. Each time, I arrived after the fact. As with the birth of my daughter, my emotional reaction to the birth of my son was pretty much nonexistent. Now we were four.

I want to emphasize that I love both of my children. I love them with all the love I am capable of giving, given my damaged brain. But I did not greet their arrival with joy. It felt more like another brick being laid on top of me. All I felt was pressure, stress, self-loathing, fear of failure, etc.

My mom came to the apartment every day to make sure we had food and essentials for the baby. I wasn't always awake when she came. I would only find out later from Deena that she had been there. That was how unwell I was.

* * * * *

A year passed in the blink of an eye. During this time, my mental health struggles continued unabated. No relief. No remission. No peace. I continued to spend much of my time sleeping. Occasionally, I would have a panic attack. Usually, I was able to survive these episodes without going to the hospital. In this foggy state of mind, I would often go days without really seeing my wife or my kids. I've been told that when you're around your kids on a daily basis, you don't notice them growing up and getting bigger. In my case, even though they lived with me, because of my frequent episodes of mental absence from their lives, it seemed as if they had grown two feet between each time I saw them. Given that my son was younger, it was especially noticeable with him.

"I know you're disappointed by how your settlement went," my mom said one day.

"Yes, very," I sighed wearily.

"Don't worry about it," my mom said with a smile. "Your father has a surprise for you."

"What's that?" I asked.

"He's going to open a business," my mom said. "Everything is going to be okay. He's going to buy a gas station with land."

"I'm happy at least one of us will have made it," I said with a hint of melancholy.

"He's buying it for you," my mom retorted.

My dad had spent nearly thirty years in the United States, trying to make and save money for the express purpose of buying his own business. This had been his lifelong dream.

My mother explained that recently he had met a businessman by the name of Saad Ahmed. This man had expressed interest in selling my father a gas station and convenience store in Meriden by the name of Friendly Mart. Ahmed was going to sell him the business as well as the surrounding property, but he wanted over a million dollars for this deal.

My father did not have that much money. As a result, my dad was pressuring my mom to sell her beautiful house in Jordan to raise money to purchase this business.

"They're going to give me a good price for the place. I have some money, but I need more," my dad told my mom. "So I need you to stay in one of the apartments and sell your house." He paused. "Ahmed is bringing along a very nice guy named Osama Tarik. He's like an angel," my father said. Osama Tarik was effectively going to be my dad's business partner.

* * * * *

When I began hearing about this deal, it made me very nervous. It was one thing for my father to start pushing my mom to sell her house. But it was another thing entirely when I also got wind of Ahmed pressuring my father to sell his own house as well. I felt that I needed to say something.

"I don't know, Dad," I commented. "This seems kind of fishy. Why are they trying to get you to sell your house?"

My father was very smart. But he was also very trusting and naive. In fact, at times, it seemed as though he would trust anybody. I was very suspicious, and I began to believe that Saad Ahmed and

Osama Tarik knew about my father's trusting nature. It also became apparent that they knew details about my father's finances that they should not have known. They knew how much money he had in his bank account. They knew how many properties he owned. They seemed to know how many pennies he had in his pocket. Everything.

At this point, the entire family was becoming upset with my father. Nobody thought that this was a legitimate deal. My mom kept putting my father off. Every day, my dad would call her, and she would say she would get around to selling the house the next day. Or the day after. Or tomorrow. Or soon. My mom was every bit as suspicious as the rest of the family was. But she was unwilling to directly confront my father on the issue. As it turned out, my dad, who loved my mom and never disagreed with her, did not ever push her on this issue.

But this little charade went on for quite some time—into the next year. Finally, my father told us that he was going to pay Ahmed $300,000. Apparently, this was enough money for them to turn the business over to my father.

* * * * *

Shortly after my dad gave my mother this news, he called me. Deena was sitting next to me when he called.

"Adam, I wanted to talk to you about something," he said excitedly.

"What's up, Dad?" I asked curiously.

"I don't care what you're doing. I need you with me," he started. "I want you to come back home to America and bring your family."

"I can't live in America, Dad…" I sighed.

"I think if you come here, you will be much better," he said. "You can work when you choose and just sit in a chair if you want. I need you. I want you to come next week," my dad implored, his voice filled with heavy emotion. "I bought this business for you. I want to help you, and I need you."

"Dad, I can't make it next week. I need a little time," I said with tears in my eyes. I was greatly moved by his words, moved at what he had done for me. As always, it was never about himself. There was no man more unselfish than my father.

"Take as much time as you need," my dad said, and I could hear the smile in his voice. "Tomorrow I'm going to buy and send you a plane ticket. It's open-ended. You can come when you're ready. Don't worry about the cost." He paused. "You know what? I'm seventy years old. I want to enjoy my life now," he said. "I signed up for a gym membership the other day, and I want to use it."

"You did what?" I laughed.

"Yes. I signed up for a gym membership," he continued. It felt good to hear him laugh, and it felt good for me to laugh. "How much time do I have left? Ten? Twenty years?" he chortled.

I wanted to say he had forever, as I didn't want to contemplate a life without my dad in it.

"I want to enjoy that time," he repeated. "I did it, son. I got my own business in America." I could hear and feel his cheer radiating through the phone.

* * * * *

Osama Tarik got wind of my father's plan to bring me to the United States to work with him. He was not happy. My father said that when Tarik got wind of me coming to work in the store, he took his shoe and threw it at my father's face. In my culture, this is an act of extreme disrespect. When my mother told me this story, I was enraged. However, things got worse.

After taking his $300,000 and promising that this was enough money for them to sign over ownership of the business to my father, Tarik and Ahmed refused to give my father a bill of sale. This outrageous behavior made my family very angry. Why did they take the money if they were not intending to give him a legal business contract and bill of sale?

In addition, for some bizarre reason, Tarik and Ahmed said that until he was given a bill of sale, he must work third shift. He was supposedly the owner of this business, and they were making him work third shift? An owner doesn't do that. Owners are supposed to work during the day so they can actually run the store. We couldn't help but wonder what in the world was going on.

"Adam, I screwed up," he said to me on the phone.

"Oh?" I said with confusion, not really knowing what he was talking about.

"They don't want me to bring anybody to work here. So you can't come," he said, sounding very sad and regretful.

"It's okay, Dad," I said, trying to reassure him. "I was never that invested in the idea in the first place."

"No, son. It's not okay," he said. And he sounded like he was crying. "I screwed up."

"We all do…," I replied. "You've forgiven me for my screw-ups many, many times. More times than I can even count."

"I'm broke. They took all of my money, and they won't give me the bill of sale," he said.

Unfortunately, he called me during one of the days when I was not really with it. If I had been more with it, I would have tried harder to make him feel better. I didn't know that when I was talking to him that day, it would be the last phone conversation I would ever have with him. If I had known that, I would have said much more. I would have told him how much he meant to me, how much I loved him. I honestly don't even remember how that conversation ended. It seemed like just another phone call with no more meaning than that.

* * * * *

Two weeks later, on June 27, 2012, I was sleeping when the phone rang. My wife was home, and she quickly rushed to the phone to pick it up, hoping I wouldn't wake up. It was Raafid. This alone put Deena on edge. His tone, right away, worried her. Something was going on, and whatever it was, it wasn't good.

"Can I speak to Adam, please?" Raafid said in a hurried, urgent tone.

"He's sleeping now. Can I take a message?" Deena asked.

"No! I need to speak to Adam!" he insisted.

"Well, he's sleeping—" Deena started but was cut off.

"Then wake him up!" Raafid yelled urgently.

"What's going on?" Deena asked worriedly.

"Just wake him up!" Raafid said, sounding increasingly desperate.

"Tell me what's going on!" Deena insisted, her voice rising.

"Our father…," Raafid started. And it was clear he was fighting back tears. "Our father was shot. He died…"

Chapter 22

On June 6, 2012, my father was led to believe that he had finally purchased the business he had sought for nearly thirty years. Finally, his dream to own a business in America had come true. Finally, all the blood, sweat, and tears that he had poured into trying to make this dream come true had paid off.

Once he believed he owned the store, he didn't waste any time. American flags were placed everywhere around the property. He was proud of his accomplishment and proud to be an American. Quickly, my father became a well-respected member of the Meriden community. He started a charity drive for locals who were less fortunate than him. Customers who came to the store were greeted by his friendly, happy demeanor. He became the highlight of some of his regulars' day.

Three weeks later, while most of the family was in Jordan attending the wedding of one of our relatives, he was hard at work in the store. But increasingly, he was becoming worried about the business.

"They're screwing me up," my father commented to my sister at one point. "They're going to kill me."

It started with his partner, Tarik, getting wind of my father's intention of bringing me to America to work in the store. Tarik became so irate that he threw his shoe in my father's face. The disrespect did not end there. He and Ahmed started to make my father's life extremely difficult.

This did not impact my father's attitude toward customers one bit. But when my father was forced to work third shift, countless regulars would express disappointment and surprise that their favorite business owner was no longer there to greet them first thing in the morning. Those customers began asking why my father was working third shift.

They would ask, "What owner of a store works third shift? The owner of any store should be working in the morning."

On June 27, 2012, my father was working the night shift with his friend Walt. For some reason, Walt was nicknamed Mac by my father. At some point, a rather large Hispanic-looking man with tattoos entered the store. The man demanded that my father give him all the money, and he told Mac to lie down on the ground.

"Just give it to him," Mac told my father calmly. My father did as he was instructed to do, without hesitation. My father's behavior was in stark contrast to how I had reacted when I was in the same situation. My father handled it in exactly the manner you are generally supposed to. In response, the man calmly raised his gun, aimed at my father, and fired. The bullet struck my father directly in the chest. Then the man ran out of the building. The man in question was a man I will never forget for as long as I live. The man was Lorenzo Camacho.

Within twenty minutes, the police and medical crews were on the scene. My father was rushed to the hospital where lifesaving measures were attempted. Unfortunately, these measures were unsuccessful, and he was declared dead at just after 2:00 a.m. on June 28, 2012.

* * * * *

My father was an amazing man. He never lived for himself, never bought anything for himself, just saved. If one of his kids needed something, he would not hesitate to give it to us. He virtually never spent money on himself. It was always for us. Everything he did was to make the family happy. He truly loved my mom. It seemed as though he worshiped the ground she walked on. Even buying the gas station was not really for himself. He bought it to help me. He intended to secure my future once it became clear that the insurance case settlement had not worked out as hoped. Aside from it helping me financially, he had hoped it would give me a renewed meaning and purpose. Maybe bring me back to being the son he once knew. Never once did he give up on me. Not once.

To this day, it kills me that he never really had the chance to enjoy his life. He had just begun to think about relaxing, believing that the gas station would provide meaning and financial security for me and the entire family. Sadly, he was gone too soon to be able to reap the rewards of his life's work.

* * * * *

While my father was dying in America, I was in Jordan, sleeping, blissfully unaware of anything, completely unaware that I was losing the man that meant so much to me.

Deena did not believe that my father was really dead. Maybe it was shock. Maybe it was because it was Raafid who was delivering this news. In any case, she did not believe it. She believed that my father had been shot but not that he was dead. After she hung up the phone, she quickly came into my room to wake me up.

"Adam," she said quietly, gently shaking me. She tried for several minutes before I began to wake up.

"Deena?" I said as I rubbed my eyes.

"Something's happened...," she began hesitantly.

"What?" I asked, feeling my chest tightening already.

"Your father..." She paused and gathered her emotions, trying to keep from crying. "He's been shot."

"What! When? Where?" I asked in shock as I quickly sat up in bed.

"Tonight. At the store," she said quietly. "He's in the hospital."

"It's okay. It'll be okay," I said. "The doctors—they'll save him. He'll be okay."

* * * * *

My mother was in Jordan when my father was shot. Upon hearing the news, she started screaming and freaking out. She was brought to the hospital and given a sedative to help her calm down.

When I heard about my mother, I quickly rushed to her side. I wasn't crying. I wasn't upset. I didn't believe my father was dead.

"It'll be okay, Mom. Dad will pull through," I said, trying to be reassuring.

This drew a confused look from my mom as she lay prone on the hospital bed.

"What are you talking about?" she asked me, sounding disturbed.

"He will be okay," I said while grabbing for her hand.

"Adam…he's gone," she said through tears.

"Don't talk like that!" I snapped. "Dad's strong. Strongest man I've ever known. He will pull through!"

"He died!" my mom shouted at me. Her heart rate monitor started shooting up. This did not go unnoticed by the nurses, who were quick to come over and make sure she was okay.

"Have faith, Mom," I said quietly.

She grabbed my face and pulled me closer. "Listen to me, Adam. Your father is gone. He is dead. He isn't coming back," she said with quiet desperation.

"No! You lie!" I shouted at my mom, startling her.

"Sir!" The nearby nurse finally piped in. "I'm going to have to ask you to leave!"

"No, it's okay," my mom said. "This is my son. He's just upset."

"My father isn't gone. He'll be okay. You'll see," I insisted. And I quickly departed the hospital, leaving my very upset mother behind.

* * * * *

At this point in time, my sister had been the only member of my family, aside my father, who was in the United States. Hearing the news, she quickly made her way to the store and was horrified by the sight of emergency vehicle lights, lighting up the streets surrounding the store. Tarik arrived at about the same time as my sister. The store was alive with activity. Several cops were surveying the scene. My sister wandered over to the counter. The sight of our dad's freshly spilled blood nearly made her pass out. She almost fainted a couple of times while she was there. Eventually, she became so emotionally distraught that an ambulance was called for her. But she refused to even be examined by them.

According to the police reports, Tarik stated to the police on the scene that he believed the murder of my father was a planned murder and that it might have had something to do with two former employees who had recently been terminated. These ex-employees were Maritza Ortiz and Khalid Al-Hamad. Tarik claimed that he had these suspicions because of death threats that the two former employees had made.

I had met Maritza about a year before when I was visiting my dad briefly in America. This claim from Tarik turned out to be nonsense.

* * * * *

After leaving my mom at the hospital, I found myself walking the streets of Jordan. Several people who recognized me tried to offer me sympathy for my father's death. But I wasn't having it. I brusquely brushed them aside, still not accepting the truth of the matter. Eventually, I happened upon a local bar where I started drinking rather heavily. Drinking was something I rarely did since alcohol and my medications were a dangerous mix. But now, I said, "Screw it." I was drinking and toasting to my father's safe recovery.

"Adam?" I heard from behind me while I took a big swig of my drink. I turned to see Sharaf looking at me with concern.

"Old friend!" I yelled. "How are you?"

"Good." He paused. "I heard about your dad…"

"He'll pull through. He's strong!" I said and took another swig from my drink.

"Pull through?" he said, sounding confused.

"You think a single bullet will kill him?" I laughed. "My father is strong. Plus, they love him in America. The police and the doctors will take care of him."

"I heard something different…," Sharaf began to say hesitantly.

"And what's that?"

"I heard he was already pronounced dead," Sharaf said with a wince.

"Whoever told you that is a liar!" I said, sticking a finger in his face. "My dad is fine."

"Okay," Sharaf said, sitting next to me, not wishing to argue with me. "If there's anything I can do for you, don't hesitate to ask."

"Right now?" I asked.

"Sure. Right now," he answered.

"Drink with me!" I said, raising my glass cheerfully. Sharaf shrugged and joined me.

"Let me tell you something!" I shouted at the top of my lungs. "I am very proud of my father!"

"Proud?"

"Yes, proud!" I paused. "He finally achieved his dream of owning his own business." I looked down at the bar. "I wish he could be proud of me too."

"I'm sure he is."

"No. No way! Proud of what? I am nothing now. A loser. There's nothing to be proud of," I said loudly.

"That's not true, Adam...," Sharaf protested, but looked uncomfortable.

"It is the truth!" I insisted boisterously. Sharaf again went silent. We spent the rest of the time drinking in silence together.

After drinking until nearly two in the morning, laughing with the random people in the bar, I returned home with the help of Sharaf. I collapsed into bed, blissfully sleeping, while chaos in my family's life reigned.

* * * * *

In our religion, when someone dies, we have a three-day period of mourning. Typically, we all gather in one of the families' homes—in this case, it was my sister's house. Food and coffee are generally served to the guests who come to pay their respects. Deena slept there for the entire three-day ordeal. She was helping to serve the guests and do her best to keep them happy.

My sister, having been in America, having seen where my dad had been shot, and eventually having to identify the body, was emotionally wiped out and stained with memories that she would never be able erase. Nonetheless, a part of me envied her because she got to see my dad one last time. She had returned to Jordan to attend one of the three days of mourning that were being held at her house. She was around to see me continuing to be in denial. I sat on the couch, irritated by the entire affair. I was a black, dark cloud in the middle of the room.

At one point, I yelled, "You people are liars! My dad's going to be fine."

"Why isn't he getting it?" my sister asked Deena wearily.

"Just give him a few days...," Deena replied knowingly.

* * * * *

My sister returned to Massachusetts to make the funeral arrangements. All the while, I still believed that my father was in the hospital and that he was going to make a complete recovery. It was not until day three that the truth finally hit me. I was sitting on the couch when I got the call from my sister.

"Hello," I said.

"Adam, say goodbye to your father," my sister said, clearly drained.

"What do you mean say goodbye?" I retorted with a hint of hostility in my tone.

"We are burying him today, Adam," she said. "It's time to say goodbye."

"But...," I began, "the doctors are going to save him. He can't die."

"They didn't save him. He's gone. This is for real. No joke. No lie," my sister said.

"Okay...," I said, tears welling in my eyes.

I hung up the phone and just sat there, staring at the floor. It was finally dawning on me that he was really gone, that he wouldn't be coming back. A tear dripped from my eyes and fell to the floor. I sniffed, sat back, and rose.

"Everyone!" I drew the attention of the assorted family in the room. "I have news," I said sadly. "My father"—I paused—"he was shot and killed." I wiped tears from my face. Nobody said a word. They just looked at me in stunned silence. My uncle stepped forward, looking extremely annoyed and shaking his head.

"Adam," he said, his voice filled with quiet anger, "your father died a week ago. What are you talking about?" I just stood there for a moment. Finally, I couldn't take it. I left the apartment, storming out, my emotions becoming too much for me to handle. He was gone. Really gone…

* * * * *

I went home. Entering my house, I was upset. I was overwhelmed by emotion, so much so that it physically seemed to hurt. Images of my father flashed through my mind. In my mind's eye, I saw my father pushing me on a swing. My heart started beating out of my chest. I saw my father picking me up and throwing me into the air. We both laughed. I took some of the medication that my doctor told me to take if anxiety was overwhelming me.

Increasingly, I became alarmed by my chest tightening, my breathing becoming difficult. Each breath seemed petrifying.

"He's dead," I heard an unfamiliar voice say to me. "You killed him."

"No." Tears were streaming from my eyes. "I didn't kill him!" I shouted to no one.

"He killed himself for you."

"Noooooooo!" I shouted at the ceiling. I fell to my knees, the tears burning my eyes, practically blinding me. My heart pumped faster and faster. *Thump. Thump. Thump.* I tried to stand, and as I did so, I lost balance and fell hard, felt excruciating pain in my head. And darkness claimed me.

* * * * *

I woke up hours later. My head throbbed. My entire body felt cold and numb. I was lying on the floor. I couldn't see. I brought my hand to my face, and I felt wetness. I didn't understand what it was. I rubbed some more and still felt wetness. I made my way to Deena's room. I opened the door and called her name. She turned to me, and her eyes lit up in terror. She screamed a loud, high-pitched scream that startled me so much that I took several steps backward. My entire face was covered in blood!

* * * * *

Deena rushed me to the hospital. As it turned out, the injury was not as bad as it looked. The doctor told me that it was likely that I had had a panic attack and had hit my head while falling down. He said I should be thankful that I didn't crack my skull on something, which could have killed me. Of course, I didn't mention that I wasn't thankful for that at all. Death would have been just fine with me. After a battery of tests to rule out the possibility that I had had some kind of heart-related episode, I was released from the hospital.

I returned home and stared out a window while Deena held me from behind. I was looking up into the clouds. I was wondering if it was possible to look hard enough into the clouds to see my father.

"I need to go to America," I said after a few moments of silence.

"Why?" Deena asked.

"I need to know what happened to my father. I need to know who killed him," I answered.

"The kids will be done with school soon. We can go then," Deena said. I turned to face her, my eyes filled with regret.

"No. I need to do this now." I sighed. "I'm going now. I'm going to use whatever energy I have to find out what happened to my father. I'm going to find out who was responsible for this!" I said with quiet, seething rage. "I'm sorry, but I have to do this on my own. I divorce you..."

Deena reacted as if I had hit her. She took her arms off me and took a few steps back. She said nothing, simply walked out of the room and out of sight. I wasn't sure if I would ever see her again. I didn't care. The only thing that mattered to me was finding out what happened to my father and making sure justice was done.

CHAPTER 23

I arrived in America once again by way of JFK airport. This was the first time I arrived in America without being greeted by my father's warm, smiling face. Instead, I saw the sad, distraught visage of my younger brother, Zahir. We embraced, holding each other for a long time. I felt as though I was giving a very cold hug. I had no idea what to say to him at that moment as he started crying. We had lost our father. What could I possibly say to make that okay for him? What could possibly be said to make it okay for me?

"We lost our father," Zahir said, almost sounding like he was talking to himself.

"I know," I sighed. "I'm here to find out why..."

* * * * *

We went directly to my father's house in Massachusetts. The house looked the same. Everything was still there. But the house felt like it was missing something. It felt cold and empty. The spark of life that once inhabited the house seemed gone now. I walked around, running my hand over the furniture, trying to connect with my father's essence in any way that I could. I found myself looking at a picture of my smiling father with the rest of our family. It was taken well before I was nearly beaten to death all those years ago—simpler times, when the future still looked bright for us all. Even though I had felt as though my heart had been ripped out when I was attacked, I now realized that a small part must have remained because I now felt that what had remained was also vanquished.

I went into his room and sat on his bed, looking about, seeing things that had meant the world to my father. Out of the corner of my eye, I noticed something. I smiled at the sight of a small vase that I had made in school back when I was a kid. I picked it up and marveled at it. Despite it being misshapen and hardly a professional job, he had kept it all these years. I stood up and opened his closet. For many years, my father had never really bought very much. But recently, since buying the gas station, he had begun to buy himself some winter clothes. I noticed that the clothes in this closet were recently purchased. A lot of them never had a chance to be worn.

When I was younger, I had frequently accompanied him to clothing stores. "You see this?" he would say as he pointed at the price hanging over the clothes. "This is a good deal!" He didn't believe in buying expensive clothes just for the sake of it. He took pride in finding the best deal possible.

I left my father's room and went downstairs, down to the basement. I found the old mattress that I used to sleep on. It hadn't moved from its spot. I lay down, and I quickly went to sleep.

* * * * *

I have no idea how long I slept. When I woke up, I went upstairs. It had been so quiet that I was startled to see that my mom was home, sitting on the couch and staring off into space. As I approached her, she seemed just as surprised to see me as I was to see her.

"Mom? What are you doing?" I asked.

"I'm waiting for your father," she said, sounding drained.

I just looked at her, stunned, completely uncertain of what to say. What could you say to something like that? I knew that she knew that he was gone. She wasn't in denial the way I had been. But oddly enough, she was in a state of mind in which even though she knew he was gone, a part of her still expected him to walk through the door any minute. I sat down, waiting with her for a few moments.

"Mom...," I started. But then I was silent.

* * * * *

As we drove to the Enfield Street Cemetery, I couldn't help but notice how beautiful the weather was. It didn't seem right. It didn't seem right that the temperature was so warm and the sun was shining so brightly. The weather did not fit the mood of the moment as we approached the spot where the resting soul of my father resided. I spent most of the drive with my mom in total silence. Neither of us really knew what to say. And I was no longer any good at small talk.

The car came to a full stop. Not wasting any time, I jumped out of the car and quickly made my way over to my aging mom to help her out. I offered her my arm to grab on to, and she accepted. As we walked, I stared at the many tombstones ahead, trying to see if I could spot my dad's. But this was a ridiculous exercise. My dad's grave was so far ahead that I couldn't possibly read names from that distance.

"He never got to see your children," my mom said, breaking the long silence.

The comment made my heart explode with pain as I realized the truth of her words. On more than one occasion, he had asked me to bring my family back to Massachusetts. But I never had.

"I know," I said in absence of anything better to say. My voice was barely above a whisper and filled with bottomless regret. I scanned her face for blame or anger. But I saw none. Only sadness. Looking into her eyes, they seemed almost as lifeless as I'm sure my father's looked. A good portion of her soul had died along with my dad as had mine.

We started walking through the cemetery. My arm was wrapped around my mom, helping her walk. The walk seemed to take an eternity. Then my mom raised a finger, pointing off at a spot in the distance. She was pointing at a square patch of dirt surrounded by endless grass.

"He's there," my mom said as she stopped in her tracks. Without speaking, she communicated a desire to go no further. I untangled my arm from her and quickly ran to the spot. I stood over the small swath of land, staring at the spot for several moments. Slowly, I was overcome by utter despair. This was the moment during which my father's death finally became real for me. I had come to know the truth, but this was the moment in which I knew in my soul that he was gone. I cried, broke down into tears, sobbed as I had never allowed myself to. I fell to my knees and then collapsed on to the dirt over my dad's grave. I lay there prone on the ground, sobbing uncontrollably. My mom watched me, internally debating about whether or not to come and comfort me. But she seemed paralyzed, unable to move. After a few moments, I slowly got up. Kneeling on my dad's grave, I started to dig. I desperately started digging the dirt away from my dad's grave. I wanted to see him. I wanted to touch him. The desire was overpowering.

"Adam!" my mom called from where she stood. I ignored her. "Adam, what are you doing?" she demanded, startled.

"I want to see him!" I yelled without turning around. My mom was paralyzed no longer. She moved as quickly to my side as she could, putting a hand on my shoulder.

"You need to stop," she said firmly.

"I need to touch him," I said, my voice cracking. I was practically blind from the tears filling my eyes.

"Adam. There is nothing to see," my mom said quietly but firmly. "He's gone. Let him rest."

I stopped digging, wiped the tears from my eyes, and slowly stood.

"Of course, you're right, Mom," I said quietly and more calmly, without looking at her. "I'm going to find out who did this to you, Dad," I said to the ground. "I'm going to find out why you're here!"

I intended to live up to my promise. I intended find out who killed my father. And why. I suspected that the people my dad once called his best friends were behind it somehow. I had no proof of their involvement. But I was determined to find it. I would find justice for my father. This was what my life was all about now.

Chapter 24

After the cemetery, I dropped my mom off at the house and went to pick up Zahir at his hotel room. I had noticed that since I returned to the United States, my brother didn't seem like his usual self. He was more down beat than usual. Very depressed and despondent. I certainly hadn't expected this to be permanent. But as time passed, it appeared to be. My dad's murder had crushed his soul. My dad's death had affected me just as much as it had affected Zahir. But at this point in my existence, there was hardly much left of my soul to kill.

When Zahir opened the door, it was almost as if I was being greeted by a mirror image of myself. He looked as though he had just spent a night drinking heavily, and he hadn't showered. I didn't ask him about it. But I'm sure he had a nasty hangover. He squinted as the sun flashed in his face. The only thing that differentiated him from any random homeless person (or me, for that matter) was that he was wearing a perfectly tailored suit. Seeing him in the suit caught me off guard a little.

"You dressed nicely today…," I said with a tilt of my head.

"We're going to see the store, right? The store which our family owns," he explained. "Figured I should dress for the occasion."

The store was about a ten-minute drive from the hotel. We pulled into the parking lot, and I marveled at the decently-sized white brick building. On the facade, it read: Friendly Mart in golden letters. I felt a surge of pride. This was my dad's business! Temporarily forgetting about his death, the smallest of smiles came across my face. It didn't take long for me to remember he was no longer with us. The smile faded from my lips, replaced by a look of cold determination.

"Let's go," I said to my brother, who nodded.

We entered the store and saw an Arabic-looking man with gold spectacles at the counter. He greeted us warmly. But once he noticed the expression on our faces, he began to look nervous.

"Osama Tarik?" I inquired.

"Yes," he started defensively. "Who are you?"

"Adam Noor. This is my brother, Zahir," I said with an edge in my tone. A look of recognition came over his face.

"Mr. Noor's kids…," he said.

I nodded. What I wanted to do in that moment was punch Tarik in the face and beat the living crap out of him. I restrained myself, even as my blood boiled just looking at him. Out of the corner of my eye, behind Tarik, I noticed a red stain.

"My dad's blood…," I said aloud to no one in particular.

"Yes…blood is hard to clean up," Tarik said quietly. I went behind the counter without thinking, causing Tarik to stiffen visibly. Zahir also looked uncomfortable.

"This is where my father was when last he was alive," I said, talking to myself.

"I'm sorry about your father. He was one of my best friends." Tarik said quietly as I stared at my father's blood.

He didn't sound sincere to me. "I don't believe you," I said angrily, standing up quickly.

Tarik flinched as if he expected me to hit him. "Excuse me?"

"I don't believe that you're sorry!" I shouted loudly, this time only inches from Tarik's face. Zahir was now looking very nervous. "You threw a shoe in my father's face! That's how you treat your best friend?"

"I did no such thing," Tarik said, sounding offended.

"My father said you did!" I shouted. "You calling him a liar?" Then I started yelling and shouting at Tarik in a hysterical manner.

At this point, Zahir had had enough. He dragged me out from behind the counter and away from Tarik. We moved deeper into the store while I shouted at Tarik all the way. "I know where you're from!" I shouted as Zahir continued pushing me away. "Where you're from, your dream is to own a bicycle!"

"Calm down!" Zahir said as he continued pushing me away. "Calm down! We don't have the bill of sale."

"What are you talking about?" I yelled, unable to think clearly through my rage. Zahir held up his index finger to indicate that he wanted me to quiet down. He kept an ironclad grip on me to make sure I didn't try to lunge at Tarik.

"They never gave our father the bill of sale. There's no proof we own this place," Zahir said to me quietly, trying to keep himself from being heard by Tarik.

"So what?" I asked angrily, but more quietly.

"They can kick us out. We need to play nice for a little while…," Zahir said, practically whispering.

"Why?" I demanded.

"You want to find out what happened to our father? We have to play this smart. Running off at the mouth isn't smart, brother," Zahir said. "Our father purchased this business for us. For you! To help give you a future. Getting yourself kicked out will destroy what our father worked for."

"How would they kick us out?" I laughed skeptically. "These people are Muslim. Our brothers! How would they do that to us?"

"The way you're acting, he's well within his rights to call the police and have you removed…," Zahir said. "And these people believe in nothing! They aren't like us, brother." He paused. "So calm the heck down."

I looked at my brother. Even before my incident, he had always been the smartest of us. I thought hard about what he was telling me.

"Very well," I said with a resigned tone. "We'll play it your way."

"Good," my brother half smiled. "You calm?"

"I'm calm."

Zahir let me go. For a moment, I didn't move. After the moment passed, I slowly made my way back to Tarik. "I apologize, sir," I said, hating the words coming out of my mouth. "My condition sometimes makes it hard to control my temper. But please, sir, I would like to work here."

"Work here?" Tarik chortled.

"Yes, sir, like my father wanted me to," I responded, trying to control my annoyance.

"No way!" Tarik yelled incredulously.

"Why not?" I asked, feeling my temper start to flare up again. Zahir was staring at me intently. He once again looked very nervous.

"What could you possibly do? You're a crazy person!" he said, laughing.

"My father bought this business for me…"

"And he's gone now. He has no say here anymore," Tarik said quietly.

I was seconds from punching him in the face. Zahir stiffened, almost expecting my explosion. I took a deep breath and calmed myself down.

"Fine," I said, calmer. Zahir seemed surprised by my measured response. "I don't need to work here. I just want to come here every day. Hang out. Talk with the people. I just need to be close to my father."

"No…" Tarik said, shaking his head. "I don't need you hanging around the store. And I don't need him either." He indicated Zahir.

I was about to start shouting when suddenly the door to the gas station opened to reveal a man in a rumpled suit. It was another person who looked like us. I knew exactly who this man was.

"Saad…," Tarik said with surprise, confirming my suspicions.

Into the room walked Saad Ahmed, my dad's former best friend. This was the man who sold my father the store. I recognized him on the spot. Unlike Tarik, I had actually met Ahmed a few times.

"As-Salaam-Alaikum," Ahmed said, offering his hand to me. This was the standard Muslim greeting. It translates to "Peace be unto you."

"Wa-Alaikum-Salaam," came my response, meaning "And unto you peace." This was hardly what I wanted to say to the man. But as Zahir had told me not that long ago, we had to play this smart.

"I would like to ask you a question…," I started.

"Ask away, brother," Ahmed said jovially.

"Whose business is this?" I asked.

"Your family's, of course!" Ahmed answered.

"Then where is the bill of sale?" I demanded.

"Not yet...," he said.

"What do you mean not yet?" I asked with an edge in my tone.

"We're not ready yet to give it to you. We will in due time. But you are the owners of this business," Ahmed answered.

"Do you believe in God, Ahmed?" I asked randomly with my eyes narrowed.

"No," he replied.

"No?" I asked, surprised. This wasn't the answer I was expecting. Perhaps Zahir was right. These people really didn't believe in anything...

"I don't believe in God. That's English, brother. I believe in Allah," Ahmed clarified.

"Well, I believe in nothing anymore. The only reason I live now is to find out what happened to my father and why," I said.

He didn't respond to that. He just looked back at me with no expression. Out of the corner of my eye, I noticed another person wandering out from the back of the store. He was a large black man, and I had a feeling I knew who it was.

"Is this Nazel Gak?" I asked.

"Yes, it is. What of it?" Ahmed asked while Gak gave them a questioning look.

"I want him gone," I said simply.

"Gone?"

"Fired," I clarified.

"What the—" Gak started to say. But Ahmed raised a finger indicating that he should be quiet.

"Why?" Ahmed asked.

"My father had issues with him, and we don't need him," I answered with an edge in my tone.

"We need him. He's very important to the business," Ahmed said in a matter-of-fact tone.

"Why?"

"He just is," Ahmed said with a shrug.

"I don't want him here!" I said, shouting.

"Tell you what...," Ahmed said. "When we give you the bill of sale, you can do what you want with Gak. Until then, he stays. Deal?"

I glanced at Zahir, and his expression suggested that I should leave it be for the moment and move on.

"Fine," I sighed. "But this business belongs to my family?"

"Absolutely, brother," he answered.

"Tarik doesn't want me here. Doesn't want me to work here," I said, pointing at Tarik, who looked at me with disgust.

"Perhaps he's just worried about your health, brother," Ahmed said amiably. "Your mental health issues are no secret."

"I don't care. This is my father's store, and it's all that I have left of him. I want to be here," I said irritably.

"You can be here," Ahmed said wearily. Tarik looked like he was about to protest but was silenced by a single look.

"Excuse me, sir," Zahir piped up. It was the first time he had spoken in a while.

"Yes?" Ahmed said.

"Since this is our family's store, I would like to check out the books, keep an eye on the business," Zahir said. "I have a full-time job, so I won't be able to be here often. Maybe every weekend."

I looked at Zahir, a little surprised that he was willing to do that. I nodded and smiled.

"As you wish," Ahmed said with a small respectful bow. Without further word, Ahmed left the store. Tarik looked extremely angry.

This was enough to make me happy. I was convinced that Tarik was my enemy. I believed that he knew something about my father's murder, even though I had no proof.

"Adam, why don't you go home and get some rest? I'm going to stay here a while and take a look at the books," Zahir said. He gave me a look that indicated that I should just do as he suggested.

"Very well," I said and gave my brother a hug. Without another word, I left the store. Once outside, I saw a man smoking. I recognized him immediately. It was my father's longtime friend, Mac.

"Adam?" Mac asked.

"Mac!" I shouted, giving him a hug.

"Thought you were still in Jordan…"

"I came back because of my dad." I sighed wearily.

"I'm sorry about your father," Mac said, looking like he was on the verge of tears. "I was there that night…," he said, his voice sounding haunted and hollow.

"What happened?" I asked.

"The last thing your dad did was to ask me to get him a coffee…"

CHAPTER 25

According to the police report, on the night my father was killed, Osama Tarik arrived at the store with my sister. My sister was very upset and almost fainted several times. But she refused the offer of medical attention. This was only the beginning of my sister's long and draining night. She would later be required to identify our father's body at the hospital.

Both she and Tarik told the detective working the case that they believed it was a planned murder. My sister believed this because of a phone call received by my mother not long before my father was shot.

"They're going to kill me," my dad had said to my mom that day. He didn't elaborate any more than that. However, it was clear that he felt his life was in danger. Given the treatment he was getting from his "partner," Tarik, as well as Ahmed's refusal to give him the bill of sale, my dad's fear seemed justified.

On the night of my father's murder, Tarik cast suspicion on two former employees that he claimed had issues with my father. He said the recently terminated employees, Maritza Ortiz and Khalid Al-Hamad, had made death threats directed toward my father. I knew Maritza from a few years back. She had been at my father's house more than a few times.

First, the police interviewed Maritza. She said she hadn't spoken to my father since the first of June, when she had had surgery. She added that five days later, it was Ahmed who told her she no longer had a job. According to her, Ahmed said that he had sold the store without telling her. During the police interview, she said that she had no problem with my father. But was she telling the truth?

Later, the police interviewed Khalid Al-Hamad. He also alleged that Ahmed was the one who fired him after selling the store. He told the police that he had never experienced any hostility toward my father. He specifically said that both he and Maritza were aware that Ahmed was the one behind them losing their jobs. During the interview, Khalid mentioned that he didn't feel like Ahmed handled the sale of the property very well. Was Khalid being honest?

The police concluded that these two ex-employees harbored no animosity toward my father. My question is, why did Tarik insinuate that there was? Why did he claim there was hostility toward my father when my father was not even the one who fired them? It appears someone did not tell the truth.

Frequently, I called the police to talk to the detectives that were on my father's murder case. Each time, I asked them about their progress. Their answer was usually the same.

"I'm sorry, Mr. Noor, but I can't give you any information on an ongoing investigation," the detective would say politely but firmly.

"Do you have any leads?" I would ask.

"I can't answer that, Mr. Noor. What I can tell you is that we are hard at work, trying to locate your father's killers."

"Please, sir, please work hard to get the people who killed my dad. I'm begging you," I said.

"We're doing our best to do just that, sir," the detective said.

"God bless you, sir. Thank you."

* * * * *

After much dickering with Ahmed and Tarik, my family began working in the store. Once they did, the support from the people of Meriden was amazing. People started coming to the store just to show their support. Many people who knew my father, as well as many who did not, were stopping by to express their sympathy regarding what had happened. Every time someone came in to talk to me, I was overcome with emotion. Without fail, I would cry.

"Are you one of Mr. Noor's kids?" I remember a middle-aged woman asking me one day.

"I am," I answered with pride.

"I came here every day to see him," she started. "I'd buy my coffee, and he would warmly greet me. Always brightened my day." When she finished, she had tears in her eyes. I grabbed her hand and gently kissed it.

"Thank you," I said with a tear in my eye.

"I miss him," she said sadly.

"As do I. There was no better father." I paused. "Thank you. You're an angel," I said, kissing her hand one more time.

* * * * *

One day while I was taking a work break outside the gas station, I noticed my other brother, Raafid, approaching. He approached me with a serious expression. He did not seem happy.

"Hello, brother. What brings you here?" I asked.

"Visiting the store that I'm part owner of," Raafid answered.

"That you are," I sighed. "Listen, I wanted to talk to you…"

"About what?" Raafid asked.

"Our father is gone," I began. "This business with Tarik and Ahmed is going to be difficult. To keep this business going and find out what happened to our father, we will need to really work together."

"I know. You're right. And I think this is going to get very messy before it is over," Raafid answered with the sound of dread in his voice.

It had been a long time since I had had the opportunity to really talk to Raafid. But I felt that the next topic of conversation had to be processed.

"I know you're in love with my wife," I said without turning around. I threw the cigarette on the ground and stomped on it. Raafid stopped dead in his tracks. He turned to look at me while I faced away from him.

"Oh yeah?" he asked.

"You were in love with her before I even knew she existed," I said with certainty. I glanced in his direction. "Don't bother to deny it. I've seen the way you look at her. I'm damaged in every way imaginable, but I'm not a stupid man. I know I'm right."

"Okay, I admit it," he sighed with a resigned tone of voice.

"If you were in love with her, then why did you work so hard to get me with her?" I asked.

"Mother wanted her for you," Raafid answered simply while approaching me. "We do as our parents want."

I nodded in understanding.

* * * * *

"Adam?" I heard a voice that sounded familiar as I slept in my bed in the basement of my parents' house. I wasn't sure if I was hearing a real voice or if it was just a voice in my dreams. "Adam…" I heard, this time followed by the feeling of someone shaking me. My eyes opened to darkness. I slowly turned my head and found a person standing over me. It took a while for my eyes to clear. When they did, I realized it was Zahir. He was dressed in a full suit and held a manila folder with what looked like a bunch of papers in it.

"What are you doing here?" I asked groggily.

"Sorry for waking you. Mom let me in," Zahir replied respectfully.

"Okay. Why are you here?" I asked, realizing he hadn't really answered my question.

"We need to talk," Zahir sighed.

"About what?" I asked.

"Get up and get dressed. I'll be waiting upstairs for you. I need you awake for this," Zahir said. Without a further word, he left the basement and went upstairs. As I lay there, I felt my heart pounding and my chest tightening. I wasn't a man who appreciated suspense. I slowly breathed in and out until my heart slowed down. Over the years, I had picked up some strategies from Dr. Rick to get my anxiety under control. It wasn't something that I was able to do in all situations, but this time I was successful.

* * * * *

After about a half hour, I wandered upstairs and found Zahir in the kitchen, drinking coffee and reading the newspaper. The TV was on. He saw me and gave me a small smile. Without asking, he poured a cup of coffee and handed it to me. Zahir must have been reading my mind. I took the coffee gratefully and started drinking it.

"So why are you here?" I asked.

"I've been going through the business records at the gas station. In addition, I have been looking through our stock. We have problems...," Zahir started.

"Such as?"

"Ninety-five percent of the food that they sold our father is out-of-date by two years," Zahir said with urgency. "The food they sold him is basically garbage. But we're selling it."

"People are coming to our store just to show their support, and we're selling them expired merchandise?" I asked with dismay.

"Exactly," Zahir said, sighing.

"Someone is going to get sick...," I said, shaking my head.

"Not only that. I looked further into the stock. It pretty much seems like the ice cream we're selling melted and then refroze. It's no good, brother," he said, slamming the folder on the counter.

"Unbelievable," I said, shaking my head.

"There's more...," Zahir said hesitantly.

"There's more?"

"The store used to be a brand-named gas station. When they sold the store to our father, they renamed it Noor Mart and started selling generic gas," Zahir said, indicating the file he had been carrying.

"What's that?" I asked.

"Dirtier gas. Less good for your car. And you get less gas mileage from it. On top of that, they're selling the gas at the same price as brand name gas," Zahir exclaimed.

He was about to continue talking when he suddenly became transfixed by the television. He slowly moved toward the TV with a look of shock on his face. I eyed him curiously.

"What's wrong?" I asked.

"They caught him...," Zahir answered with his mouth hanging wide open.

"Caught who?"

"The man who shot our father...," Zahir said distantly. This startled me enough to cause me to start paying attention to the television. I turned the television way up as they were discussing it.

"Lorenzo Camacho," I said, echoing the TV.

There on the TV was the face of my enemy, the face of the man who took the rest of what remained of my heart and soul. I stared at the TV with my blood boiling, wishing I could leap through the television and kill the man with my bare hands.

"Tahtariq fi nar jahannam," my brother said as he stared at the television, his eyes burning with anger and hatred. He seemingly echoed my own thoughts. I turned to look at my brother, whose eyes never left the screen.

We both watched the television for a while. They arrested Lorenzo Camacho, but they had yet to catch his driver from that night. I turned back to Zahir and stared at him for a few moments.

"We need to talk to Ahmed."

CHAPTER 26

Zahir arranged for a meeting at my mom's house. This meeting included Zahir, Raafid, my mother, and myself. My sister wasn't present as she was in Jordan at the time. We sat at the dining room table, and it felt odd. It was the first time in a long time that we were all together like that.

"I'm sure you're all curious why I asked you to be here today," Zahir started.

"Yes, I have been wondering what is on your mind lately," Raafid said, looking very serious.

"I know that this has been very hard, and we are all under a lot of stress," Zahir said. "But we have important things to discuss about our family's future. Point blank, Ahmed is never going to give us the bill of the sale," Zahir ended sharply.

"Ahmed told me the other day that he would," Raafid said in mild protest.

"We are being played…," I said, standing up and starting to pace.

Meanwhile, my mom sat at the table, looking increasingly distressed and agitated.

"We need to put all of our minds and hearts together for the good of the family," Zahir said quietly. "We all have a stake in what happens to our father's store. Dad wanted this business for the family to give us all a better future," Zahir sighed, "a future that's in jeopardy."

"You're that certain of that?" Raafid questioned skeptically. "You don't believe we can take Ahmed at his word?"

"No. We can't. Nothing about this situation makes any sense," Zahir replied passionately.

"What do you mean?" my mom asked. "What about it doesn't make sense?"

"Any of it! Look. I've spent more time in this country than you guys have. I'm telling you there is absolutely nothing about this situation that makes any sense! Where do I even start?" Zahir paused. "Why is Ahmed constantly hanging around the store? You sell something. You're done with it. You buy a car from someone. You shouldn't expect to see him coming back to drive it. We have no control over the store whatsoever. We don't have control over the stock, over the money. Nothing!"

Zahir paused and opened a manila folder that was sitting on the table. "In addition to the out-of-date stock being sold, I've also discovered that we're behind on every conceivable bill," he said, holding up a bunch of bills. "They haven't paid their property taxes in at least a couple of years. No idea what they spent Dad's money on, but it wasn't the business."

Zahir paused once again for emphasis. The silence was deafening. "Furthermore, there is no way the property is worth as much as Dad paid for it. Or what they were trying to get him to pay for it. They wanted Dad to sell his houses, remember?" Zahir looked at our mother, who merely nodded. "This entire situation is a load of crap."

"What are you suggesting we do?" Raafid asked.

"We need to take this matter to court," Zahir said emphatically.

"Court! No, we can't do that," Raafid said with shock.

"Why not?" I spoke up defensively.

"Because, brother, we would lose!" Raafid yelled. "Zahir, you may understand the people better than us, but I am the lawyer, and I understand the law. Our name isn't on a damn thing. We have no proof of anything. If we take this to court, we lose."

"Maybe so…but if we don't take it to court, we'll eventually lose anyway," Zahir said quietly.

"No, no…," our mother said, breaking her long silence. "We need to play nice. Eventually they'll give us the bill of sale."

"With respect, Mother, you are wrong," Zahir said gently.

"I am tired," our mom said with clear anger. She apparently had had enough of the conversation unfolding in front of her. "I need to rest now." Mom stood up and slowly walked away from us. Zahir slumped in his chair and started rubbing his temples. He knew he wasn't winning this argument.

Zahir shook his head and looked at me with my slumped, despondent shoulders. The meeting hadn't gone the way we had hoped. Without the family's approval, we could not proceed with bringing the matter to the courts.

* * * *

Zahir and I approached the Friendly Mart, both walking briskly and with determination. He stopped me for a moment, which took me by surprise.

"You should let me do the talking," Zahir said.

"Why?" I asked, feeling a little defensive.

"You tend to get overheated. We need to stay cool…," Zahir said with a bit of a wince, clearly expecting me not to take his words all that well. I was about to protest but then thought better of it. He was right.

"Very well. Lead on…," I said with a small reassuring smile.

We entered the store, where we quickly spotted Ahmed chatting with Tarik. When he spotted us, his expression was one of annoyance.

"As-Salaam-Alaikum," Ahmed said with an annoyed-sounding huff.

"We need to talk," Zahir said, skipping the pleasantries.

"Oh, dear. This sounds serious," Ahmed said mockingly. "What about?"

"You sold my father bad merchandise," Zahir said with an edge to his tone.

I did as I was told and remained silent.

"Bad merchandise?" Ahmed said, sounding surprised. "In what way is it bad?"

"On the shelves is expired candy and food," Zahir answered.

"Don't worry about that," Ahmed said dismissively.

"What do you mean don't worry about that?" Zahir asked, beginning to become more strident. I struggled to keep my silence. My fists were clenched, but I remained silent.

"Exactly what I said," Ahmed said with a fake smile, a smile I really wanted to wipe from his face.

"With all due respect, sir," Zahir began with a tone that suggested something quite different from respect, "somebody is going to end up getting sick!"

"Who cares?" Ahmed retorted.

"Who cares!" Zahir repeated with disbelief.

"They are Americans. They are *kafir*," Ahmed said dismissively.

"People are coming here just to support us, and we are selling them garbage?" I finally piped in, drawing a look from my brother. But he simply nodded. I couldn't keep my mouth shut any longer.

"The American people are stupid. They'll buy whatever. If they get sick, who cares?" Ahmed said. "They probably won't trace it back to us."

"When are we getting the bill of sale!" I demanded, having heard enough of what Ahmed was saying.

"In time," Ahmed answered.

"You keep saying that. When?" I said, drawing closer.

Zahir was no longer really paying attention. He was pacing behind me, getting more and more heated by the second.

"When we're ready," Ahmed said. Then he walked behind the counter to be next to Tarik. Tarik had been watching the entire conversation but had yet to say a word. He just sat there staring at me with obvious hatred.

Zahir just walked out of the store without saying another word. I started to do the same and then stopped, looking back at Ahmed, who eyed me curiously.

"They found my father's killer," I said.

"I heard," Ahmed answered indifferently. He looked away while I continued to glare at him. Realizing I was still standing there, he decided to say something else. "Justice is finally served..."

"Somehow I don't think it is," I said, and then exited the store without another word.

I saw Zahir standing on the sidewalk with his hands at his side. He was clearly agitated. "You think these people are playing some kind of game with us?" I asked.

He turned to me, surprised to hear my voice. "Definitely," Zahir said in exasperation.

"What's going on?" I asked.

"Wish I knew. They're up to something, and I don't like it one bit…"

* * * * *

A couple of days later, Zahir and I drove to the store, where we noticed something interesting. The name had been changed from Friendly Mart to Noor Mart. We stopped dead in our tracks and examined the sign, which was clearly made of very cheap material. The door to the gas station opened, and bounding out of it towards us was Ahmed, who wore a jovial smile.

"You see what I did?" Ahmed said enthusiastically. "You see! The store belongs to you! That's your bill of sale!"

Zahir and I looked at each other, both with the same dumbfounded look of disbelief on our faces. After several moments, we started walking toward the store without saying anything. Zahir turned back to Ahmed, who looked disappointed.

"Nice try, but we still need an actual bill of sale."

* * * * *

I was working at the gas station during the afternoon when a well-dressed man entered the store. He was an older-looking white man wearing a business suit. I eyed him curiously as he approached. In appearance, he kind of reminded me of Mr. Peterson, whom I worked for all those years ago.

"Excuse me…," he began.

"Yes, sir?"

"My name is Chris Smith," he said with a professional air. "I'm actually a state senator…"

"A senator?" I said in surprise.

"Yes, sir!" Senator Smith said with a warm smile. "I was actually wondering if you could put me in touch with the Noor family. I heard what happened to Mr. Noor and wanted to meet with them."

I eyed him with curiosity and with a bit of paranoia. I had no idea who this person was, even though he had just told me.

"I'll ask them...," I answered.

"Great!" Senator Smith said in response. "Here's my card." He handed me a business card with his name and phone number on it. "If they're interested in meeting with me, have them give me a call."

* * * * *

Senator Chris Smith was not the first politician to visit my family. A few weeks earlier, Senator Smith's challenger, Eleanor Truman, had visited with us. I was touched by her support and even went as far as to say that she was "a very nice lady" in the press.

I brought the request to the family as I said I would, and my mom agreed to meet with the senator. Arrangements were made for him to visit my mom's house in a few weeks. Both my sister, who was back from Jordan, and I were present for this meeting.

When he came to the house and saw me, he greeted me with confusion.

"You were the one I talked to at the gas station...," Senator Smith said with a quizzical look.

"Yes, sir. I'm one of Mr. Noor's sons," I confirmed.

"You didn't say anything when I was talking to you," Senator Smith said, sounding amused.

"I apologize for that, sir. I have issues. Don't trust people too much," I explained. He seemed to accept that explanation without further comment. He made his way through the house to where my mom and sister were.

"Mrs. Noor," he greeted my mom with a handshake. I started to translate for her because she neither speaks nor understood much English. "I wanted to offer my condolences on the loss of your husband. I've talked to many people in the Meriden area, and many

235

speak highly of him." He kneeled down in front of her and took her hand.

"Rabbaba yamik," my mom responded through tears.

"She says God bless you," I translated. Senator Smith smiled and then stood, addressing everyone.

"I did some digging, and I learned that Lorenzo 'the Razor' Camacho was released from prison sooner than when his sentence was scheduled to be up because of the early release program," Senator Smith said.

"Early release program?" I asked.

"Yes, sir. It's a Massachusetts law that I have been a major opponent of since the law's inception. Your father is just the latest in a long line of victims of this program," he replied. "In a few weeks, I plan to hold a press conference to speak out against this program. You guys are welcome to join me and to talk about your father if you would like." Neither my sister nor my mom seemed interested in doing so. I, on the other hand, was intrigued.

"With respect, sir, I would be interested in doing that...," I said, stepping closer to the senator.

"Fantastic," Senator Smith said with a smile. "I believe you have my card?" he said with an amused tone.

"Yes, sir, I do," I replied, smiling back.

"Very good. Give me a call, and we'll set up a time for you to come to my house to talk more about it," Senator Smith said.

* * * * *

The early release program was a Massachusetts law passed in 2011. It's also known as the Risk Reduction Earned Credits program. The idea is that you can earn up to five days off from your sentence for each month of a combination of good behavior and taking some classes.

Lorenzo Camacho had earned the nickname the Razor from his time in a gang. A razor blade was his weapon of choice. He went to prison in 2006 for armed assault. He was eligible for parole in May of 2011, but he was denied. Then in February of 2012, he was approved for parole, but no one could be found to sponsor him. Two months later, he was released from prison, on time served. He had earned 199 days of credit due to his involvement in the early-release program.

He had qualified for early release despite the fact that he had engaged in all kinds of shenanigans in prison. For instance, during one incident, he burned a mattress. According to Senator Smith, who obtained firsthand information from a prison guard, Lorenzo Camacho was one of the worst-behaved prisoners that he had ever seen. How did this man earn so many credits for good behavior if that was the case? Two months later, he went to where my father was working and killed him, forever destroying my family.

His original sentence was scheduled to run out in October of the same year. Granted, that was only a difference of six months. However, if he had served his sentence the way he should have, without the credits from the early-release program, he wouldn't have been around to kill my father in June.

CHAPTER 27

I met with Senator Smith at his house a week later. Much to my surprise, his house was not that far from my father's gas station. It was a decent-sized house, bigger than my parents' home. It was clear to me that the senator came from some serious money. He greeted me at the door with a warm smile.

Together, we walked to the living room. I was surprised by the sight of another man standing there. This other man was a bearded, redheaded, wiry-looking man. The man wore a cardigan sweater, a light-brown overcoat, and a pair of glasses. He reminded me of the cliché of what an American college professor might look like.

"Adam Noor, this is Senator Nick Allen," Senator Smith said as Senator Allen held out his hand.

"Senator," I said somewhat awkwardly as I took his hand.

"Please just call me Nick ," Allen said with a smile.

"So, Adam, tell me a little bit more about yourself," Senator Smith instructed as he gestured for me to sit down on the nearby chair.

"Not sure where to start…," I said.

"Do you have a wife? Kids?"

"I have kids. Regarding whether I'm married or not, the answer is complicated," I said vaguely. The question made me miss my kids. It had been at least a good month since the last time I had seen them.

"Oh, one of those stories," Smith said with a chuckle.

"Yes." I nodded in agreement.

"Where are they? When do I get to meet them?" Smith asked kindly.

"In Jordan."

"It must be lonely to be separated from your family," Smith commented sympathetically.

"Life is lonely," I again answered vaguely.

"Well, as we talked about previously, next week I am organizing a press conference regarding the early-release program. In addition, I am starting a petition to have the law completely abolished," Smith said with a businesslike tone.

"A petition?"

"Yes, sir. We have quite a few signatures so far, though I don't have exact figures," Smith said.

"Do you want me to write a speech?" I asked.

"That's the last thing we want you to do," Allen said. I glanced at him with a look of surprise then back at Smith.

"No, Adam. What we want you to do is talk about your father, talk from the heart about what he meant to you and what it meant to lose him. We want you to put a human face on someone whose family has been affected by this awful law," Smith said.

"I see," I said, feeling somewhat confused. "Forgive me, sir, but I don't actually know anything about this law you're talking about."

"No forgiveness needed. You should know something about the law you're going to be speaking out against." Senator Smith laughed, and I favored him with a half smile. The senator began to fill me in on the specifics of the law. I didn't understand much of what he said. But the one thing I did understand was the fact that Lorenzo Camacho was released early, and because of that, my father was dead.

"The law is an absolute joke. Everybody is eligible for this thing—those that have committed sexual assault, armed robbery, you name it. The classes that are part of the program have absolutely nothing to do with rehabilitation. I looked into the classes and one of them was The History of the Philippines. What does that have to do with anything?" Smith asked skeptically. "Oh! My favorite item was that the law made the credits retroactive. Camacho was released because credits were added retroactively. This program is supposed to be an incentive program for good behavior and to rehabilitate yourself. How can there be retroactive incentives? Makes no sense…"

I didn't understand everything, but he sounded like he knew what he was talking about. And the fact that my father died because of a man being released due to this program automatically put me against it.

We talked for a while longer. Then Senator Smith told me that he had a meeting to go to.

"I know I could never replace what you lost," Smith said as we started walking out of the house, "but I'd like you to think of me as a father figure."

I looked at him with surprise. The words hit me hard. My eyes welled up with tears, and I couldn't help myself. I gave him a big bear hug that I think took him by surprise.

"Thank you, sir," I said emotionally.

"You need anything, you call me. Day or night," Smith said as all three of us left the house.

* * * * *

The senator would certainly regret making that offer. He was not yet totally familiar with my mental health issues. But he would learn about them. I treated him as I did anybody I considered a father figure. I called him day and night, sometimes calling him to scream and swear at him. Thankfully each time, the man was kind and forgiving.

As the day of Lorenzo Camacho's first court date neared, I became increasingly agitated. Tensions at my dad's store had only increased as time went on. Zahir and I would get rid of the expired merchandise, and somehow it would end up back on the shelf the next day.

* * * * *

The day of the trial, I was sporting an all-black suit with sun shades. I was really nervous when entering the court room. The last time I had been in a court room was the day that my insurance case ended. And that was hardly a great memory. Before my family went to the court, I got a call from Senator Allen. He told me that he wasn't going to be able to make it but that his heart was with us. However, Senator Smith would be at the court house with us, escorting my mom. Senator Smith would appear at every court appearance related to my father.

I sat nervously on the uncomfortable wooden benches at the courthouse, waiting to see my enemy. All my family members were there, silently waiting for the proceedings to begin.

I was scoping out the place, trying to see if there was any way that I would be able to attack Lorenzo Camacho when he was brought into the courtroom. The level of security was too great for me to even get close. Maybe I'd be able to touch him, but that was about it. I didn't want to do something just for show. If I was going to get to him, I wanted to do some damage, maybe even kill him. I didn't care if I'd end up in jail forever. However, I knew that I wasn't even going to get close.

Finally, Camacho's name was called, and I instantly sat up straighter, staring at the door I knew he would come from. He came into view with his shaved head, a big Hispanic-looking man. I stared at him with my eyes blazing, hatred in my heart for the man who took our father from us. My mom burst into tears as soon as she saw him. Smith grabbed her hand to comfort her.

"You're going to hell!" I shouted when I saw him. Zahir started shouting as well, briefly causing a ruckus that almost got us removed from the court. We settled down and just stared at him with quiet seething hatred. Senator Smith had prepped us. We understood that this was the beginning of a long, hard journey before we could finally see justice done.

* * * * *

On a hot day in August, the day of Senator Smith's press conference arrived. It was decided that the press conference would be held in front of my dad's store. The senator felt that having the event at the scene of the crime would be a powerful symbol.

"You nervous?" Smith asked me shortly before we were going to talk in front of the many cameras that had planted themselves outside my dad's gas station.

"No," I answered.

"Liar." He laughed.

"It's been a long time since I performed in front of so many," I started, looking out into the assembled crowd. "But I'm not nervous." For a moment in time, I was briefly experiencing the joys I had once experienced in the nightclubs, singing for the people. I was the center of attention once again. I was once again the one everyone was looking at.

"This is your chance to stand up for your father," Smith said to me, clapping me on the shoulder.

Senator Smith talked first. What did he say? I honestly don't remember. It was seemingly forever before I had a chance to talk. All of a sudden, my face was in front of the microphone. I could hear the clicking sounds of pictures being taken as I stood there in front of them. After what seemed like an eternity, I started speaking. The words just poured out of me. All the emotions, everything I had been feeling for months, all was now just pouring out of me, booming out of the microphone at the assembled crowd. I didn't know what I was saying. I just kept talking and talking. It felt amazing to say everything that I had wanted to say for the last couple of months, to talk about my dad, the man I had missed dearly and would have done anything to get back, the man that took care of me after the incident that destroyed my life. I cried right there in front of everyone. I cried. When I was done, I hugged Senator Smith. And he told me that he was proud of me. The words meant so much to me.

* * * * *

Not long after the press conference, I got an angry call from Saad Ahmed.

"Why were you just on the news in front of the gas station, talking about your father?" Ahmed demanded.

"You have a problem with that?" I asked in disbelief. "Why? How could you possibly have a problem with me talking about my dad?"

"You were blocking potential customers from getting in...," Ahmed said weakly but with an edge in his voice.

"Nobody was being blocked. He was my father, the man who meant so much to me! He was your best friend!" I shouted at him. "Why do the cameras make you nervous? Why?"

"I'm not nervous!" Ahmed yelled back. "The press was in the way of customers getting to us. It's costing us money!"

"I don't care," I said to him, laughing, and just hung up. Later, I would see him in person at the store, and we did not resume our argument.

"You know, seeing you talking about your dad nearly made me cry...," Ahmed said.

"Why?" I asked suspiciously.

"I miss him...," Ahmed said, turning to me, surprised by the question.

"I don't think so," I said, shaking my head. "I don't think that's the reason you cried.

"Oh, then why?" he asked.

"I think it's because you feel guilty...," I answered and then walked away from him.

CHAPTER 28

A couple of weeks later, I drove to the gas station. Waiting outside was Raafid, smoking a cigarette. He seemed tired. I stepped out of the car and went to greet him.

"You know I keep getting calls from our sister. She is amazed that you're on TV all the time." He paused. "You do seem to be constantly on the news lately."

"You could be on the news too. People are interested in learning about what happened to our dad. They want to know who killed him," I remarked.

"But the killers have already been caught. You know this because you were in court not that long ago, facing one of them...," Raafid replied.

"The person who pulled the trigger may be on trial. The person who drove him that day also. But not the people responsible for it," I said, drawing closer to him.

"The people responsible for it?" Raafid asked me, confused.

"That's right. The ones that hired Camacho to do it...," I said quietly.

"What the heck are you talking about, Adam?" Raafid asked, shaking his head.

"Tarik and Ahmed," I asserted. A stunned look came over Raafid's face. "They are the ones that hired Camacho."

He ran up to me, drawing me closer, throwing the cigarette away. "Do you have proof of that?" he asked with intensity.

"Not yet," I said quietly. With that, my brother let out a long sigh and then slowly backed away.

"Zahir will find the proof...," I said.

"Where?"

"He's been looking through the store files. He will eventually find something that proves my theory," I retorted with passion.

"There is probably nothing to find," Raafid said and then glanced around to make sure he wasn't drawing attention to us. "If they did what you think, they aren't going to leave evidence around. These people aren't that stupid."

"I will prove it," I insisted.

"You have to promise to keep quiet about this for now," Raafid said emphatically. "If you let your theory slip, it could be very dangerous around here. I've got to get back inside before they get suspicious." He quickly went back into the store to work.

* * * * *

"When exactly are you planning on paying these bills?" Zahir asked one day during an argument in the gas station with Ahmed. He was so frustrated that he slammed the folder that he always seemed to be carrying around with him when talking to Ahmed. Zahir often told me that he thought his carrying it around would make Tarik and Ahmed nervous.

These days, the duo had plenty of reason to be nervous. Reporters were constantly camped out around the gas station, wanting to talk to me. They were trying to talk to other members of my family as well, but I was the only one who liked the spotlight. It gave me back a little piece of what I had lost all those years ago.

"Don't worry about it," Ahmed replied, agitated.

"I do worry about it…," Zahir said with annoyance. "The business isn't going to do very well with no electricity."

"Pay the bill yourself if you're so worried about it," Ahmed said with an edge in his tone.

"You know what?" Zahir retorted, "Some of this I could actually pay. But I'm not going to do it until I have a bill of sale in my hands. So when's that coming?" Zahir sneered with hostility. I was watching from behind the counter. In front of me was my mom, who decided to visit the store that day.

"Soon," Ahmed said dismissively.

"The same exact answer I've been getting from you all year," Zahir replied.

"But forget that for a moment," he added with a wave of his hand. "The property taxes you haven't paid in years is a much bigger problem…"

"The bills will be paid," Ahmed said, clearly losing his patience.

"Before or after the government takes the business from us?" Zahir responded sarcastically.

"Preferably before," Ahmed answered.

Zahir was beyond frustrated at that point. He threw up his hands, walked behind the counter and into the office.

Ahmed watched him go, his face tight and his anger visible. He turned to my mother, who had silently been watching the conversation. Of course, she had not understood a word since the conversation had been in English. But she had been recognizing the body language and ascertaining the general tone of the conversation.

"Mrs. Noor…," Ahmed said, approaching my mom.

I stiffened a little, not sure of Ahmed's intentions. But I was prepared to pounce. He put a piece of paper in front of her, and she looked at it with confusion.

"Sign this please," Ahmed said, putting a pen in my mom's hands.

"What is this?" my mom asked.

"It's just paperwork to help you get the bill of sale," Ahmed said and waited expectantly.

"For the bill of sale?" she asked.

"Yes, ma'am." Ahmed smiled.

My mom smiled and quickly signed without further comment. Satisfied, Ahmed walked out of the store.

"Mom." I gulped, wishing I had spoken up just a bit sooner. "What did you just sign?"

"I don't know…something to help us get the bill of sale…"

* * * * *

As one could probably guess, what Ahmed had instructed my mom to sign was not something to speed up the process of getting the bill of sale. In reality, it was a legal document making my mom solely responsible for ordering all the merchandise for the store and paying for it. Everything in the store was now legally my mom's responsibility, including the gasoline. My mom didn't speak any English. She didn't understand a single thing about running a business. Furthermore, she didn't have any actual money. Our dad gave what was left of the family money to Ahmed to purchase the business. My mom had visited the store a half-dozen times within the month. And Ahmed instructed her to sign a document making her legally and financially responsible for *everything*. Ahmed knew full well what he was doing. He made sure Zahir was nowhere to be seen. He counted on me having enough respect for my mom to not interrupt. I really should have. When confronted about the matter, Ahmed simply said it was a series of steps being taken to turn the business over to us. In fact, it was just another in a series of steps for continuing to play games with us.

* * * * *

In reaction to this latest move by Ahmed, I sought a lawyer. I took this action for two reasons. First, I was receiving the money from the insurance settlement a little at a time over a number of years. I was attempting to get this money in one big lump sum in order to help out the business. The second reason was to start proceedings to legally remove Tarik from the business. I remember sitting in a lawyer's office, nervously waiting for him to finish looking through the documents that I had given him.

"Okay, sir," he started, "I don't think I can help you with your insurance company settlement."

"Why not?" I asked.

"Simply put, your settlement is a legal document which you signed. There's no way to change it at this point. Your only avenue at this point is to talk to a representative of the insurance company to see if they'd be willing to give you a lump sum payment," the lawyer said.

"I don't think they'll do that...," I said hesitantly.

"Neither do I," the lawyer added with a small amused smile. "However, as far as removing Tarik as a partner from your family's business, I think that's something I can help you with."

"Really, sir?" I said, surprised.

"Really," he answered.

"Thank you, sir!" I exclaimed.

"Don't thank me yet. It's not a guarantee." The lawyer paused. "Let me ask you a question. Your brothers, sisters, and mom are all part owners of the business, correct?"

"Yes, sir. Correct..."

"Then in order to proceed with this, you need to get them to approve legal action against Tarik as well...," the lawyer said.

"I need to get my family to agree?"

"That's correct, yes," the lawyer said.

"That may be a problem..."

* * * * *

Zahir was a smart guy, and the family knew it. Even if he wasn't at the head of the table as Raafid was or I should have been, they respected him. If he couldn't get my family to go along with taking the matter to the courts, I (whom nobody listened to anymore because of my mental health issues) had no chance. Where Raafid went, my mother followed. She loved and trusted him very much. If he told her it was time to jump off a bridge, she would do so. The only family member who supported my idea of going to court was Zahir. My idea, at least for the time being, had died a quick death.

* * * * *

I was working third shift with Nazel Gak, the guy that my father never liked. Because of my father's feelings, I never liked the guy either. I was tolerating him, waiting for the day when Ahmed and Tarik went away so I could officially get rid of him.

"You should really just leave…" Gak said to me.

"Excuse me?" I asked defensively.

"You don't get it, do you?" Gak said with an unpleasant smile.

"Get what?"

"This business isn't yours. It isn't your father's. This business is ours. Sooner or later, you will be gone," Gak said.

"You're wrong," I said forcefully.

"You should go now, or this is all going to get ugly," Gak said.

"I'm not leaving. This *is* my father's business. You guys will be the ones to go," I said angrily.

"Suit yourself," Gak said, laughing. "By the way, in case you think it's a secret, Ahmed and Tarik know that you met with a lawyer to get Tarik removed…," Gak said and then walked away.

* * * * *

During a wintry day in early December, I was working at the gas station. Even inside the gas station, it was a little bit chilly since the heat didn't work very well. Next to the counter was a heat fan that helped a little bit. I was working by myself that night because no one else was able to come in to work. I was staring off into space when suddenly I heard a tap at the door. In order to feel safe, whenever I worked third shift by myself, I always locked the door. I walked in front of the counter to look outside. There, I saw a man named Sean. He was a homeless white guy. Because I empathized with his plight, I occasionally let him do some work in exchange for food and cigarettes. But on this night, as soon as I saw him, he started yelling and shouting incoherently at me. I was startled and scared. He started banging on the window as hard as he could with a large piece of wood. Surprisingly, the window did not break. I quickly made my way to the door and opened up, pushing Sean backward.

"Man! What the heck are you doing!?" I asked angrily.

Before I realized what he was doing, he grabbed me and pulled me outside. I reacted quickly by taking a swing at him. He fell hard backward. My heart was pounding out of my chest. I had no idea what the heck was going on, but at this point, I was acting on pure instinct.

"Sean, what the hell!" I shouted as he quickly jumped to his feet and moved toward me. He was clearly not done fighting just yet. He swung the big piece of wood at me, completely missing. Undeterred, he swung at me again, hitting the arm that I had put up to protect myself. I grabbed his arm and violently pulled him toward me. I delivered a quick punch to the face, and I followed him down as he fell. I repeatedly punched him over and over again to make sure he was down for the count. When I was confident he was done, I slid off him and on to the sidewalk. I lay there exhausted and breathing hard, hoping that I wouldn't have a panic attack in that moment.

The police arrived soon after the fight ended. Sean told the police that he attacked me because I owed him fifty-five dollars. This was nonsense. I never paid him in cash. I didn't understand. I had always helped the guy out. And he paid me back by essentially trying to kill me? I had no proof, but I suspected, given what transpired later on, that Sean had been paid to attack me. This was Ahmed's opening salvo against me.

* * * * *

Meanwhile, Zahir continued to be a thorn in the sides of both Ahmed and Tarik. He did this by questioning everything he could about the business and their business practices. This included con-tinually insisting that they cough up the bill of sale. He had taken on an increasingly hostile and less diplomatic air. Eventually, Ahmed had had enough, and he took steps to deal with the threat that Zahir represented.

I remember this day as clearly as if it had happened yesterday. It was the weekend. Zahir was in the store with me, talking business. Neither Tarik nor Ahmed were at the store that day. This was highly unusual. The door opened to reveal a police officer in full uniform. I thought nothing of this since police officers frequently shopped at the store.

"Excuse me," he started in a businesslike tone. "I'm looking for a Zahir Noor...," he finished, mispronouncing Zahir's name a little.

"That's me," Zahir answered with a worried look on his face.

I was just looking at the cop with curiosity. *What the heck is this about?* I wondered.

"What can I do for you?" Zahir asked.

"We got a complaint about you from a Raafid Noor...," he replied.

"Raafid Noor?!" I shouted in disbelief, drawing a look of disproval from Zahir. He clearly didn't want me getting involved in whatever was going on here.

"Raafid filed a complaint against me?" Zahir said suspiciously.

"Yes, sir. He said you were threatening him..."

"That's—" I started to say angrily. But a single finger from Zahir was enough to silence me. Very few people could get me to be quiet. Zahir happened to be one of them.

"There must be some mistake. I have never threatened Raafid," Zahir said with a respectful air.

"Several witnesses confirmed the account," the police officer added. "You're not under arrest. But I'm going to have to ask you to leave the store and maintain a respectful distance from it," the police officer finished.

Zahir looked like he had been punched in the stomach. But his face registered that he knew exactly what was going on here. He seemed to nod with understanding.

"This is bullshit!" I shouted. "Zahir did no such thing!"

"Brother! Zip it!" Zahir commanded. He didn't want me to end up getting arrested.

"Your choices are you leave the store now, or we could put you under arrest," the police officer said calmly but forcefully.

"I'll leave peacefully," Zahir answered quietly with a resigned tone.

"No, you can't be serious!" I shouted once more.

"Adam, it's okay. Kindly shut the hell up," Zahir said lightly, turning his attention toward me. "Doesn't do the business any good if we're both kicked out today." He turned back toward the officer with a nod.

He quietly walked to the door and slowly left the building. I stayed behind with my rage building by the second. I was going to make someone pay for this. And I knew exactly who that someone was.

CHAPTER 29

As soon as someone replaced me at the gas station, I was in my car, driving with anger toward my mom's house. Barely parking the car, I jumped out and started running toward the house. I didn't knock or anything. I was happy to see Raafid right there in the dining room. His eyes widened at the sight of me. He didn't have time to react before I pushed him up against the wall, hard.

"How could you do that to Zahir?" I shouted at him ferociously.

"Brother, I kicked your ass once, and I can do it again! So I suggest you get your hands off me!" he shouted back at me. I gave him a little shove and then backed off.

"How could you do that to him? Your own brother!" I said, still in his face.

"I didn't want to. I feel badly about it…," Raafid started.

"Then why?" I asked in angry disbelief.

"Ahmed told me that if I removed Zahir from the business, he would give me the bill of sale," Raafid explained with a hard look.

"And you believed him? You betrayed your own family on his say so?" I yelled.

"I did what I did to protect our father's legacy!" Raafid shouted back at me. "As soon as we have the bill of sale and Ahmed is gone, we'll let Zahir back in!"

"That will never happen! You just cost us our best chance to keep the business!" I yelled. "Zahir was our only chance! And now you did Ahmed's bidding and got rid of him. Good job, brother!" I yelled sarcastically.

"I'd watch your step, brother!" Raafid said, drawing closer to me. "They aren't happy with you either."

I sighed sadly. "Now we are going to lose everything."

* * * * *

That night, as I closed my eyes and attempted to sleep, my phone rang. I quickly answered it.

"Hello?"

"Hey, Adam…," I heard Deena's voice echo through the phone.

"Deena, it's late here," I said, rubbing my eyes.

"I forget what time it is there," Deena said with a trace of humor. "Want me to call back?"

"No, no. It's fine…" It had been a couple of weeks since I had last talked to her.

"How's everything going?" she asked.

"Fine," I lied. "It's going fine."

"Did your family agree to take Ahmed and Tarik to court?" she asked.

"No." I paused. "No improvement on that front." I sighed. "How are the kids?"

"They're good. They miss you," Deena said quietly.

"Really?" I asked, feeling surprised.

"Of course, they do. That surprises you?" Deena asked in an astonished tone of voice.

"Yes," I answered simply.

"Why? They're your kids. Of course, they miss you…"

"I'm not always…any good," I answered quietly.

"That doesn't matter to them," Deena said. "Listen, we've been talking about coming to live in America with you…"

"Yes?" I intoned somewhat uselessly when she went silent.

"What do you think about us coming now?" Deena asked.

"I'm going to be honest with you…," I started. "Now is not the best time." I was understating the situation drastically.

"The kids would really love to come and see America…," Deena said quietly in response.

"I know, I know," I sighed. "Things are just crazy now. Maybe in a month or two," I said.

"Okay," Deena said, the disappointment evident in her voice. I felt tears welling up in my eyes. There had been plenty of low points in my life, but this seemed like the lowest of the low. I couldn't bring myself to tell her the truth so that she might understand why I was saying no. If she saw my family and me in this condition, she would lose respect for me, and I would lose even more self-respect.

"Kiss my kids for me," I said and hung up the phone. I suddenly realized that I was physically and emotionally depleted. After a few moments, I put my head down and fell asleep.

* * * * *

Given how things were going at home, I spent more time at the gas station. But this was no safe haven for me. In the wake of learning that I had tried to have Osama Tarik removed from the business, Ahmed had instructed Gak to give me a hard time.

My main memory for the beginning of 2013 involved constant calls to the police. Gak started to threaten me, telling me I needed to leave and go somewhere else, to not come back. At one point, although I have no police report to back me up on this, they brought in a guy with a gun who told me to leave. I wasn't scared of death. I was perfectly fine with dying. I had been for some time. The scariest enemy of all was the one that had nothing left to lose. The man left without shooting me that day.

Over the next several weeks, again and again, the police were called. Sometimes by me and sometimes by Gak. They never really did anything. Eventually, they took longer and longer to respond. At one point, they started giving us stern warnings to stop wasting their time. They were getting calls very frequently. The police were pretty confused as to exactly what was going on.

* * * * *

I became exhausted by the constant harassment. So one night I called Gak. "Don't come back. We don't need you here," I said.

"You're the one who isn't needed," Gak said, laughing.

"You're fired, Gak," I said forcefully. "Don't come back."

"Fine," Gak said, laughing. "I could use a day off."

I hung up the phone with satisfaction, celebrating my little victory. It would be the last one I would have in our battle.

* * * * *

Night turned into morning. I was looking forward to Tarik arriving so I could have my fight with him over firing Gak. Tarik was late that day. As I was waiting, I was surprised by the sight of someone very familiar, someone that I was shocked to see walking through the gas station doors. In walked the elderly visage of Maritza Ortiz. She was the one that had been fired by Ahmed and accused by Tarik of possibly having something to do with my father's murder.

"Gak!" she mistakenly said, not getting a good look at me. "Where's my best friend, Tarik? Where's my coffee?" she asked warmly.

"Maritza, you still come here?" I asked incredulously.

"Yes, why wouldn't I?" Maritza asked, startled.

"They fired you, accused you of having something to do with my father's murder…," I said, trying to wrap my brain around what I was seeing before my very eyes.

"Your father?" Maritza asked slowly. "You're not Gak!" Her eyes slowly registered recognition, and I could see a building horror in her eyes. This was the exact moment when Tarik walked through the doors. He saw me and saw Maritza standing there. His face lit up with complete terror.

"Did you bring her here to kill me?" he shouted.

"What!" I asked, totally confused.

Tarik started freaking out, shouting hysterically, acting completely crazy. When I think someone is acting crazy, that's really saying something. He finally declared that he was never coming back and sprinted out of the store as fast as he could.

* * * * *

At this point in time, Tarik and Ahmed withdrew their involvement in the business. They didn't give us the bill of sale, but they also didn't participate in ordering stock or buying gas. That responsibility was now legally my mom's, thanks to the paper they had her sign. Nobody that was still an owner in the business had money to actually run the gas station. It wasn't long before we started running into serious problems.

"It's horrible," I remember saying to my brother Zahir over the phone. "We can't buy gas. We can't buy anything!"

"I can imagine," Zahir said with a weary sigh.

"And we don't make any money from credit card transactions. That money is directly deposited into Ahmed and Tarik's accounts," I said as I was ringing up customers in the store. The few that remained loyal were trying to demonstrate their support for my father.

"Yes. I remember being pretty angry when I discovered that fun fact," Zahir said. I imagined him shaking his head as he spoke.

"You need to come back. The business needs you, brother," I said.

"Oh no. I don't think so," Zahir said, almost laughing.

"Why?" I asked.

"Because legally, I'm not allowed to be there. Don't want to risk being arrested," Zahir replied.

"You think Raafid would do that? Do you think he still thinks that Ahmed will give him the bill of sale and he would be saving the business for the family if he has you arrested?"

"I have no idea what our brother would do, and I'm not about to take that chance," Zahir said with an edge in his voice.

* * * * *

With the business still running but effectively shut down as we ran out of gas, both the mayor of Meriden and Senator Smith met with Ahmed to discuss what it would take to reopen the business. Ahmed targeted me in those meetings. They accused me of taking stock and money from the register, accusations that were completely false. During the meeting, which I would later learn about from

Smith, their agenda was fairly clear. They wanted me gone. They feared me because they thought I could damage them in some way. At least that was my take on it.

Two weeks later, they offered Raafid a deal. They would come back to the business and work to eventually turn it over to our family in exchange for one thing. My complete removal from the business. Raafid agreed to their conditions, and he convinced my mother and sister that this was the only way to get the bill of sale. Learning of this crushed my soul in ways that I didn't think was even remotely possible. Of course, my mom, who was elderly, didn't speak any English and didn't really know what she was signing.

Raafid truly believed that this would lead to the business finally being ours. He was mistaken. Ahmed and Tarik went right back to their old tricks. Finally, Raafid woke up and decided it was indeed time to bring the matter to the courts. Alas, it was too late. The only real chance the business had of staying in the family's hands, Zahir, had been banned from the business thanks to Raafid's belief in Ahmed and Tarik's word.

CHAPTER 30

My wife continued to call me, pressuring me to let her and the kids come to the United States. I kept putting her off with one excuse after another. I was doing everything I could to avoid telling her that the business had failed and that I did not have enough money to support her and the kids the way I had hoped to. I felt an overwhelming sense of shame about my current situation, and I wasn't about to give her more evidence that she had married a weak man.

I considered going back to Jordan but decided to stay in the United States for two reasons. First, I didn't have the funds to make the trip. But even more importantly, I still wanted to make sure that the people responsible for my father's murder were punished, not just the two who carried out the crime but the ones behind the scenes who planned it. I believed I knew who was responsible for my father's murder. But I needed to figure out how to get proof.

* * * * *

One night, I found myself looking in the mirror. It had been ages since I had last done so. I had not really looked at myself in the mirror for over a decade, when my life had been taken from me. I was startled by the image looking back at me. In some ways, it seemed as though it had not been long ago that I had been a young man coming to this country with his new wife, expecting to really be something. I was energetic and youthful. That was not the face I saw in the mirror now. My hair had traces of gray in it. My face was starting to get wrinkles. So many of my years had been stolen from me. What was this old sick man going to do with his life? What work could he possibly do with his severe mental health issues? How could he make his life have any meaning, now that his father's gas station was gone? What was the point of being alive? I was no good to anyone. There were only two reasons for staying alive that I could think of. Deena frequently called and reminded me of the first one: my children. The other reason for living was so that I could do everything in my power to make sure justice was done for my dad.

The money I was getting each month from my insurance case settlement wasn't enough to allow me to do what I needed to do. It was just enough to barely get by. But it was not enough to enable me to save money and get a place of my own. It was certainly not enough to support a family. I tried to get back to work, with disappointing results. Nobody wanted to hire a man with as severe a mental disability as I had. I knew that I was a nobody now. I knew that I couldn't obtain and retain a normal, regular job because of my mental health symptoms. But I kept trying. I was begging anybody I could to give me a chance at a job. I did this despite it causing me to feel deeply shameful. But I could no longer afford pride.

* * * * *

One day, I walked into a local family-owned gas station and went immediately to the counter. The elderly-looking man behind the counter looked at me curiously, waiting for me to ask for something.

"Can I help you?" he asked.

"I'm looking for a job," I answered, sounding tired.

"You want a job?" the man said skeptically, looking me up and down. "You look like a homeless man."

"For all intents and purposes, I am," I answered with a flat tone. "Please, sir, I need a job. I'll do anything you ask…"

"Wait a second," he said, eyeing me more intensely. "You look familiar."

"You might have seen me on the news," I suggested.

"You were on the news?" the man said, laughing again and sounding skeptical.

"Yes, sir. My father was murdered at his gas station," I started. "Here in Meriden actually…"

"Here in Meriden…," the man said absentmindedly. For a moment, it looked as though he had forgotten that I was standing there. He looked deep in thought. "You're not"—he paused—"a son of Mr. Noor?"

"Yes, sir. That's me. Adam Noor," I said with a weary sigh.

"Ah yes," the man said with recognition. "You didn't lie. You have been on TV!"

"Great, so you know me," I said with hint of sarcasm. "Can I have a job?"

"I've heard whispers that you're not exactly the healthiest guy in the world, mentally," the man said hesitantly.

"Yes. My dad's former partners have been spreading rumors about me," I said, feeling my chest tighten as I began to think about it. My heart started beating a little harder.

"Are you saying the rumors aren't true?" he asked.

"Some of them are. Some of them aren't," I said defensively.

"Your health?"

"I have mental problems, yes. But I'm not dangerous. I've never hurt anyone with anything other than my tongue," I answered.

"Your tongue?" the man repeated.

"Yes, sir. My mind is diseased. I lash out with my mouth. Sometimes I can't help it," I said honestly.

"What could you possibly do here?" the man asked skeptically but with a hint of sympathy.

"I can do odd things. Whatever you need. I just need money for my kids…," I replied.

"You have kids?" he asked surprised.

"Yes, sir. Two of them. Both in Jordan. They want to come here to be with me. But they can't if I can't make more money," I said, my voice tightening up as my emotions bubbled to the surface.

The man sat there, looking at me for a while, continuing to size me up.

"Fahmi," he said, sticking out his hand. I took the offered hand, giving it a firm shake. "I'll give you a job, doing whatever I can think of to have you do. I'll pay you under the table."

"God bless you, sir," I said gratefully.

The money wasn't enough by any means. But it was a start. It was also better than having no job.

As it turned out, Fahmi actually owned a number of gas stations. Early on, our relationship seemed to be pretty good. He was very supportive. However, like all my other relationships, it gradually deteriorated.

* * * * *

Most of the time, I was working at the gas station, I was mainly there hanging out, talking with the people. When conversing with the customers, I almost always discussed my father and what had happened to him. Eventually, this annoyed my new boss to no end, and several customers complained to him about me. He would frequently admonish me, telling me to stop badgering the customers. I would rarely listen. I didn't want anyone to forget about what happened to my father.

After months of my avoiding discussing what was really going on with Deena, she had finally had enough. She started demanding to know why I was stalling. It was clear that she was no longer buying any of my excuses. She probably hadn't believed them from the beginning.

"Do you not want to see us? Do you not want to see your children?" she asked through tears.

"It's not that," I said, sighing heavily.

"Then what? What's going on?" Deena demanded. She continued to demand an explanation while I sat on the phone, saying nothing. Finally, she pushed me so hard that the truth exploded out of my mouth.

"I don't have a suitable home for you guys to come to!" I yelled.

"Okay, let me think…," Deena said, trying to process what she had been told.

"I'll sell everything," Deena replied.

"Excuse me?" I asked, trying to figure out what she was referring to.

"I'll sell all the furniture in the apartment and anything else I can sell," she said quietly but determinedly. "I will send you the money, and you will rent a place for us to live."

"My dad bought us some of that furniture...," I said absent-mindedly, feeling my heart spasm with pain.

"It's just things, meaningless things. Your kids want to see America. And they want to see you," Deena said gently.

"If that's what you want to do, then do it...," I said wearily and then hung up the phone without saying goodbye.

* * * * *

Around this time, I had started to withdraw from the few people that remained in my life. These people included Dr. Rick, Senator Smith, and Senator Allen. They were the only people with whom I had continued to have consistent contact. And it had been several months since I had talked to Senator Smith.

Then in late 2013, Smith called about my father's murder case.

"Lorenzo Camacho just rejected a deal," Smith said to me after exchanging a few pleasantries.

"What deal?" I asked.

"The judge, Justin Gladhand, offered Camacho a deal which would have sent him to prison for forty years," Smith said in his businesslike tone.

"Why would he do that?" I asked, feeling anger building in my chest.

"The judge said that he felt obligated to offer him the deal because in all likelihood, the case is headed to trial," Senator Smith answered.

"And Camacho rejected this deal?" I asked.

"Yes, sir," Smith said.

"Good," I said, relieved. "Forty years is not enough for what he did to my family. The rest of his life isn't enough. He needs to burn for all of eternity!"

* * * * *

When Camacho rejected this deal, it caused the media to have renewed interest in my father's case. They started coming to the gas station where I was working. This did not please Fahmi one bit. He was already getting increasingly annoyed with me, and the media's presence did not help matters. Fahmi was involved in some less-than-reputable business practices, including paying me under the table. He was scared that the media would start examining. As a result, our relationship became increasingly fractured.

It was around this time that I met a reporter whom I will never forget. Jackie Huntley, from Channel 3, came to the store. While talking to her, I suggested that I thought there was more going on with my father's murder than met the eye. I explained my suspicion that Camacho was hired to kill my father. I mentioned the documents I had in my possession that proved how much my father had invested in the business. By this point in time, given all the turmoil that my family had experienced over dealing with Ahmed and Tarik, they sold the business for a tiny fraction of what had been paid for it.

Having listened to all this, Jackie Huntley agreed to do a story about my dad's death and what eventually became of the business. She went to Osama Tarik at the gas station, but he refused to talk to her. He actually threw her out of the store. Next, she went to Ahmed's home in Massachusetts and was not allowed entry. Nor were her phone calls returned. When the segment aired on the news, I cried. Seeing my father's story presented by her tugged at my heart. She did an amazing job. She had tried very hard, though unsuccessfully, to discover the truth. My question was: why didn't Ahmed and Tarik want to answer questions? My father was supposedly their best friend. Why didn't they want to talk about him?

* * * * *

Jackie Huntley's report and the increased media attention on my father's case inspired me. I put up signs all over the place around the gas station about my father.

"They took $300,000, and then they killed him."

"Who killed my father?"

The words were set against a backdrop of my father's smiling face. When Fahmi saw the signs, he was furious.

"What is the meaning of this!" he yelled. "They know who killed your father!"

"They don't know who paid him to do it," I said calmly as Fahmi continued yelling at me.

"I give you a job when no one else will, and this is how you repay me? With this nonsense?" Fahmi yelled, a vein practically popping out of his head. I honestly thought he was going to end up having a heart attack or something. But I didn't care about his anger or his feelings.

"You take these signs down now!" he screamed.

"No," I said quietly.

"No!" he yelled in disbelief. "What do you mean no?"

"My dad's story is more important than anything, more important than me, more important than your business! I need the people to know what happened to my father!" I shouted passionately.

"You're taking those signs down, or I will!" Fahmi demanded, jabbing an angry finger in my direction.

"You take them down, and I will just put them up again," I said with a shrug.

"That's it. I can't take it anymore! You're fired!" he yelled.

"What?" I asked, shocked.

"You heard me! Get the hell out of my store!" Fahmi yelled, approaching me fast and getting in my face.

"Don't pay me if you don't want to. But I'm not going anywhere. I need to talk to the people," I said. At this point, I walked away from him to start a conversation with a random customer who had walked into the store and was observing our fight.

Fahmi just stared at me and fumed. There was no chance that he was going to leave it at that though. There was no chance of him walking away, leaving me with a win over him.

* * * * *

A couple of days later, a group of men who hailed from the same country as Fahmi and Saad approached me while I was sleeping in my car. Unwisely, I did not have the car door locked. They opened the door and dragged me out of the vehicle. I was terrified when I saw the group surrounding me. I honestly thought they were going to kill me. The man who seemed to be the leader punched me in the stomach, which made me collapse to the ground. The pain seemed to radiate all throughout my body. I gasped for air as I fell.

"You need to leave the store and not come back!" the one closest to me said as he pulled my head up by my hair. Then he punched me hard in the face. I felt my face explode with pain. I was certain that either my nose was broken or it would be bleeding a great deal. "Do you hear me? Leave and don't come back!" he said with a quiet menace.

I started to see flashes, flashes that I didn't initially understand. The parking lot and the men around me seemed to disappear, replaced by fuzzy, blurry images. These images turned out to be flashes of myself standing in the gas station all those years ago on the day when my life ended.

"No…," I said quietly, feeling terrified.

The man holding on to my hair took my words to be an act of defiance, mistaking what I was reacting to.

"No?" he said, laughing. Then moved his fist back, preparing to strike…

* * * * *

What I experienced next was like a movie being played in my mind that I could hear and see as vividly as though it was really happening. I heard "Give me your money."

I didn't understand what was going on. My head throbbed and my mind was cloudy.

"I SAID GIVE ME YOUR MONEY!" the man yelled again, louder and shoving the gun even more into my face.

Panicked and not really thinking, I quickly reached for my wallet and handed it to him. He threw the wallet against the floor, his face registering anger and total disgust. "I WANT WHAT'S IN THE DRAWER. DON'T GET CUTE WITH ME!"

* * * * *

"Tell me you understand, or I will keep going," the man above me said. I was aware of the pain in my face and throughout my body. What I had been unaware of was that the man had continued to punch me...

* * * * *

The movie in my mind continued.

"You got any kids?" the fuzzy image asked me. I couldn't talk with the gun shoved in my mouth, so I merely shook my head no.

"A wife. No kids. Just one person to miss you?"

I wondered what was taking him so long. Why he didn't just pull the trigger and end my life right then and there? End it as I knew he was going to? In my mind, I begged for that last kindness from a man who showed me nothing but heartless cruelty. My heart and mind raced. My breathing was unbearable and shallow. Every part of my body ached in pain. I just wanted it to be over. I just wanted him to end it. I barely noticed that he was tying me up against one of the shelves.

"Lie down on your stomach and kiss the floor," he demanded. I did as I was instructed without comment. I barely had the strength to keep myself upright any longer anyway. "Close your eyes," he said, and I did so.

* * * * *

"Tell me you understand!" my attacker demanded of me as his friends cheered him on, telling him to hurt me more.

"I understand...," I finally rasped, barely aware of my surroundings. My attacker released me, and I fell to the hard payment. The pain of the collision barely registered with me.

"I'm going to go now, and I'm going to piss on your father's grave," the man said. These words sparked me back to awareness. I wanted to lunge for him, to cause him pain. However, at the moment, I didn't have the energy to move a single muscle. I lay on the ground and fell asleep!

CHAPTER 31

Meanwhile, in Jordan, my wife managed to sell off everything she could and sent me the money. She saved enough money to buy a plane ticket for herself and the kids. I was able to put a deposit down on an apartment in Middletown, with the Jarvis Company. To put it mildly, my place was sparsely decorated. But it would definitely be a better environment for my family than my previous situation. I was supposed to pay a thousand dollars a month. In Jordan, a thousand dollars a month would net you a pretty decent apartment. Here in the US, that same amount of money afforded us a place that really wasn't fit for dogs.

I realized I had no chance of keeping this new apartment without a job. With my wife and kids soon to join me, I really had no choice. So I went back to Fahmi to beg for my job back.

"No. No way," Fahmi said as soon as I came through the door. "I thought my friends would have helped you get the message."

"Please, sir. My family is coming here soon. I need a job. I'll keep quiet," I promised. He and I both knew that there was no real chance that I would be able to hold up my end of the bargain.

"Fine. I'll move you to one of my other stores. The customers here are sick of your harassment," Fahmi said. "I'll give you a call and let you know where to go."

I smiled and went to shake his hand. He made no move to accept my hand, so I dropped it and simply left the store without comment.

* * * * *

My new boss had me doing any crappy job he could get me to do. I was basically in charge of keeping the bathrooms clean as well as helping customers find things. The toilets would get disgusting quickly since my boss made them available to the general public. When I cleaned those bathrooms, I sometimes saw it as symbolic of just how far I had fallen from my dreams of being a famous singer.

One day I saw Gak enter the store. The moment he saw me, he started laughing at me. He was smoking a cigarette. No other customer had ever gotten away with smoking in the store, but my boss just let him do it without comment. From this observation, I gathered that he had had plenty of unpleasant experiences with Gak. In the town of Meriden, Gak was a known troublemaker.

"You think me being here cleaning bathrooms is funny?" I asked him.

In response, he just puffed smoke in my direction.

"Doesn't matter if I'm standing in this bathroom. I'm still going to find out what happened to my father. When I do, there will be no business or job for you anymore," I said with a bitter smile.

The smile dropped from Gak's face. He looked like he wanted to take a swing at me. Instead he dropped his cigarette right in front of me. Then he stomped on it while glaring at me. He left without saying another word.

* * * * *

As satisfying as it was to get a win over Gak, in the final analysis, it really meant nothing. My mental health, which had always been precarious, seemed to be getting worse. I started to have more panic attacks, and I had no idea why. But it was scaring the heck out of me.

Dr. Rick speculated that the reason I hadn't been having as many panic attacks when I initially arrived back in the United States was that I had had a purpose. Something meaningful to focus my energy and attention on. I had been focused on finding out exactly what had happened to my dad and to bringing those responsible to justice. In addition, I had wanted to take care of my father's store. But now, the store was gone. And I was in no real position to pursue evidence about what really happened to my father. I had to hope the police would dig something up.

* * * * *

One day I found myself waking up on the floor at home with medical personal surrounding me. I had no idea what had happened. I felt groggy and confused. All I knew was that there were men in white uniforms all around me.

"Sir! Do you know who you are?" one of the men asked me as he flashed lights in my eyes.

"Adam…," I answered weakly.

"Adam, a neighbor called us when she heard a big bang coming from your apartment. It looks like you collapsed, sir," the emergency medical technician said.

"I did?" I asked in confusion.

"Yes, sir. It appears so, sir," the man said with a mixture of professionalism and empathy.

"I must have had an attack…," I said groggily, rubbing my temples.

"An attack?"

"Yes…panic attack," I answered.

"Sir, I would like to take you to the hospital to have you checked out. Make sure everything is okay," he said.

"No. Not going to the hospital," I answered.

"I would feel more comfortable if you went, sir," the young man replied, wincing.

"I don't have insurance. I don't have money," I explained.

"This is your life, sir. Worry about money later…," he said compassionately.

"Easy for you to say," I replied sarcastically with a bitter laugh. "It was just a panic attack. No need to go to the hospital."

The person taking care of me did not look happy at my response. But he accepted my response nonetheless. Legally, he couldn't force me to be treated.

"All right, sir," he said with a shake of his head. "But please be careful."

* * * * *

I wasn't being assigned many hours to work at the new gas station, and I was making very little money. So right off the bat, I was struggling to pay rent.

One day, while at the gas station, I started to feel my chest squeeze, and my breathing become labored. Once again, I was experiencing a panic attack for no reason that I could deduce. My heart was beating hard, and I became more and more worried. I tried to get my mind to focus on something pleasant, but it wasn't working. I was leaning against the wall, trying to calm myself. My heartbeat seemed loud enough to drown out all other sound. A person entered the bathroom and saw me sitting there with my hands clutched against my chest. He tried talking to me. I saw his mouth moving. But all I heard over the blasting sound of my heartbeat was the muffled sounds of a barely audible voice. The man assumed I was having a heart attack and called 911.

By the time the ambulance had arrived, the panic attack had passed. I told the medical personnel what had happened. They told my boss that I had had a panic attack and that I was okay. They added that there was nothing to worry about. My boss, not being from this country and not being particularly bright, thought that a "panic attack" meant that I had tried to physically attack them. So as soon as the medical personnel were gone, the boss fired me.

This was followed by another round of my begging Fahmi to give me another job. He could not have looked angrier to see me walk through his doors once more.

"My family is coming soon. Please let me come back...," I begged.

"No! Sorry, Adam. But I don't want any trouble. And you, my friend, have been nothing but trouble since I hired you," Fahmi said irritably.

"Please..."

"No!" he snapped. "You're done. Get out of my store and don't come back. You know what will happen if you do."

And then he stopped acknowledging that I even existed. I threw up my hands and simply left the store.

At this point, my wife and children were only one week away from arriving in the country. I had no job, and I was already falling behind on the rent. I was in deep trouble. Of course, I told my wife none of this. I lied to her, telling her everything was fine. I honestly thought it would be. I thought my mom would be able to rescue me. But this turned out to be wishful thinking. In the past, my mom would have figured out some way to do this. But now, with the death of my dad and everything else she had been through, she was unable to throw me a life raft.

* * * * *

A short time later, I met a man from Iraq named Saleem, who was living in my building. He had been granted US citizenship after having done work for the United States military. He was a young man with a nice family. After we had a number of conversations, he knew my story.

"Don't worry, brother. If you get kicked out of there, you can come and live with my family and me," he said with a comforting smile.

I honestly wasn't comforted much by his words, but I pretended to be. Saleem had some understanding of my mental health issues, but he had no idea what it was like to live with me. If I moved in with him, he would be taking on the burden of taking care of not only my wife and kids but me as well. That was the last thing in the world I was willing to do to anyone.

Saleem came to JFK airport with me to pick up my family. Many memories of being in that airport came to me all at once. But this was the first time I could recall welcoming someone else here. It had always been the other way around.

Nervously, I waited in the terminal to catch a glimpse of my family. After what seemed like an eternity, I finally saw Deena. She looked just as beautiful as the day I met her. But at the same time, she appeared to wear the burden of the life I had created for her. She looked more run-down, tired, and haggard. Despite all this, when she saw me, she smiled. Next, I spied my kids walking side by side with her. It had been two years since I had last seen them. They had become so big! This was the first time I had ever seen my son walking! Suddenly, I was hit with the realization that my mental health issues and the death of my father had cost me the ability to experience my children's early development, including seeing my son's first steps.

Deena gave me a hug when she finally got close enough to do so.

"Welcome to America," I said with a sad smile. My words were an echo of the words my father extended to me when I first set foot in America so many years ago. So much damage had been done to me since.

"This is Saleem," I said, pointing to my friend once we parted from the hugs. My kids were jumping up and down, hugging my legs with excitement. Deena greeted Saleem warmly. Then a look of confusion came over her face.

"Where's your mom?" Deena asked.

"She couldn't come," I answered hesitantly.

"Why not?"

"She hasn't been very well for many months," I sighed heavily.

"I am very sorry to hear that," Deena responded sadly.

"Come, you should see the apartment…," I said, knowing full well that she was not going to be happy with what she would see.

CHAPTER 32

Upon seeing our new home, my wife was aghast. Saleem had helped me clean the place up. But that did not cover up the fact that there was no TV, no internet, and barely any furniture. She went to the kids' room. There she saw only two small mattresses lying on the floor. Nothing else.

"Where am I going to sleep?" she asked.

It had been a long time since we had slept in the same room together. She had always preferred to sleep alone. And so had I. I pointed to one of the two mattresses without saying a word. A look of disgust came over her face. When she looked into my room, she saw that it was no better.

"You said everything was fine!" she screeched.

I cringed. Hardly a joyful feeling. After all this time, she still trusted what I said to her. She probably should have known better.

"We shouldn't have come," she said out loud.

"I told you that," I said sadly. "And there's something else I should tell you..."

"And what's that?" she said, her tone dripping with dread.

"I no longer have a job," I said, looking at the floor.

"You don't have a job?" she asked but barely sounding surprised.

"And I'm falling behind on rent here. We are in trouble," I said plainly.

"I'd ask why you didn't tell me any of this before we got here, but you never tell me anything," Deena said sadly.

"I'm going to get a job!" I insisted. "And if not, Saleem said we could live with him."

* * * * *

Meanwhile, my family was told that Lorenzo Camacho was planning on pleading guilty. Or at least that was how we initially interpreted it. I called Senator Smith, excited about this. But he seemed less than enthused. He didn't think it made any sense. Senator Smith went to talk to the people in charge of the situation and got the full story. Senator Smith, being a highly educated man, found himself confused by what he was hearing. It was all very technical. But what he discovered was that my family didn't quite understand the truth.

"Adam, he isn't going to plead guilty. He's entering a plea using the Alford Doctrine," Senator Smith told me.

"What's that?" I asked, mystified.

"Basically, it means that he acknowledges that the state has overwhelming evidence against him, but he is maintaining his innocence. In exchange for entering this plea, he will probably get a lighter sentence," Senator Smith said.

"What sense does that make!" I yelled, outraged. "How can he say there is enough evidence against him but he's innocent?"

"I agree. It doesn't make much sense. Quirk of the law," Senator Smith said.

"Why are they doing this? Why are they letting this happen?" I demanded.

"If I had to guess, it's because the architects of the early release law don't want this thing going to trial. They don't want the embarrassment. I don't have any proof of this, but I think it's possible that the governor's administration made some kind of deal with Camacho," Senator Smith said.

"Okay, bye…," I said, hanging up the phone in anger. I sat there with my breathing becoming harder. I wanted this man who killed my father and destroyed the life of my family to burn for all of eternity. I didn't know what a "lighter sentence" meant. But whatever it was, it was going to be less than what Lorenzo Camacho deserved.

* * * * *

"Daddy, why don't you have any furniture?" I remember my daughter asking. "Is this the American style?"

"Yes. It's the American style," I answered sheepishly while trying to disguise my shame. I looked down at my daughter, who had grown so much since the last time I had seen her. I had missed her so much that my heart hurt. I had missed much of my daughter and son's early years because of my mental health issues and because of my crusade to find out what truly happened to my father. I knew I had made a mistake when letting them come to the United States. I knew that my kids deserved better than me: a man who couldn't take care of them in even the most basic way. With me, these kids were just a step away from living on the streets.

"My mattress is too small, Daddy...," my daughter said as she hopped around the living room. She was so full of energy! I envied her.

"When I get some money, I'll buy you one. I promise," I said, kissing her on the forehead. Of course, I had no idea when that was going to be. It was a week into the new month, and my insurance check was already gone. I had no job and my food supplies were dwindling. I was feeling more and more ashamed of myself by the minute. My wife suggested that she get a job. But she was here on a visa and wasn't allowed to work in the US.

Since losing the family business, times were difficult for all my family. Much as they might have wished to help, they were having trouble keeping their heads above water.

* * * * *

I became so desperate for help that I made a phone call to someone I had not talked to in over a decade. This was a man that I was supposed to begin singing with before my life was turned upside down.

Since I had last talked to him, Abdulla Ghani had turned into both a successful musician and a successful businessman. He owned a bunch of gas stations. I called in hopes that he would both remember me and be willing to help me out with a job.

"Who are you again?" he asked, and my heart sank.

"Adam Noor. I was supposed to sing with you...," I answered quietly.

"Oh, Adam! I heard about your dad. I was so sorry to hear about that, man," Abdulla said, his voice filled with regret. "What can I do for you?"

"I was hoping you would be willing to give me a job...," I answered.

"A job? As a singer?"

"No. In one of your gas stations. I can't sing anymore," I said.

"Hold on a sec...," he said and pulled the phone away from his ear. But I could still hear him.

"Kelly!" he called. I assumed Kelly was his wife, girlfriend, or even his daughter. I never did figure out which. "How many gas stations do I own now?"

"Twenty," I heard the woman's voice say. She sounded youngish.

"Find my friend here a spot!" Abdulla yelled, and he put the phone back to his ear. "I'm going to find a job for you. Don't call me though. I'll call you!"

"Thank you," I said, feeling relieved. But I never heard from him again.

* * * * *

"I don't get it," my wife said as her frustration grew. "We can't even get help from our own people!"

"I know. They change when they come here." I sighed, nodding my head.

"Why?" Deena asked.

"Some of them come here with maybe a dollar in their pocket. They come here and work until they own a gas station. They become wealthy. And then they forget. They forget what it was like to be the man with only a dollar in his pocket. The dollar blinds them. America changes them," I said with sadness.

I reached out to an old acquaintance whom I knew was not very compassionate. But he owned his own business, and I hoped he would help me in some way. The bills continued to pile up, and the food became more and more scarce. He told me that if I showed up at his store every day, I could have the stale donuts that he was going to throw out. Stale donuts are better than no food, I suppose. But this did little to make me feel better about our situation. He also gave me permission to dig through his trash to find cans to cash in. Terrific! I was now acting like a homeless person. My pride didn't stop me from doing it, but this only increased my shame. On a good day, I dug up five dollars' worth of cans. That did not go very far.

One day, while picking up the donuts, I noticed a man wearing a Papa John's hat and shirt. He was an older Arabic-looking man. You can say a lot about me, but I am definitely not shy. I approached the man quickly.

"Excuse me, sir," I began. "Do you work for them?"

"Actually, I own a Papa John's in Middletown," he said, eyeing me curiously.

"Any chance you could use some help?" I implored.

"I just had a guy quit the other day…," he responded.

"Please, sir, any chance you could hire me? I need a job for my family," I said in a pleading tone.

He eyed me up and down. He couldn't have been too impressed by what he was seeing. I looked like hell.

"Come in Monday, and we'll talk," he offered.

"Thank you, sir!" I said gratefully. Maybe, just maybe, I had found a way out of my crummy situation. But when in my life was anything ever that easy?

CHAPTER 33

I did as the man told me. I showed up at Papa John's early in the afternoon. My new boss looked me up and down and clearly didn't like what he saw. He handed me some clothes to put on. Other than the hat, there didn't seem to be a standard Papa John's uniform. It was clear that this man knew that my situation wasn't good and was electing to help me out.

"Okay, you are going to deliver pizzas. Pizzas need to be delivered within ten minutes," he instructed.

"Yes, sir," I said cheerfully.

My first day did not go very well. It took me an hour to deliver each pizza. I was desperate to do well here. But my brain wasn't any less damaged now than it had been before. Sheer willpower didn't make me any more capable of working.

"Don't worry. It's your first day," my boss said with a reassuring smile. "You'll get better."

Unfortunately, he was wrong. The second, third, and fourth days did not go any better. In fact, I seemed to be getting worse. My boss evolved from reassuring me to berating me. Every other person who worked for this man managed to make a ton of tips. Not me. Unless you consider having a pizza thrown at you by an irate customer counting as a tip! And this happened more than once.

After one particular bad day, I remember going to the bathroom and just sobbing. If I couldn't even handle the most basic job, how was I ever going to get out of my bad situation? How was I ever going to be able to take care of my kids? I felt useless. I felt pathetic. I began to feel that I could only survive in this life by accepting the charity of others. I feared that this could also be my children's fate.

I began to hear my dad's words echoing through my mind, saying, "When I am gone, there will be no one to help you, take care of you." As always, he appeared to be right.

* * * * *

One day, a parent called Papa John's, looking to feed her kids. My boss had no other delivery guy at the time, so reluctantly he sent me. I knew I didn't have that many more chances. I tried to concentrate and pay attention to where I was going. But my damaged mind was not letting me. I begged God to show me the way, to help me find the place in a timely fashion. But my prayers went unanswered. Then I heard my phone ring. As you could have guessed, it was my boss.

"Where the heck are you?" he said, clearly agitated.

"I don't know…," I answered truthfully and nervously.

"Stop the car. Pull over and tell me the street you are near," he said.

I did as I was instructed.

"Terrific. If you turn around right now, it will take you only two hours to get to your destination," he said, his voice dripping with sarcasm.

"Really?" I asked, naively.

"Really! You know what? Take that pizza and just eat it!" he said, laughing derisively. "And get your ass back here."

* * * * *

I walked into the pizzeria with my head bowed, expecting to get yelled at. My boss looked extremely unhappy to see me. He glared at me as he helped a customer at the register. He waited for the customer to disappear before addressing me.

"Terrific job as usual, Adam," he said, continuing with the sarcasm. "That's another dissatisfied customer. Lost another one for me."

I said nothing and just looked at him.

"You know what we're going to do?"

"What?" I asked.

"Forget driving. From now on, you are going to walk the pizzas to their destination. Pretty sure they will get there faster," he said.

"Excuse me, sir. Are you making fun of me?" I asked.

"Am I making fun of you?" he roared. "I think I'm entitled."

"Are you saying you don't need me?"

"Adam, you have cost me over seventy customers. I hired you despite the fact that you looked like a homeless bum and despite your reputation…"

"You knew about that?" I said, surprised.

"Of course, I did! I had this guy Saad calling me and telling me not to hire you. I gave you a shot. But if I keep giving you chances, I'm not going to have a business anymore. So, no, Adam. I'm sorry, but I don't need you," he continued angrily. "Please get the heck out of my store."

I stared at him, tempted to protest. But he didn't give me a chance. He left the register and walked farther into the store. I was thinking about following him, but I decided against it. This was the end of my brief Papa John's career.

I went home and told my wife the news. She shook her head with clear anger and disappointment. At the same time, she looked unsurprised. She "congratulated" me on another lost job.

"What are we going to do now?" she asked.

"I don't know…"

* * * * *

The phone, cable, and internet were now all disconnected. The court date regarding my eviction case loomed. I was having more and more panic attacks, not bad enough to land in the hospital, but severe enough to be scary. Deena and I were fighting almost every day now. It was like old times. Hardly a nostalgic memory that I wished to revisit. Sometimes we fought because of the situation. Other times, we fought because it was hard to live with me. My mental illness made me a tiring person to be around.

Out of desperation, I visited a friend who owned a restaurant. He was a wheelchair-bound man whom I had known for a long time. I didn't go there to ask for help. I was going there to demand it. I told him I needed a hundred dollars as we stood there in the middle of his crowded restaurant. I told him I wasn't leaving until he handed me the money. He looked around at the customers and realized that a crazy man creating a scene might negatively affect his business. So reluctantly, he handed me the money. I knew I had lost a friend that day. But I was so desperate, I didn't care. I needed the money.

* * * * *

That night, I woke my daughter out of a sound sleep. I had absolutely no idea what time it was when I did so. She looked up at me groggily, noticing that I was uncharacteristically excited. Given how rare this was, it made her very curious.

"Wake up! We're going to Walmart to buy some food!" I said excitedly. Thankfully, the nearby Walmart was open twenty-four hours per day. It turned out to be the middle of the night!

I spent a good chunk of the money on food. But I saved enough to be able to take the family to the beach. Since arriving in America, my kids had been begging me to take them there. At the beach, they were happier than I had ever seen them. They ran around on the hot sand, picking up seashells and letting the ocean waves crash into them. I sat on the beach, watching them, feeling wistful. I couldn't remember the last time they seemed so carefree or happy at all for any extended amount of time. Despite the crappy situation we were in, life had yet to take its toll on my children.

My kids love America. They love everything about it. My daughter enjoys going to an American school because it is so much less strict than the school in Jordan. Once they were here, my kids worked hard to learn the language. Now, they speak it better than I could ever hope to.

At some point as I watched the kids running through the sand, I looked in my wallet and realized that all my money was gone. And I was still weeks away from getting my check from the insurance company. I tried to forget about that and just enjoy the sun while lying next to my wife. But this plan failed. The thoughts began to plague me. I still had no idea how I was going to improve things for my family. But at least I had given them a day of happiness.

* * * * *

Two days later, I opened the refrigerator door and was greeted by a nearly empty fridge. I stood there frozen, just staring into the nearly empty, cold box.

Suddenly, out of nowhere, I heard, *You can't take care of them. You can't provide for them. You can't be the man they need you to be.*

My heart started beating faster. I recognized the voice. It was one I hadn't heard for a long time. One I hadn't expected to hear again while I was still alive.

"Dad?" I whispered.

That's right, son.

"I miss you," I said with a tear forming in my eye. "I need you now more than ever."

I can't help you any more than you can help them, he said. *It's time to join me.*

"Join you?" I repeated.

Yes, in the afterlife, my father's voice continued. *They are better off without you. You are useless to them. Join me, and we can be together again.*

"I should kill myself?" I asked out loud.

"Who are you talking to?" I heard my scared wife say from behind. I turned to her, and she was looking at me nervously.

"My father," I answered softly.

"Your father?" she asked incredulously.

"Yes. I'm talking to my father," I said, closing the refrigerator door.

"He's dead...," she said, slowly approaching me.

I walked over to the kitchen drawer and opened it. Taking out a knife, I held it up, moving it so the light would reflect off its metal surface.

"I know," I said quietly. "Deana, do me a favor…"

"What favor?" she asked, her eyes widening at the sight of the knife. She had no way of knowing what my intentions were. Was I going to stab her and then kill the kids too?

"Take care of the kids for me…," I said with a thin smile.

"Adam, what are you talking about? You are scaring me," she said, her voice cracking.

"There's no need to be scared. Everything is going to be okay," I said, calmly walking toward the bedroom.

She seemed frozen in fear, uncertain of what to do, uncertain of what I was going to do. I remember walking into the bedroom. After that, I honestly don't remember anything.

* * * * *

I woke up hours later, lying on the floor, clueless once again as to why I was there. Once again, there were a bunch of ambulance workers walking around me. Among them was the one who had visited my home before.

"I don't wish to go to the hospital," I said immediately, still groggy.

"I'm sorry, but this time, you don't have a choice," Mr. Nissan said to me sympathetically.

"What do you mean I don't have a choice?" I asked, trying to sit up. Mr. Nissan held me back.

"You tried to kill yourself. By law, you have no choice. You're going to the hospital," he said. At that moment, a couple of the ambulance personal picked me up and placed me on the gurney. I didn't see my wife or children as I was carted off to the hospital. I imagine they were scared out of their minds.

* * * * *

I sat alone in the emergency room for hours. I wasn't a priority. The only thing stopping me from eloping was a single security guard. As I sat there, I thought about how every step I tried to take only seemed to make me feel worse and worse about my life. I had no desire to live. I just wanted to die and join my father. After what seemed like an eternity, a female doctor finally came and talked to me.

"So what's going on? Why did you try to kill yourself?" the doctor asked in a sympathetic tone.

"It'd be a shorter answer if I told you all the reasons I would want to live." I sighed, not even looking at her.

"Are things really that bad?" she asked.

"Yes…," I answered plainly.

"You have a beautiful family," she said, looking down at the file.

"Whom I can't protect, whom I can't feed or take care of, who will soon be out on the street because I am no good," I said bitterly. I told her my story—all of it—from the moment I was attacked until the present day. By the end, we were both crying. The professional air she had initially projected was gone. She hugged me. It felt good.

"I can see why you would want to…," she started and didn't finish her thoughts. "Have you looked into food stamps?" she asked.

"Food stamps?" I paused. "What is that?"

"Government assistance to help pay for food," she answered. "It won't help with your other problems. But at least your kids will be able to eat." She handed me a pamphlet with information about the program. I could barely read it because I couldn't concentrate. I'd have Deena look at it when I saw her next. She was better at that stuff than I was.

"Is there anyone who could pick you up?" she asked.

"No," I said quietly.

"Anybody you could call?"

"My phone is shut off," I answered.

She looked at me for a while, trying to decide what to do. She ended up calling a cab for me and giving me fifty bucks. I'll never forget the kindness of that woman…

* * * *

Lorenzo Camacho's sentencing was scheduled for the end of 2014. My entire family was there. It was the first time I had seen my mom for quite some time. Senator Smith escorted her to her seat. Despite not being far from each other, it felt like there was an ocean between us. I sat in the court room, anxiously waiting for Lorenzo Camacho's case to be called. This was the day I had been waiting for ever since my father had been gunned down, the day my dad would get some measure of justice even if it wasn't yet complete. (Hector Ruiz's case—Camacho's getaway driver—was still ongoing, and the people I thought to be involved had yet to be implicated.)

"Please, sir, don't let the killer ever see the light of day," I pleaded with Judge Gladhand when the court case began. I told the court that I wished Massachusetts still had the death penalty. Nothing less than death was a severe-enough punishment for what he had done to my family. "When this killer came into our lives, he destroyed everything," I said emotionally. Lorenzo Camacho looked back at my family with no emotion.

Senator Smith read a statement for my mom since she didn't speak any English.

"My husband of over forty years was violently ripped away from me while I was nine thousand miles away. I could not be at his side," her statement began.

I started crying as her statement was read. I often wished I had been with my dad on the day he was killed, had been with him and comforted him in his final minutes, had made my dad know that he was not alone, had paid back a little bit of his many years of kindness toward me, or even to have taken the bullet instead of him.

"We are condemned to a lifetime of suffering that will only end in our deaths," my mom's statement concluded.

Lorenzo Camacho tried to claim that the shooting was an accident, that the gun went off by accident. This claim was ridiculous. I saw the surveillance footage. He took his time, aimed the gun, and fired. It was not an accident. He shot my dad with intent to kill. Although I believe he was probably acting at the behest of the people who paid him, he was still the one that pulled the trigger. Judge Gladhand agreed with me.

"I don't agree that it was an accident. I don't agree with the defense counsel," Judge Gladhand said. "What I saw in the video was an elderly gentleman turning over his hard-earned cash and the defendant calmly shooting him."

In the end, Camacho was sentenced to fifty-three years. Fifty-three years was not nearly good enough to make up for what Camacho did. No sentence could be. Judge Gladhand, in his closing statement, said that there was no sentence that he set that could equal the value of what was taken from us. He was right. Nevertheless, nothing less than a life sentence seemed appropriate to me.

"Not enough," I said to the press afterward. "It's not enough." I repeated it as I stood next to Senator Smith. "I'm sad now. My father's gone, and all he gets is fifty-three years?" My only consolation was that one day, Lorenzo Camacho would receive ultimate judgment from God.

CHAPTER 34

I spent the day with my wife at Dunkin' Donuts, taking advantage of their free Wi-Fi. We were signing up for food stamps, and much to our surprise, we were approved. This was something about which I was ambivalent and somewhat embarrassed.

"So this is my dream now? Simply to be able to eat?" I asked, shaking my head.

My wife pointed out that the ability to feed our kids was a significant improvement over our current situation. She was right, but still I didn't feel that great about it, especially since it was likely that none of us would have a roof over our heads pretty soon.

Not long after Lorenzo Camacho's trial ended, I once again found myself in court. This time, I was battling for the lives of my family. The case that would determine the fate of my family. I didn't think there was much chance that this was going to end up in my favor.

"Please, sir, don't make my kids sleep on the street," I pleaded with the judge.

"What's the reason for you being behind on the rent, sir?" the judge questioned.

"I cannot work. I'm damaged," I answered.

"According to this file, you haven't been to Social Services yet. Is that correct?"

"Social Services? No, sir," I responded.

"Why not?" the judge asked, surprise in his voice.

"I don't know about them…," I answered.

"Okay. I'm going to send you down the hall to talk to Social Services. Hopefully, they will be able to do something for you and your family. When you're done talking to them, come back here," the judge finished, dismissing me.

* * * * *

It took me a while to find Social Services. The person working at Social Services was an attractive woman in her forties named Pat. I sat in front of her desk as she read over my file for a few moments.

"Adam Noor...," she said aloud. "Why does that name sound familiar?"

"I've been in the news," I replied wearily.

"The news? For what?" she asked innocently.

"My dad was murdered at his gas station," I answered.

"Murdered!" she gasped. Then she spent some time thinking. "You aren't...are you a son of Mr. Noor?"

"I am," I said with a small smile, happy that she was aware of him.

"I'm so sorry about your father," she said sincerely. She began reading the file. "It seems you're behind on rent. Why?" she asked, her tone free of judgment.

I began to tell her the long story of how I got into this mess, the story of the last decade or so of my life. When I was finished, I could tell she was holding in tears.

"You break my heart," she said quietly. "Okay, I have your information. I'm going to work very hard to see if I can do something for you. Go back to the court. You'll hear from me in a few days," she finished.

I thanked her, stood up, and started to walk toward the door. She called after me. I turned, looking at her curiously.

"If you get kicked out, your family can stay with me," she said.

I grabbed her hand and thanked her again sincerely. I left her office to go back to the court room to face an uncertain fate.

* * * * *

After arriving back in the courtroom, it wasn't long before I was once again in front of the judge.

"Okay, here's the deal. The landlord is willing to work something out with you," the judge began.

"Thank you, sir," I said.

"The arrangement they are willing to make is as follows: you will pay $150 per week in addition to your monthly payments. And you will be responsible for paying the court fees," the judge added.

"Excuse me, sir," I began, startled. "But that's not possible."

"Find a way," the judge said dismissively.

"How?" I asked skeptically.

"Don't you have family or friends?" the judge asked.

"Nobody will help me." I shook my head.

"Then my suggestion is that you look into charities or hope that Social Services comes up with a solution for you," the judge said. "Do you accept the terms?"

"It's impossible."

"Sir, if you don't accept the terms, you will find yourself out on the street today. It is my recommendation that you agree to the terms," the judge said.

"Then I don't have a choice," I said, shaking my head and feeling my shoulders slump.

"No, sir, you really don't," the judge said. "Do you accept?"

"Yes," I said with a resigned tone.

"Very well. It is my duty to inform you that if you are late by more than a week, the marshal will be at your house, and you will be out on the street. You are dismissed."

Just like that, my day in court was over. I was despondent and depressed. I figured that at best I had bought my family a week. There was no way that we were going to be able to come with the money needed to pay what was expected of us. All that had happened was a delay of the inevitable.

* * * * *

I went home and waited on pins and needles for a call from Social Services, hoping against hope that they would come up with a last-minute plan to save us. In the meantime, I gathered up everything that wasn't bolted down and sold it. Everything. Clothes, furniture—everything except the clothes on our backs. I don't remember the amount of money I made selling everything. But it didn't amount to much, certainly not enough money to keep us in the apartment.

A couple of days later, we got a call from Pat, asking us to come down to Social Services. My heart practically exploded when I heard her voice. My wife and I rushed down to the office as quickly as we could, hoping that our prayers were about to be answered.

"How are you?" Pat asked with a big smile as we entered the office.

"Terrible," I answered. "Please tell me you have good news."

"I do actually," she said with a smile. "I believe we have found a way to fix your problem."

"How?" I asked excitedly.

"I've talked about your case with several people, and I found someone interested in helping you out," she answered.

"Who?" I asked.

"He doesn't want you to know. He doesn't wish to be contacted or thanked. He was moved by your story, and he just wants to help," Pat said in a professional tone.

"Thank you! Thank you so much!" I said, laughing and hugging my wife.

"No problem." Pat smiled. "In a few days, you should be getting something delivered to your house.

* * * * *

A few days later, while I was fast asleep, there was a knocking at the door. Given the medications I was on, when I was asleep, I was dead to the world. It took quite a bit of effort to wake me up. My wife quickly made her way to the door. It was a FedEx delivery. She gratefully took the box and found herself excited. She didn't know for sure, but she thought she knew what was in the box. Deena hoped that it contained our salvation. She quickly ran into the bedroom.

"What is it?" I rasped.

"It's here," she said excitedly.

"What's here?" I asked. Then it suddenly occurred to me what she was talking about. I jumped out of bed and followed her to where the package was sitting. I eyed it nervously, hoping that Deena was right. I opened the box. Slowly. What was inside was a very nice professional basket. I opened the little card inside. The card said that my debt to my landlord had been paid. In addition to that, we were given an additional $2,000 to buy stuff for the kids. I called for my daughter excitedly. She ran into the room, curious about the commotion. My son followed her.

"What?" my daughter asked excitedly.

"Guess what!" I said, picking her up and practically throwing her in the air.

"What!" she repeated, giggling.

"We're finally going to get you that bigger mattress. Hell, you're going to have your own bed!" I said excitedly. I hugged my wife happily. I couldn't remember the last time I felt anything like this. For once, my problems had been solved. For once, something had gone right in my life. Maybe, just maybe, there was hope for this family after all. Nothing had really changed. But for this moment in time, the darkness had been lifted.

EPILOGUE

Present day

On a warm spring day, I find myself walking amongst the tombstones in the cemetery that rests my father's soul. I move slowly, leisurely. There is no urgency in my steps. I'm taking in every sight. Every tombstone I walk by, pondering the now silent voices of the dead.

Where am I now that I am concluding my story? Have I finally conquered my mental illness? Have I discovered the whole truth regarding what happened to my father? Am I at peace? Am I living a prosperous and comfortable life? Sadly, the answer to each and every one of those questions is an emphatic no. I'd like to be able to finish my story with a happy ending. But this is not a movie or a children's book.

Dr. Rick convinced me to write this book. He believed that writing about my life would be a powerful and helpful therapy exercise. In addition, he said that others would find this to be a remarkable and inspiring story of perseverance. I am the one who has lived (and am living) this life, and even I can't quite believe all that I have been through. But the recounting of my story has been a way to find some healing and to honor my father, to bring life to the man I miss with all my heart, the man I hope to be reunited with one day. I hope that my story can also serve as a legacy for my children.

At this point, I wish to shed light on an issue that is often swept under the rug and ignored. In my home country of Jordan, there is great stigma attached to those with mental health issues. Although there is stigma attached to those with mental health issues in the United States, it is less severe here. But even here, not enough attention is paid to attempting to alleviate the suffering of those with severe mental health issues such as mine. It has been said that a country and a culture can be judged by how they treat their most vulnerable members. It may be that the health and happiness of a society are positively correlated with the care and compassion that members show toward one another.

If there is a single message that I wish to deliver to those who suffer as I do, it is this: If you have serious mental health issues, don't hide. Don't lie. Be upfront about the problems that you have. One of the most self-defeating mistakes I made in my life was to hide my mental health problems from others—most significantly, from my wife. It was a grievous mistake to not be totally upfront about just how damaged I was. I believe I ruined her life in the process and made mine quite a bit more difficult.

Senator Smith is still crusading against the Early Release Program, trying to get it repealed. He was recently reelected to the state senate partly due to his stated hopes of accomplishing just that. I still talk to him often. He is one of the few people still in my life on a regular basis. Occasionally, I still participate in press conferences to tell my father's story and talk about this horrendous law that lead to his death.

In June of 2015, Hector Ruiz accepted a plea bargain that gave him fifteen years in prison. My family and I were not happy. I begged the judge to bring this case to trial. I believe that Ruiz has information regarding the possibility that Camacho might have been a pawn who killed my father at the behest of another. I believe that Ruiz was connected with Maritza Ortiz, who had worked with my father, and knew Osama Tarik. Unfortunately, the judge refused my request, and Ruiz was officially sent to prison for only fifteen years. And with him might have gone our last chance to uncover the full truth regarding the circumstances of my father's murder. But I haven't given up hope, and I never will. I hope that one day the full truth will be revealed.

Subsequently, I wrote the following letter, which was published in our local newspaper:

Dealing with Grief

To the kind people of Meriden:

The response of the people of Meriden to the murder of my father showed me a side of the community that people rarely see. My family received much sympathy and support from so many people. It helped us to deal with our grief. The Meriden police were fantastic, too.

We really appreciate their appearance during the hearings at court. One person in particular I want to thank is Senator Chris Smith, who has supported the family for the last three years. My family is disappointed that the criminal justice system has no intention of pursuing others who we believe were involved in the murder of my father.

We believe there are others involved because, among other reasons, the day before he was murdered, my father called my mother (who was in Jordan) and told her, "They are going to kill me."

We had hoped that the judge would reject the plea bargain agreement and force Hector Ruiz to undergo trial for felony murder.

We wanted this to happen because we believe it is the only way Ruiz might cooperate with investigators and confirm that others were involved in the planning of the crime. Sadly, the judge approved the deal. Now there is no way of putting pressure on Ruiz to disclose the entire story. Perhaps someone reading this letter will know the identity of others who planned this crime. We would welcome any information someone in the community may have to help police reveal the entire truth of the crime.

* * * * *

You may have been assuming that after all I have experienced in the United States, I would no longer love this country. That is absolutely not true! Despite its flaws, which all nations have, this is still a great country. I love America and its people. In fact, I found that the people who helped me the most were not the people from my own culture. It was Americans! Since 9/11, tension between the Muslim communities within the US and the American people has increased. The high-profile attacks from ISIS have inflamed matters. One of the reasons I felt that this book was important now was because of recent events and the political climate. The attacks in Paris and San Bernardino, California, have led to an increasing anti-Muslim sentiment in this country. I felt it was important for a Muslim who is not a terrorist to speak up. As I've said in this story before, any religion that advocates killing others is not a religion I would have any part of. That's not what Islam is all about. ISIS represents the high-jacking and perversion of my religion. It is a radicalized version that I could never stand for.

What has hurt me about this has not been people's attitudes toward me. What hurts me is when I look at my daughter and son. I know that they will get looks in public when they are out and about. I know some people will see them and think that they are terrorists or are simply up to no good. People will look at my children through fear-tinted glasses. I know that my children will end up facing this ordeal. They will have to face the reality that many people will hate them even without knowing a thing about them. They will be unfairly judged simply because of how they look and due to incorrect assumptions about who they are. This breaks my heart to no end. It hurts to realize that this will be a source of pain for them. My hope is that they will meet people, like I did, who will not judge them in this way, that they will meet some of the many great people who call themselves Americans.

* * * * *

After a long leisurely walk, I finally arrived at my father's tombstone. There appeared to be some newly planted flowers that I assumed came from my mom, my sister, or one of my brothers. In my own hand was a small potted plant that my kids picked out, insisting that I bring it with me on this visit to my father.

"Hello, Dad," I said with a smile. "Your grandchildren and my wife say hi." I kneeled down before his grave and placed the plant as close to his grave as I could get it. "I wish I could tell you things were great. That I'm awesome. But I'm not," I said sadly. "We're stable. We're caught up on bills. We're not going to get kicked out of our apartment. But things are just so hard." I sigh. "I stay with my wife and kids because I don't want to be a disappointment to you. I know it's what you'd want," I continued. "But I am a drain on them. I see it in my wife's face. Just like I did to you, I tire her, constantly having to battle me and my sick mind, taking on twice the workload because not only does she have to take care of the kids but me too." A tear formed in my eye. "I feel guilty, Dad. Constantly. Every day of my life." I sighed and then remained silent for a long while. When I spoke again, it was about something else.

"Dr. Rick convinced me to write a book about what happened to us. I found someone to help me write it. I'm going to make sure the world never forgets what an amazing man you were. What I wouldn't give, Dad, to see you for a day. Or even an hour. I'd pay anything, any amount of money, to sit where we used to have barbecues with the family in the old house, to talk to you about everything that's going on in my life, to get your advice." I paused. "Advice I wish I'd followed more often. Because most all the time, you were right and I was wrong." I laughed.

I found myself overcome with emotion at that moment, and I started crying. I reached out to the cold tombstone, feeling its slightly rough surface. "I have never found the full truth of what happened to you, but I'm never going to stop trying, not till the day I die," I said through sobs.

"I miss you so much," I haltingly whispered. "But you know what? One day, Dad. After I've fulfilled whatever God's purpose is for me, I will join you. I will walk through the gates of heaven, and I will see your smiling face. I will run to you and give you the biggest hug I can possibly give." I smiled, still with tears in my eyes. "And then I will walk hand in hand with you. I will do something that I haven't done in what seems like many lifetimes." I tried to collect myself once more. I was both smiling at the thought of being reunited with my father and tearing up to the point where I could barely see. "I will sing for you."

THE END

Author's post script

I finished writing this book in 2016. But I almost did not publish it. When I completed writing the book, my children and wife were living with me. However, since then, my wife left and insurmountable barriers were put between me and my children. This last traumatic experience drained me of all hope. I became severely depressed and ended up homeless. My suffering multiplied exponentially. There were some dark years and I nearly lost my life.

But I am on the rebound again. I thought long and hard about whether or not to publish this book. Ultimately, I decided to go ahead with the publication. Although in 2016 the former-entertainer part of me still enjoyed the spotlight, I now no longer like to draw attention to myself. For this reason, I have not used my real name and have published under a pen name. I have also changed the names of everyone in the book, except for Dr. Kenneth Selig and Dr. Rick Lautenbach.

I want to say that despite all my disappointment and suffering since coming to this country in pursuit of the American Dream, I still love the United States and am proud to be a citizen.

I want to say that I hope people will hear about how I have grappled with my difficulties and find something of value which they can use to grapple with their own challenges.

I want to say that I hope people will hear about my saintly father and keep his memory alive. Dad, I will always love you and remember you.

Finally, the most important reason I decided to publish this book is to serve as a gift to my children. I know that even when we lived together, they were sometimes confused and anxious due to my behavior. I want them to know that through all of my suffering,

I have always loved them dearly with all the emotional intensity of which I have been capable. I want them to feel that they know me and understand that in my mind, they are perfect just the way they are.

In my next book, I will discuss the events that were factors in my being separated from my children. Until then my children, know that I love you always.

Adam Noor, Middletown

I called myself Adam Noor during this book in order to honor my son, Adam, who I love very much. But I have chosen not to reveal my true name.

ABOUT THE AUTHOR

Adam Noor is a Jordanian-born Muslim man who moved to the United States to chase the American Dream. He is a man who was passionate about everything he did. He loved his family with all his heart. He created and performed his music as a way of communicating his joy and ecstasy in life. He was mystified and intrigued by the infinity of stars in the night sky. When he fell in love, it was with his entire being, no holds barred. Despite accomplishing the initial phase of his dream—moving to the United States, getting married, being auditioned to become a performer, and being invited to perform—his passion was transformed into equally intense pain and suffering just as he was about to enact his dream.

Since his unfortunate turn of fate, Mr. Noor has demonstrated an amazing tenacity to continue to survive and grasp on to hope that is awe-inspiring and inspirational. He describes his painful journey in excruciating but honest detail. In the telling of his story, Mr. Noor demonstrates a strength of character that enables him to persevere through vulnerability to transform his initial passion and exuberance for life into a determination to find personal meaning that can transcend suffering.

Mr. Noor continues his quest for meaning and hopes his story will provide emotional sustenance for others who are travelling roads similar to his own.

CPSIA information can be obtained
at www.ICGtesting.com
Printed in the USA
FSHW010842200320
68259FS

9 781684 565405